P9-BVG-768

DISCARD

WEST GEORGIA REGIONAL LIBRARY
HEADQUARTERS

IBSEN: A PORTRAIT OF THE ARTIST

Ibsen

A PORTRAIT OF THE ARTIST

BY

HANS HEIBERG

TRANSLATED BY JOAN TATE

UNIVERSITY OF MIAMI PRESS

CORAL GABLES, FLORIDA

ORIGINALLY PUBLISHED AS FODT TILL KUNSTER: ET IBSEN PORTRETT

© 1967 Aschehoug, Oslo

This translation © *George Allen & Unwin Ltd. 1969*

Library of Congress Catalog Card Number 71-124089

ISBN 0-87024-156-7

All rights reserved, including rights of reproduction and use in any form or by any means, including the making of copies by any photo process, or by any electronic or mechanical device, printed or written or oral, or recording for sound or visual reproduction or for use in any knowledge or retrieval system or device, unless permission in writing is obtained from the copyright proprietors.

Manufactured in Great Britain

Professor Rubek (defiantly): 'I'm an artist, Irene. And I'm not ashamed of that weakness that perhaps adheres to me. For I was *born* an artist, you see.—And I'll never be anything else but an artist, anyhow.'

When We Dead Awaken, Act II

H- 163/97

Foreword

THERE are probably very few of us who have given much thought to the strong influence of Ibsen's writing, or to the way in which his characters have taught us all something about ourselves, so perceptively and sensitively that many people are better acquainted with those characters than they are with their own kin.

In the history of European literature and culture, Henrik Ibsen has been given the distinguished place he deserves, both at home and abroad. So many studies of his plays have been published in so many countries that an up-to-date Ibsen bibliography would today cover many hundreds of pages.

Among the more interesting and readable contributions have been works by such eminent Norwegian scholars as Professors Halvdan Koht, Didrik Arup Seip, and Francis Bull. For my own part, since my youth I have also had a certain weakness for another and perhaps less serious Ibsen scholar, namely Gerhard Gran. His biography, written only ten years after Henrik Ibsen's death, gives a more personal picture of the writer behind the works. Gran was a near-contemporary and knew how it felt to be present at the launching of several of Ibsen's later plays.

But I have always wanted to read a biography of Henrik Ibsen as a human being—a portrait of the man before he became a mask. Many a time I have felt like the elephant's child in Kipling's famous story, who was not only interested in the crocodile's grunt, but obstinately tried to discover what it ate for dinner.

Throughout my career in the theatre I have been concerned with quite a number of Ibsen's works, and the desire to paint such a portrait has made itself felt many times. Here I have attempted it. That I have referred to Halvdan Koht's great two-volumed biography is obvious, but I know Professor Koht will forgive me from his grave since I once told him that I wanted to do so. That I have also taken much from Seip, and perhaps not least from Professor Francis Bull's wise lines of argument and

9

great fund of knowledge, I hope will also be forgiven me. I am indebted to so many others that it is impossible to list them here. To the best of my ability I have thrust my short trunk into the 'great, grey-green, greasy Limpopo river', to sniff out things about Ibsen's background and life. It may well be that the crocodile has sometimes taken a firm hold on my snout.

Henrik Ibsen's work speaks for itself to a great extent, but with new emphases and new hidden meanings for every generation that reads it. Where his writing does not speak clearly enough, many have helped us towards understanding, and will continue to do so. But of his own life Henrik Ibsen has written very little, confining himself almost entirely to indirect information through his correspondence, articles, and his few speeches.

Let it be said emphatically that this book is not intended for academics, neither does it seek to offer any additional material to the research into Ibsen's literary work. It is meant for the enjoyment of people who are interested in Ibsen himself. If this is achieved then it has fulfilled its aim.

H.H.

Contents

Contents

I

Where He Came From

WHEN Henrik Ibsen's father, a merchant called Knud Ibsen, married his childhood friend, Marichen Altenburg, in 1825, Skien was a town of between 2,000 and 3,000 inhabitants. By Norwegian standards of the time, it was by no means an insignificant town, for there were only just over a million people in the whole country, and only a tenth of them lived in the towns. Skien was much like other coastal towns, which had founded their prosperity on large timber exports to England after the Great Fire of London in 1666, exports which continued with props for coal-mines. The great days of Norwegian sailing ships began from that time.

Like other towns, Skien had its troubles; there were wars and seizures of shipping, fires and fluctuating markets. During the Napoleonic Wars, when, instead of being Norway's best customer, England became her worst enemy, when English men-of-war closed every port, Skien equipped ten small boats to fetch valuable grain from Denmark, but only two of them returned.

As a timber and sailing town Skien had its advantages and drawbacks. The waterfalls in the town meant that timber from the thickly forested uplands could be sawn into planks with the help of water-power, but the waterfalls were only big enough to use during six or seven weeks in the spring, so the sawing season was very short. The sawdust from the mills drifted slowly out over Bryggevannet and was deposited there so that the inlet from the sea became silted up.

The town did not boast any notable personalities. It had been the seat for a court of law since 1294, but this court was dissolved in 1774, more than fifty years before the time this book is concerned with. The town was the county town for Bratsberg County, but the nobleman and sheriff, H. Wedel Jarlsberg, resided on one of his estates outside the town, and later on an estate which lay even outside the county boundary.

A number of prosperous merchants lived in Skien, and the most notable of them was Diderik von Cappelen, who owned Gimsøy Cloister, seven sawmills on Kloster Island, Stormøllen, and fourteen of the inland sawmills. He had represented Skien at the new National Assembly in Eidsvoll in 1814, and was married to a sister of Knud Ibsen's mother, so the Ibsen family had good connections.

It may be of interest to take a look at the social composition of this community. In the year 1835, the year the writer's father, Knud Ibsen, suffered a financial disaster, there were in Skien thirty-eight shopkeepers and merchants, thirty-one chandlers, provisioners and innkeepers, sixty-seven seamen and fishermen, ninety-three craftsmen, 181 day-wage earners, 369 servants and 111 paupers. In other words something less than a hundred households living off trade and shipping, a few of them wealthy, like Cappelen, others quite prosperous, and some insolvent, like Knud Ibsen—but evidently with plenty of servants.

During the first quarter of the century Skien went through severe trials, which it survived, sometimes with glory. The first six years of the century in Skien was a time of considerable enterprise. Dredging of the harbour was carried out so that vessels lying fourteen feet deep could sail right into the town instead of constantly having to go farther on to Porsgrunn, the neighbouring rival town. And Skien had got her own shipyard by 1806. Then the bad years followed with the blockade until 1814—fateful years in the history of Norway.

It is not possible to give a brief outline of the spiritual, econo-mic and social background behind Henrik Ibsen without looking back to 1814. The life of Norway during the nineteenth century owes its character to the events of that year.

Europe was exhausted after Napoleon's attempts to make himself the ruler of the world. In the farthest hidden corner of this world was a dominion of Denmark—Norway—which for seven or eight years had had to look after itself, cut off from the absolute and unremitting power and patronage of the Danish king; a dominion which for several hundred years had been easy to rule with the help of a small number of officials, some Danish, some Norwegian, but all educated and trained in Copenhagen. Many of these officials married daughters of officials and produced children who followed in their footsteps.

The country had been easy to rule from Denmark because it had been wholly without ambitions of its own. The handful of noblemen were Danish, closely bound to their own country and seldom mixing with the native population; and the bourgeoisie which grew up later also consisted to a great extent of immigrants from Denmark and other North Sea countries, who clung to the privileges in respect of farming and trade which accrued to them from the Crown. The peasants could not even sell butter and meat in the nearest town without paying taxes at the town boundary.

Nine-tenths of the population consisted of owner-occupier peasants, but most of the farms were small, spread over more than 300,000 square kilometres, lying in long, isolated and thinly populated valleys. It was, in short, a province where the administration seldom had any alarming problems to deal with—an ideal province for a distant absolute monarch.

Nevertheless, throughout the eighteenth century, Norway was obviously making economic progress. Whereas before she had mainly produced furs, skins, dried fish and oysters for Denmark, she now produced valuable raw materials, such as silver, copper and, not least, timber. And the country, inspired by the ideals which had found expression in the American Declaration of Independence and in the French Revolution, was beginning to show signs of an increasing thirst for freedom.

In January, 1814, when Napoleon was tottering to his fall and his Danish ally, Frederik VI, had to make a separate peace, Denmark was made to pay for backing the wrong horse by surrendering dominion of Norway to Sweden, who, being on the winning side this time, had to be compensated for the loss of Finland to the tsar in 1809.

These facts are elementary history; but few people realize how foolhardy it was of the Norwegians not only to declare themselves independent, but also to adopt a constitution which was in principle democratic in direct opposition to the victorious great powers. Politically all ended well: the Swedes accepted a compromise instead of carrying on the war to the end, as had happened with the former French revolutionary, now the Swedish Crown Prince, Carl Johan Bernadotte; and the great powers put up with this. That, one of the rare miracles in history, is outside the scope of this book.

But it soon became evident that the independence that Norway had won by union with Sweden was poorly founded from the economic point of view. The country had been reduced to starvation level by the war. Trade with England, which earlier had more or less formed the backbone of Norway's economy—or at least had given the Norwegians the courage to straighten their own backs—had been destroyed by seven years of war, and it took almost that time to get it going again. And on top of that great demands were made on Norway, which the optimists in Eidsvoll had not reckoned with. When the Danish king had handed over Norway to Sweden at the Treaty of Kieler, he had stipulated that Sweden should also take over Norway's share in the national debt, for which he was responsible. And Frederik VI insisted that that part of the treaty should be kept.

But Sweden had not received the dominion she had bargained for, and naturally considered it out of the question that she should pay for acquiring only an independent partner under a common king. The result was that Norway herself had to accept this debt to Denmark. The debt was not great by standards of today, but it proved almost catastrophic to the empty Norwegian treasury; the young Norway was made keenly aware of the cost of being a man. To prevent the State going bankrupt, a State bank, the Bank of Norway, was inaugurated in 1816. Citizens were required to take shares in this bank to the tune of two million speciedalers.[1] If they had no money or valuables of other kinds, they could pay in *silver*. And Norway was a country rich in silver. The mines in

[1] The speciedaler was worth about 5s.

Kongsberg had not only supplied Denmark with silver for two and even three realms, but had also benefited those in Norway who were able to pay. Possession of silver was thus more usual than in other countries. The rich ate off silver plates, had tankards, bowls, candlesticks, forks and spoons of silver, and the peasants had fine silver ornaments with which to decorate their wives.

It is the measure of Norway's desperate economic plight that this obligatory purchase of shares in the Bank of Norway was not implemented until four or five years after the statute was passed, and then it was not only the little people's hereditary silver which was melted down into riksdalers in the Bank of Norway; and it took ten years finally to squeeze their quota of shares out of the laggards.

Nevertheless by the early 1820s, life was considerably easier; there was an optimistic feeling that the hard times had been lived through and overcome. It was no doubt with bold plans for the future that in 1822 the twenty-five-year-old Knud Ibsen started his business career in Skien.

Knud Ibsen's paternal grandfather was a master mariner in Bergen. He was only thirty-nine when he died; and his widow married again, taking with her the only child of her first marriage, a boy christened Henrik after his father, to Solum, a neighbouring parish of Skien, where her second husband was the parish priest.

When this Henrik grew up, he chose his father's profession and in 1789 at twenty-four became a master mariner in Skien. He married well—Cathrine, daughter of the merchant Plesner, whose other two daughters married the wealthy Diderik von Cappelen and the prosperous Skien merchant, Johan Blom. He was thus well placed in the best society of Skien. He was soon given a ship, the *Caritas*—owned by his brother-in-law, Cappelen. He was drowned, however, in 1797, when his ship went down with all hands on the rocks at Hesnes outside Grimstad. He was only thirty-two years old, and his Cathrine had given birth to a second son, Knud. Their first-born died in 1805, at the age of nine.

So in this generation too, a young Ibsen widow found herself alone with dependent small children; she was then twenty-seven years old. Soon after her year of mourning was over, she married again, another Skien skipper, Ole Paus. Knud grew up in his stepfather's house, together with a number of younger half-brothers and sisters who became the writer's aunts and uncles.

Thus Knud Ibsen was surrounded by solid merchant stock. After serving his apprenticeship he became head clerk to his uncle, N. Plesner. He took his commercial examination and qualified as a merchant in 1825, in which year he married Marichen (Marken) Altenburg, whose father was also a merchant and master mariner in Skien.

Before I introduce Henrik Ibsen the writer, it is perhaps of interest to take one or two samples from the environment, the soil from which he came; not in order to find characters on whom he modelled himself, or scenes which later formed the frames for his dramatic works, but rather to understand a little of the spiritual and social climate in which he grew up. Much has been written to show that the world's most famous loft, that in *The Wild Duck*, is the loft at Venstøp, where Henrik lived from the age of seven until he was fifteen. This is undoubtedly true; but that tells us little about the loft or *The Wild Duck* or Skien, for the Edal family's loft is not a real place. It is Ibsen's and our own psychological loft, where we dream and live our dream life and rescue ourselves from reality—it is anywhere in the whole world, a visionary concept brought to life. When, on the other hand, Hedvig talks about the great illustrated folio she found in the loft—Harrison's *History of London*, written in the year 1775, then there is no doubt that here we have one of the earliest sources of Henrik Ibsen's imaginative world, a work which is typical of the milieu and the place. This was just the kind of book which Skien master mariners brought back home after unloading their cargoes of timber in England.

What did they talk of in his childhood home? No doubt, in those days of difficulties which had been overcome, of the silver tax and the many crises and crashes of 1820; of Norway's independence and of world politics. But there was probably not so much talk of politics then as now, for at that time there were no parties or party programmes, only casual groupings which divided on simple matters. They discussed the timber trade and ships; but perhaps Ibsen's memory is at fault when in 1881, at the age of fifty-three, in his extremely meagre statements on his childhood, he gives the impression that he was always surrounded by the whining of saw-blades. No doubt, however, the sound was deafening during the short season, when about fifty saws were working at full tilt.

There was undoubtedly much talk of food and drink. The times had improved enough for Knud Ibsen to launch out in the bankers' world, with a consequent enlargement of his social life. Servants were cheap and plentiful and most other leading families were related to one another, so there was plenty of opportunity and excuse for lavish entertaining.

There was no real intellectual life then. The town was dominated by those who looked upon themselves as the patricians of trade, and one knew from experience that practical matters were more important than Latin or Greek. Most people's ambitions were commercial and in this town it was not considered the best thing for one's children to be trained to become officials. In this the trade and shipping towns along the coast differed from the 'cathedral-towns', where the ranking order was centuries old and ruthless. There the senior officials dominated, with authority from God and the King. There were bishops' palaces, courts of law and garrisons. The senior potentates needed good grammar schools, which would educate their children to become senior officials like themselves. There was an abyss between this social class and ordinary citizens, and in many towns this was apparent right up to the beginning of the present century.

Not so in Skien. There were practically no officials there to play at being gentlemen, and the school situation was not much to boast about either. The town had had a grammar school, but it had been closed nearly a hundred years before Henrik Ibsen's time and re-placed by a 'Danish school' governed by a 'Danish school-deacon and parish clerk'. In short, a school which taught citizens the barest essentials of reading, writing, arithmetic, and the fear of God. The rest people learned in the school of life. In 1822, a grammar school was once again opened, but Henrik Ibsen did not attend it.

2

Childhood Years and Bitterness

In his very meagre *Childhood Memories* of 1881, Henrik Ibsen gives a description of his birthplace, where he lived for the first three or four years of his life:

'I was . . . born in a house in the square, Stockmann's House as it was called then. This house lay directly opposite the church with its steep steps and handsome tower. To the right of the church stood the town pillory and to the left lay the police station with its cells and "lunatics-chest". The fourth side of the square was taken up by the grammar school and the ordinary school. The church lies right in the middle.'

He was born on March 20, 1828, and must have been sickly at birth, as he was baptized at home a few days later. (He was baptized again in church in June.) He was not the eldest child: eighteen months earlier Marken and Knud Ibsen had had a son, Johan Paus, but the boy died in April, 1828, a little more than three weeks after Henrik Johan was born.

Four more children were born. First Johan Andreas, who emigrated when he was nineteen years old during the great America-fever after news of gold strikes in California. He did not get as far as California, but reached Wisconsin, where he is thought to have died a few years later. He wrote home regularly until his letters suddenly ceased. Then came the sister, Hedvig, the only one of all the brothers and sisters to become close to Henrik, and with whom he occasionally corresponded in his later days. After her came Nicolai Alexander, born in September, 1834. He became an invalid when a nurse dropped him on the floor as an infant. When he was grown up and his father could no longer keep him, he made a living for a while by mixed trading, but went bankrupt in 1863 at the age of twenty-nine. Then he went to America and ended up in Iowa, where he died unmarried. On his tombstone is the following pathetic inscription:

'Nicolai A. Ibsen. Died April 1888, 53 Years, 7 Months, 14 Days. By Strangers Honoured and by Strangers Mourned.'

Finally came the youngest, Ole Paus, born in December, 1835. He soon went to sea and was a seaman for twenty years. Then he ran, amongst other things, a small grocer's shop in Skien, did a little farming, ran a country store at Tjøme, then became a lighthouse keeper in Stavanger. He lived until 1917, surviving Henrik by eleven years, and died in an old people's home in Frederiksvaern. Though he seems always to have been poor, he was the only member of the family who was occasionally able to give his poor embittered old father a helping hand.

The only known connection between him and Henrik is that when he wished to become a lighthouse keeper he asked his brother, then already famous, for a reference. He received one, but couched in such cool terms that one would think that it had been calculated to have the opposite effect.

The three youngest members of the family were very active in the religious field, seized by the evangelical fervour of the priest, Lammers, in 1850, and leaving the State Church together with him, but remaining in the sect when Lammers deserted it and returned to the Church. Among the many things the sect disapproved of was literature, and Ole related in his old age that the only work of his brother's which he had read was some of *Brand* and a little of *Pillars of Society*.

But it was the parents of this large family who were soon and profoundly divided—for reasons we shall come to shortly. There has been a great deal of study and research into the sources of Henrik Ibsen's genius for interpreting the human mind in a concise artistic form. His relatives on both his father's and his mother's side have been relentlessly analysed and the most insignificant verses by anyone in the family have been painstakingly dissected. It can safely be said that all finds have been negative: that his mother in her youth studied several of the fine arts was simply the custom of the times, when refined young ladies were expected to be able to play the piano, recite, embroider, take part in amateur dramatics and also perhaps paint and draw a little.

Those who believe that genius like Henrik Ibsen's is hereditary must in his case believe in some kind of mutation or in the old Skien legend that it was not Knud Ibsen, but Tormod Knudsen, the Telemark poet, later a Member of Parliament, who was the child's father.

It is true that this latter theory is a very old one in Skien and was believed by several Norwegian scholars of the last century, but it is always treated with an almost touching discretion. Oscar Mosfjeld, in his book on Ibsen and Skien, was probably the first to grasp this nettle with some realism and tear it out by the roots, though even he had some doubts at first.

The theory is based on a number of pieces of evidence of unequal worth. The fact that the portraits of Tormod Knudsen show a certain likeness to Henrik Ibsen is the weakest, for the likeness is anything but obvious and there are several witnesses to the fact that in his old age Henrik Ibsen showed a strong likeness to his legitimate father. That Ibsen in his plays often portrayed painful family secrets of a similar nature is true enough, but he himself did not necessarily experience *every* tragedy about which he later wrote. It is notorious that Tormod Knudsen in his old age had boasted in his cups that he was Ibsen's father, but this was probably after the legend had become common knowledge. The talented Tormod Knudsen was abnormally sensitive to alcohol and it often made him boastful.

Though Tormod Knudsen, despite hardships, managed to make his way in the world, in his youth he was only a clerk in the sheriff's office in Kviteseid. It was here, in 1825, that he met Marichen Altenburg, who was already engaged to Knud Ibsen and was working for the sheriff as a servant, perhaps to perfect her domestic talents. If we presume that the engagement between Knud and Marken was one of convenience, arranged by Marken's father (who died before the wedding was held in the autumn) and Knud's stepfather, and if we go on to presume that Marken fell in love with this bright Kviteseid lad of twenty-eight—and all this is very probable—then naturally we have a sad, romantic tale to tell, for Tormod Knudsen's financial and social position at that time were not such as to make him acceptable as a son-in-law to the merchant Altenburg.

Knud and Marken married. They had a child in due course—no one has insinuated anything about this child—and Henrik was not born until Marken had been in Kviteseid for three years.

It is true that Tormod Knudsen often had to go to Skien for meetings and there was no hotel there until 1833, so he might well have stayed overnight at the Ibsens' hospitable home. But by the time Tormod Knudsen had got so far that he was speaking at meetings, Henrik Ibsen was almost fully grown.

The strongest argument in support of this rumour is that Christopher Due, one of Ibsen's friends from his apprentice days with the apothecary in Grimstad, is said to have related how once when Ibsen, Due and their friend Schulerud, were celebrating in the apothecary's back room, Henrik got drunk and spoke with great bitterness of his illegitimate origins. Due's statement, however, was made many years later and it is not certain whether Due himself was present at the party, so his memory may well have been at fault, though he is usually a reliable witness. More probably, however, the truth is that Knud, after his business failure, used to fly into rages and quarrel violently with his wife and that in one of these quarrels he made baseless accusations of infidelity with the peasant boy with whom she was said to have been in love. Henrik may have heard and believed the accusation, which would have increased a bitterness towards his family for which he had already plenty of good reasons. It is not at all likely that the suspicion was well founded.

So we must accept it as a fact that Marken and Knud Ibsen were Henrik's real parents and concern ourselves with establishing that Henrik's literary skill was not inherited but painfully achieved. Obviously, he was born with a remarkably good intellect but there is nothing unusual in an average family producing an outstanding mind. In any case, Henrik may have inherited from his parents more natural intelligence than they were able to give expression to in their own lives. Marken was too soon cowed and subdued. Knud frittered his life away first in superficial success and later in bitter resignation to adversity; but even so he became known as a clever man possessed of a biting wit.

The most remarkable thing about Henrik's childhood is that though he witnessed and endured many harrowing experiences, they did not—to use the jargon of today—make him 'maladjusted' or a psychopath. They do seem to have made him unusually vulnerable and sensitive for his years: already in early childhood he was deeply lonely, a brooder, an outsider—a 'nasty fellow', a 'prickly creature' as the local people called him. But he did not have recourse to the lonely child's usual armour of injured, passive failure to respond.

Not only in childhood, but for many years afterwards, his life was plagued with incessant failures, insults, humiliations and money troubles, and if he had died before he was thirty-six he would have been remembered as a talented playwright defeated by external opposition.

His few childhood memories hardly give an inkling of what he really *experienced*, and they are mostly from his earliest years before the horizons darkened. He does not speak of his family or his home life, but he does give a few glimpses of the town which had fastened in his childish mind, a few pictures of the interior of the church, a glimpse of Stockmann's from the church tower, and a few frightening details which made an impression on him, such as the pillory, which stood in all its horror in the square. He describes this in detail, although it had then long since been out of use as a form of punishment and anyhow he had never seen it in use. He is affected by the hideous proximity of the police-station with its cells in the cellar: the pale faces which he has seen there have made a lasting impression. Most of all his imagination is stirred by the 'lunatic-chest', a dark cellar with no lattice windows, only iron plates with ventilators between the crossbars, in which insane or dangerous criminals were incarcerated. None of this was visible, but what he heard of the fears which it inspired, he never forgot.

Among the things which he was not told about by others but really saw for himself were the fights between boys from the grammar school and the ordinary school—the good school and the less good school—which were near each other. He says laconically that he did not take part in them, as he did not go to either of the schools.

Then he adds:

'Skien was in my childhood an exceedingly happy and gregarious town, almost the opposite to what it became later. Many well-educated, prosperous and respected families lived there at the time, partly in the town itself, partly on the large estates round about.'

There follow a few ordinary memories of the Midsummer celebrations and the popular amusements at the annual 'fairs'.

We have to look elsewhere for the story of the Ibsen family during the prosperous times of his first seven years of life and the years of misfortune which followed, up to the time when, just after his confirmation, he left his native town, never to return, except for a short visit when he was twenty and another in the following year.

Knud Ibsen cut a dash from the moment he married. His father-in-law, Johan Altenburg, was already dead when the marriage between Knud and Marken took place. Everything that has been found in the way of documents about Knud Ibsen's business transactions in the following years—and there is no official record that has not been minutely inspected—shows that he had his wealthy mother-in-law in the hollow of his hand and disposed freely of the family fortunes.

What was his business? At first it was simply trading. No one has described this better than Dr Einar Østvedt:

'In the spacious Stockmann's House there were no less than ten rooms, and in addition to these there were large outhouses with a hayloft, brewery, stables and byre. . . . On the ground floor of the main building, Knud Ibsen carried on his mixed retail trade in the style of the time. From Bordeaux he imported brandy, French

red and white wines, sugar, almonds and spices. From London he
had cotton materials, woollen goods and wool, and from Altona
he brought both woollen goods and unbleached linen. Otherwise
he sold a number of different articles: glassware, ivory and horn
combs, brassware, mirrors, lace, pencils, optical instruments,
meerschaum pipes and silverware. But besides his town trade,
Knud Ibsen also exported to a considerable extent. He sent brandy
to other towns, timber cargoes to Denmark, and together with
the richest man in the district, Diderik von Cappelen, he exported
large quantities of timber to London. Within a few years he had
become one of Skien's biggest tax-payers.'

Perhaps the brown horse which, about fifty years later, Henrik
recalls having seen from the church tower was at first the *only*
horse that brought all these goods to and from the shop on the
ground floor. But later there were more and bigger horses.

When Henrik was only three years old, Knud Ibsen moved with
his family to the Altenburg estate. Østvedt calls it 'the mansion of
Altenburggården, which he had taken over from his mother-in-
law the year before (1830)'. At that time he also took over,
from his mother-in-law, Altenburg, quite a large country estate
near the town of Venstøp—which became his summer residence—
and, among other things, the distillery at Lundetangen. Mrs
Altenburg must have transferred the property to her two daughters. In the early years of her widowhood she was one of the
biggest tax-payers but later on her taxes were very small.

Now, it was no longer a question of working horses for the
transport of goods. Mrs Marken had her own riding-horse and
Knud probably had both a riding-horse and carriage horses. At
Venstøp and at Altenburggården social life was on a wealthy
man's scale, with parties that might last for several days, and with
drinking sprees and more ambitious banquets at which Mrs
Marken had outlets for her talent for artistic entertainment,
forms of social life which were not only characteristic of Skien
but also of most Norwegian towns in the latter half of the
eighteenth and the first half of the nineteenth century, when they
were sailing with economically favourable winds.

Skien was in many ways quite a cheerful town during these years, with visiting theatre companies, troupes of jugglers, clowns and other amusements.

At the end of the 1830s came the great crisis in the timber market and bankruptcies among many of the richest business people followed one after another. But Knud Ibsen crashed as early as in 1835 and then he had already spent at least a year fighting with his back to the wall. Over what eventually broke him completely there is some disagreement. There is talk of a large consignment of salt to Russia which failed. It is said that he lost large sums in the many shipwrecks during the particularly stormy winter of 1833–34, but of this we cannot be certain because of the unusual structure of the Norwegian shipping and export trade at that time. Insurance as we know it did not exist, and even the big people hesitated to invest too much in one ship. They took shares in each other. 'Little people' also had a chance to take shares, and in this way mutual insurance came into existence. If the ship sank, the loss of the ship and its cargo was shared by many. If the ship was lucky through two or three summer seasons, the shareholders were able to get their money back in full, plus their share in the profits.

But one heavy loss incurred by Knud Ibsen we do know about —the Lundetangen distillery. He took this over from his mother-in-law and wanted to modernize and expand it, but was unlucky in both. When it came to the large taxes the distillery had to pay the State, it was no use asking for credit, as in other businesses. When the taxes were not paid, the distillery was ruthlessly closed by the authorities and the vats sealed; he lost the distillery— the goose that was to lay the golden eggs. He was a ruined man. The mortgages he had taken out elsewhere were at once foreclosed.

As with many other Norwegian businessmen, who also had to suffer for it, Knud Ibsen had had access to extended foreign credit, and this he had received from, among others, a merchant banker in Hamburg, C. F. A. Kragelius. He had also borrowed a great deal of money from a businessman in Porsgrunn. And the mortgages were not mere trifles: his possessions, house, property and warehouses and all 'his chattels, furniture, cattle, farm tools, etc., with no exceptions' were pledged. His other creditors followed the State's lead and the auctioneer's hammer fell with regular blows on to everything he possessed.

He did not go bankrupt, it is important to note, and this saved his self-respect for the rest of his life; for it meant that he retained his honour and rights as a citizen. With the family's help he could go on living for the next eight years at Venstøp. But otherwise there was a total change in his social status and plainly in his family life too.

He was a finished man and everyone knew it. He was not free now to be arrogant, sharp, witty and flippant as he had been in his younger days. It is clear that all along he had been a tyrant in the home; now, reading between the lines of indulgent family tradition, one can see that he visited on his wife and children his bitterness at a failure which he considered undeserved.

Relatives imply that, in private, there was a kind of separation between Knud and Marken. It is pointed out that from 1835 onwards there were no more children, and this at a time when it was common for wives to go on giving birth until their climacteric. (As we shall see later, Henrik's own marriage followed much the same lines.)

The one thing on which everyone is in agreement is that Marken Ibsen became from then on a depressed and taciturn woman. Some say that she occasionally rebuked her husband, others that she was always quiet and subdued. This is hardly surprising in the daughter of a rich man suddenly condemned to face poverty with a bitter husband who was incapable of rebuilding their home and life together; more especially if she really had been forced into the marriage simply because her mother and his stepfather were brother and sister.

When we turn to Henrik, there is complete darkness over these important years of growth from seven to fifteen. He himself has never uttered a word about them. From other people we know that he played with a puppet theatre, that he painted and drew a little, that he was insolent too—especially when anyone mentioned his fatal demotion in society. We also know he bribed the farm boys from the neighbouring farm in Gjerpen, to avoid

walking with them on the way to school. These facts in themselves tell us something of the loft he must have created in his own
secret life, during the terrible loneliness between his ninth year
and his confirmation. The drama he experienced there he kept
to himself, but he never sublimated it, as we would say today. He
never adjusted to it, never forgave and never forgot. It left him
with an open wound from which he was able to write of human
tragedy with his own life's blood.

The few other indications of what those around him thought
of him at that time are partly vague and partly contradictory.
Some say he was thoughtful and read a great deal, others that he
was quick-tempered and intractable. In any case, he was as closed
as an oyster and it is clear that he was near to no one, at home or in
the world outside.

His sister Hedvig has given a good picture of him in a letter
written many years later, reproduced by Bergliot Ibsen in her
book *The Three*:

'To us others he was at that time not a nice boy, and we were
constantly disturbing him by throwing stones and snowballs at
walls and doors. We wanted him to play with us and when he
could no longer endure our attacks, he would rush out after us,
but as he had no skill in any kind of sport and as violence lay far
from his character, nothing ever came of it and he went back to
his cubicle when he had managed to get us far away.'

Where he went to school and what they taught him there is
also of scant interest, for there is nothing from his schooldays
that can be shown to have had any fruitful results. We must be
content to know that he had to go to school until his confirmation, but that any further education was financially out of the
question. There is little doubt that his ambitions lay in the direction of an academic career. He wanted to be a doctor, and this is
borne out by the fact that after confirmation he chose to be
apprenticed to an apothecary, which would at least give him a
certain grounding in Latin. That he dreamed of becoming a painter
is more unexpected. In those days in Norway, painters went from
house to house painting family portraits of the children of good

citizens in exchange for food, lodging and perhaps a few speciedalers.

Henrik was confirmed in the autumn of 1843. It is on record that Knud Ibsen fumed with rage because, as he had had no veal steak with which to bribe the priest, Henrik had to be content with third place instead of first, on the church floor. But he was confirmed all the same, and with that, at the age of fifteen, declared grown up and mature enough to earn his own living.

He could not stay in Skien, for he could not, like his father and his paternal grandfather, rely on good connections in the best society of the town to start him on a career.

A master mariner, who was a friend of the family and plied up and down the coast, knew an apothecary who required an assistant, Reimann, the apothecary in Grimstad. So Henrik left for Grimstad soon after Christmas, 1843, arriving early in January—he stayed there for more than six years, until he was twenty-two.

3

Six Years in Grimstad

COMPARED with Skien, Grimstad was almost a village, with a population under a quarter of that of Ibsen's native town. It had received the rights of a market town some years earlier, largely because it was a kind of centre for the building of sailing ships. But for Henrik Ibsen, only fifteen years old, it must have been like coming from a large inferno to a desolate little hell.

He came to a small town where neither he nor his family had any friends or connections. The apothecary with whom he was to live and work might have been a connecting link with the town, but proved to be nothing of the sort. In the three years he lived there, he made not a single friend of his own age, was not asked inside the doors of one of the 150 families who lived in the town and did not even have any contact with the family with whom he lived.

Apothecary Reimann was a man of about forty, somewhat indolent and self-absorbed, constantly impoverished and in debt, with a steadily increasing number of children, all so much younger than the apothecary's apprentice that there was no contact there either. He had a discontented, sickly, rather plump wife, who stayed at home most of the time, boxing the ears of her children and of the apprentice whenever the mood took her. Her husband was often out drinking. In an attempt to pay off what his apothecary's licence had cost him, he also took on the village sub-post office and managed the village's newly opened savings bank. To little avail.

Living conditions for the young apprentice were the worst possible. The house was in the poorest part of the town, and on the ground floor the family had two rooms and a rather small kitchen.

The one was the family's living-room and the other the apothecary's shop and the sub-post office; the kitchen was also the
dispensary. On the next floor there were two rooms and a small
closet. The Reimann parents slept in the inner room with the
smaller children. There was a communicating door to the boys'
room, where the family's three elder boys and Henrik Ibsen slept,
and from this room a door also led into the unheated closet where
the two servant-girls—later only one—were accommodated.
From their closet a very steep staircase led down into the apothecary's store.

There was no opportunity at all for Henrik to be by himself
indoors. During the day he had to serve in the shop and boil
medicines and mix valerian drops in the tiny kitchen, and at
night he slept in the boys' room. It is said that his basic luggage
when he came to Grimstad consisted of a large bag of books. In
Skien he had at least had his own small cubicle where he could
read and be on his own. Here he had not got even that.

His financial situation was wretched. No one has been able to
find out what he earned from Reimann. During his first years as
an apprentice it was presumably nothing, which was quite usual
at that time in other professions in which apprentices received
board and lodging; and he could not have had as much as a
shilling from home. His parents had not even been able to fit him
out with clothes other than the 'frock-coat' type of confirmation
suit, which must have attracted attention in Grimstad on the few
occasions he showed himself out of doors. It was remembered as
something peculiar, and was the only thing that was remembered
at all by those inhabitants of Grimstad who were questioned by
Ibsen scholars more than fifty years later. They said that the suit
was not replaced, becoming more and more worn and shiny,
till he looked like 'a tiled stove'. He refused to take his meals with
the family when they had company.

His position, if anything, grew worse with the years. When
eventually, after three years in Grimstad, he acquired a friend,
Christopher Due, Due was astonished at his hardiness; for he
possessed neither underclothes nor socks. And this was a boy
whose father had once been wealthy and who himself displayed a

finicky vanity in later years. We have it on the authority of the Reimanns' servant, who was questioned long afterwards when Ibsen had become world-famous, that the food was extremely bad. Once there was not even any food for Christmas dinner and despite Reimann's protests the girl had to go to a neighbour and borrow some.

What was an apothecary's shop like in such a small town in those days? The right to run one was, as in so many other professions, dependent on a 'privilege'. In larger towns this right to deal in medicines was a great source of revenue, a gold-mine which could be handed down through the generations. In a remote place like Grimstad, it was anything but lucrative. The large majority of the people who lived scattered round the district died natural deaths, without the help of doctors or apothecaries, and themselves prepared—with the wise woman's help— the few medicines or other medicaments which according to old beliefs would cure most illnesses. But naturally Apothecary Reimann also had a certain trade in similar medicines, and in the summer the apprentice was sent out into the forests and fields to gather medicinal herbs and roots, which were then dried and boiled and mixed in the little kitchen, to become pills, powders and mixtures.

But there were also many spices and other goods which Reimann had to buy in the county town, and this caused him to fall more and more deeply into debt. He also sold a number of groceries such as sugar, cocoa, wine, spirits and spices.

What Henrik Ibsen really learned during those years we do not know, though we do know a little about the meagre literature to which he had access through a reading circle to which Reimann belonged. We know, too, that the stout, easy-going apothecary also helped him to learn the elementary Latin vocabulary required for the apothecary's trade and for medicinal botany, for during the winter of 1845–46 he went into Arendal and sat for an examination conducted by the then town physician—a test which was presumably a much simpler version of today's pharmaceutical examinations. Otherwise there is nothing to show that during those first three years he came anywhere near to realizing his dream of an academic career.

B

Nothing momentous happened to Henrik till 1846 when he was eighteen and had been with the apothecary for two years. Then, one of the young servant-girls, Sofie—Else Sofie Jensen—became pregnant, and the inescapable conclusion was that the young apprentice was responsible. We do not know whether the relationship between Henrik and Sofie, ten years his senior, was just a chance encounter or based on anything more stable. All we know is that in the winter the door between the girls' unheated closet and the boys' room stood open, for otherwise it would have been too cold for the girls, and in addition if someone came to the shop at night, the assistant had to go through the servants' room to reach the steep stairs. Anyhow the two of them must have kept each other warm, and the consequences were natural enough, but in the circumstances unfortunate for both of them, disgracing them in the public eye.

Sofie was quite simply sent home to her parents. There, on October 9th, she gave birth to a son, whom she called Hans Jakob Henriksen. The child's father was, by 'county resolution', made to pay maintenance for the boy until he was fourteen years of age: so he was still paying maintenance for his son after he had married his Suzannah. It is easy to understand what a humiliating burden this must have been to an impoverished, ambitious youth, who was jealous of his honour.

But other misfortunes afflicted the apothecary at this time. Financially Reimann went steadily downhill. For his debt to the apothecary in the capital, who was the supplier of medicines, he had mortgages to the tune of three thousand speciedalers, and in the autumn of 1846 his creditor had the business sold by auction, but received only 2,100 speciedalers of his outstanding debt. Soon after that the new owner of the privilege sold both privilege and shop to a young Grimstad man of well-to-do parents, Lars Nielsen, who himself had been a pupil of Reimann's, and later assistant in the apothecary in Arendal. He paid 2,500 speciedalers for it. A little while later Apothecary Reimann applied for, and was given, the post of Controller of Spirits in Kristiania, a position which must have suited his disposition and tendencies much better than running an apothecary shop.

When Lars Nielsen took over the business at the beginning of 1847, there was a great change for the better in Henrik's private life. Nielsen moved the business to new and more agreeable surroundings. He was unmarried, only four years older than Ibsen, and usually lived at home with his parents, so Ibsen ruled alone over the back room. There he could work and was left in peace and quiet, and what is more, he had opportunities for some social life with his friends. But he was nineteen before he reached that stage.

His earnings must have continued to be small, giving him little to spend after his maintenance order had been paid, for he was still noticeably badly dressed and had to show that 'hardiness' of which Due speaks. But *some* money must have passed through his hands, as he began to receive private tuition from a young theologian in the town, and in addition he enlarged the scope of his severely restricted but somewhat intense social life in his room. No doubt it did not cost him much, particularly as he was well placed for concocting his own drinks. But it must have cost him something.

He only made two friends, but they were enough to form a *milieu* in which events and thoughts could develop and blossom, in which ideas and opinions could be whetted against each other, in which spiritual growth occurred with an almost explosive force.

The first friend was Christopher Due, who had come to Grimstad in 1845 as a clerk in the customs office. A little later, an acquaintance asked him if he would like to go and look at the peculiar apothecary assistant who never showed himself out of doors. Due went in and bought four shillings worth of adhesive tape and describes Ibsen in the following way: '. . . quite a small young man, with an attractively lively face. I would like to say here that Ibsen in his youth had an unusually prematurely developed smooth brown beard, which gave his face a vigorous and at the same time harmonious expression. . . .'

No friendship was struck up on that occasion; it was quite out of the question in Reimann's house as things were. Not until the business was moved and the back room offered opportunities for company was the friendship fully developed, and as Due himself says, he became a daily visitor. Due was a year older than Ibsen.

Friend number two, Ole Carelius Schulerud, came to the town that same summer of 1847. He was also a year older than Ibsen and had begun his law studies in Kristiania. He was the son of Christopher Due's superior, Senior Customs Officer Schulerud, who had also recently moved there. A customs officer's wage must have been insufficient to keep a son studying in Kristiania, so Ole came home to his parents after the summer of 1847 to continue studying law on his own. He was successful too, for after two years' study at home in Grimstad, he returned to the capital, completed his law studies and became a barrister at a High Court; but he died in 1859, only thirty-two years old.

The three-year period that followed must have been the happiest and richest epoch in Henrik Ibsen's life, despite the fact that his circle of friends were all 'as poor as church mice'. Due was so badly paid that now and again he had to go without dinner, Schulerud was kept so short of pocket-money that it hardly stretched to a cigar at rare intervals and Ibsen was so poor that he went without a winter coat, underclothes or stockings. Opportunities for launching out were therefore very limited. But Ibsen's spirit flourished. He grew cheerful and merry, wrote epigrams and libellous verses and drew caricatures, drank punch and argued so recklessly that it echoed round Grimstad. He also took part in youthful brawls in the town. As he wrote later: 'It was not in my power to express everything that was bubbling inside me except through foolish pranks and brawls, which brought on me the disapproval of all the respectable citizens who could not put themselves in the world in which I was struggling about on my own.' Professor Koht is probably right in saying that perhaps in memory Ibsen sees himself rather too much as the leader of these youthful escapades. Others have related that while he was no doubt clever at thinking up mischief, he held himself very much in the background when it was enacted. 'He probably preferred being a spectator—in Grimstad, as in Skien', writes Koht with endearing irony.

He was anything but cowed in his relationship to his employer, the kindly Lars Nielsen, who was more like an older friend and who, having many other ploys, confidently left him in charge of most of the apothecary's business. Ibsen had dinner every day at Nielsen's parents' house, and when there were guests in the home, they liked to invite Ibsen too. They let the servant-girl watch over the shop and run the few yards to fetch the apothecary or his assistant if necessary. Through Nielsen, he was also introduced into Grimstad's better society, which hitherto had been hermetically sealed against him. Ibsen could also at times make gentle fun of his employer, whom in front of his friends he often called 'the beast'.

So they were cheerful and lively times in the evenings in the back room, over a toddy or a punch, served in ointment jars, which, when strangers appeared, were hurriedly emptied and stuffed into pockets.

Discussions ranged over every subject between heaven and earth, as other alert, well-connected Grimstad youths were later graciously allowed to join what must have seemed a revolutionary centre in the town. Due's account of Ibsen's opinion of marriage undoubtedly belongs to this, the earliest and most immature stage of their friendship. Everything was discussed: 'So not least marriage. Among Ibsen's more extravagant jokes I remember that with a certain ardour he asserted that he and his eventual wife would have to live on separate floors, meeting only at mealtimes and addressing each other in the second person plural. At that time this was his ideal of marriage.'

Perhaps the unfortunate affair with Sofie was the thorn in his flesh? Another of Due's anecdotes has an even stronger connection with Ibsen's view of life at the time, but there is a certain irony in it when one considers his later life. Due is talking of Ibsen's great talent for illustrating—a talent he later exploited in his early days in Kristiania: 'He hated all orders. One day he showed me two drawings, the first of which portrayed a plump gentleman— presumably after a good dinner—sitting asleep in an armchair, while over his head floated a cloud from which a hand, holding an Order of the Star, is protruding. The next drawing shows the new knight, who has just woken and is surprised to see the Star on his chest. He brings his hand to his head and exclaims: "What? An Order? Why? How?" He finds however, the answer very soon. "Of course, I've been asleep." '

During those years, Ibsen became not only a very rebellious enemy of the society with 'empty brains and full purses', the circles which had overlooked and despised him since he had come to the town—now he dared tread on their toes—but also an enemy of society in general, of the Church and Christianity. Revolutionary currents were running through Europe at that time. In France the February Revolution broke out and collapsed in 1848, and in Hungary the rising occurred in the same year. Ibsen had also acquainted himself with all the anti-conventional literature he could lay his hands on, from Kierkegaard to Voltaire. The opinions which he expressed in the evenings in the guardroom of the apothecary's shop surprised and shocked many people, but he was not afraid to air his views. He and he alone in Grimstad was a free thinker, the only one to dare to renounce and challenge God, society and the bourgeoisie.

Two more small items cast light on Ibsen's wholly new attitude to life at this time.

The first is recorded by Due and describes Ibsen's introduction into the social life of the town. Through the Nielsen family he had already met several people from the good bourgeoisie, among others a friend of Apothecary Nielsen's mother, an elderly Scottish-born lady, Miss Crawfurd, who was well-read and owned an extensive library, of which her young friend made constant use. It was, however, his friend Due who dragged Ibsen with him to his first ball. Due says there had hitherto been an insurmountable obstacle to getting Ibsen to join in the social gatherings which were now and again arranged by the town's more prosperous youth: he had no 'frock'. Finally the problem was solved: he got credit for a frock-coat. This surprised him considerably, and when he received the bill for it the following year, he exclaimed: 'First he's stupid enough to give me credit and then he is stupid enough to expect me to pay the bill.' The bill, however, was paid.

When he got to the ball, it proved almost impossible to get him out on to the dance-floor. He had in fact never danced before, and was also notoriously unmusical, virtually tone-deaf. 'But we managed, with his partner's and other benevolent assistance, to get the couple setting off at a swift gallop, though at first with some difficulty, but nevertheless without noticeable calamity. . . .'

Mention should also be made of his studies. We know that, since the beginning of 1848, he had been writing essays in Norwegian for a private teacher in Kristiania, Paul Stub. Three of these essays have been preserved. One is entitled 'The Importance of Self-Knowledge', another, for which he was better qualified from his own harsh experience, 'Work Has Its Own Reward'. He also began to take coaching in Latin and Greek from two theology students who lived in Grimstad—from C. S. Monsen and, above all, from Emil Bie. He also read a number of other subjects on his own without the help of teachers, his aim throughout being to embark on an academic career. So, all in all, notwithstanding that those last three years in Grimstad had been luminous and rich, and had helped to mature and inspire him, they must also have been years of incredible hardship. He must have been sustained in his labours by an iron will, irrepressible energy and indefatigable patience. He put the same sullen energy to use later on in his plays, refusing to give in until he had plumbed the depths of the human beings and human conflicts he wished to portray.

Discussions between the triumvirate in the back room undoubtedly came to centre more and more on literature, poetry and writing. Once again we must turn to Due's anecdotal and all too discreet, but fascinating, sketches of those days. Of course we must not forget that they were not written until about sixty years after; but Due is the only eye-witness we have. The other friend, Schulerud, died seven years before Ibsen became famous in Scandinavia, and has left behind no records of his time in Grimstad.

Due relates that only a few weeks after they had become real friends, he confided to Ibsen that he indulged in the secret vice of writing verse. Ibsen was at once interested and asked to be allowed to hear some of it. Not until after that did the cautious

Ibsen admit that *he* too wrote verse, and read some aloud to Due. But Due's memory is at fault when he alleges that at this early date (in 1847) as the Grimstad correspondent of the *Christiana Post* (Grimstad had no paper of its own) he sent that paper one of Ibsen's poems, and that this poem, 'In Autumn', was the first of Ibsen's writings to appear in print.

In reality, although Ibsen was already writing poetry in 1847, the first known poems from his hand dated from 1848. The poem 'In Autumn' which Due, to Ibsen's immeasurable delight, had printed in the *Christiana Post*, was not published until September 28, 1849, after he had written many poems which we now know, after *Catiline* was finished and after Schulerud had taken Due's copy of the play with him to Kristiania, in the hope of finding a publisher there.

This confusion in time is in itself of little importance, but the importance to the young poet of his first appearance in print, Ibsen has himself described in his poem 'Building Plans', written in 1853, in which he speaks of his 'blessed self-complacency'.

But he did not experience this self-complacency until a couple of years later, after the publication of several more poems. Due's own poetry was undoubtedly quenched, and he relapsed into silent admiration of the triumvirate's unchallenged intellectual and lyrical central figure, Henrik Ibsen.

The earliest poem that has been preserved is 'Resignation', written in 1847 and included in *Posthumous Writings*. It is touchingly simple; but it is derivative work, reminiscent of several other poems, including Wergeland's brilliant 'Follow the Call'. Yet in that it inaugurates Ibsen's literary life-work, it is the stirring first chord in one of the world's greatest symphonies.

Other poems were passed round among the group of friends; some have been preserved, but most have vanished and are probably no great loss. Ibsen is said to have written poems to several people in Grimstad, and circulated them beyond the apothecary's back room. He loved, from afar, several of the town's pretty girls, especially Clara Ebbell, whose admiration and favour he tried to win by the indirect approach of poetry.

But after a while the interests of this circle of friends must have turned towards *drama*, an art form more congenial to their extrovert interest in what was happening at the time, the breaches between new and old thoughts and ways, the revolutions, the struggles against authority.

There have been so many revolutions in history, both at superficial and at deeply significant levels. What is called 'The Great Revolution', in France in 1789, was the revolution of the Third Estate, the breakthrough of the citizens, which brought with it a change in the whole structure of society. The next great revolution, the Fourth Estate, began bloodily in these very years, with the February Revolution in France, later in the Paris Communes in 1870, and finally with the Russian Revolution. The Fourth Estate tried to turn the tables on the Third Estate, which had now become the rulers of society.

That Ibsen's sympathy was on the side of the February Revolution is natural enough, just as his sympathy later was with the Thranite Movement. His numbed and starved hatred for all the authorities he had met in his life, both inside and outside his home, made him identify himself with all rebels, down to Kierkegaard and Voltaire, against the Church and oppression from the authority of religion, and also against the monarchy and all that tended to enslave.

His choice of *Catiline* as his first dramatic piece was no doubt influenced by his private Latin studies, when he must have read Cicero and Sallust. In *Catiline* he found a rebel after his own heart, comprehensible alike to the upper-class boy and to the apothecary's apprentice who had come down in the world. Spartacus, the *real* slave who caused the world's most famous rebellion, lived at about the same time. In the twentieth century he became canonized as a saint and martyr for the socialist movement all over the world. But Ibsen had not even heard of him.

Ibsen conceived the idea for *Catiline* towards the end of 1848 and began to write early in the new year. How soon he imparted his great aspirations to the other members of the triumvirate is not clear. Due says that one evening they were sitting together in the apothecary's shop and Ibsen surprised his friends 'with a highly interesting piece of information, namely that he was writing a play, *Catiline*, definitely for performance'. When his friends heard Ibsen's 'fervent account of the play, in which his republican sympathies made themselves felt through the rebel Catiline's wild and audacious plans ...' his listeners naturally became infected with Ibsen's enthusiasm. It is highly likely that Ibsen, young, and drunk with the joy of creation, initiated his friends *before* the writing had begun; he had already made the brief sketch of the plot which is to be found in *Posthumous Writings*—but anyhow his friends' fervour and excitement increased as he read to them what 'between each time he had written, until—judgement'.

Due, with self-effacing modesty, has explained that the listeners only praised and admired; and no doubt they did not offer much criticism. All the same, there must have been vigorous arguments and discussions about characters, events and dramatic forms; and these must have forced Ibsen to articulate, explain and defend his ambitions and intentions. The meetings with his friends in the early months of 1849 thus played a vital part in helping Ibsen to mature.

Detailed analysis of *Catiline* is outside the scope of this book. Suffice it to say that it is not a particularly successful play. It was reasonable that the theatre rejected it and understandable that publishers refused it—though when one compares it with the contemporary work of respected writers, one would think that a publisher with a 'good nose' ought to have sensed that here was something new, and not without talent. *Catiline* is full of influence and direct loans, both from models Ibsen has since acknowledged, such as Oehlenschläger, and those he had forgotten, like Schiller, and of course, there is also the direct and indirect influence of Shakespeare. Nevertheless in some ways the play foreshadowed Ibsen's later masterpieces.

In the first place, *Catiline* obviously changed during the several hectic months of its creation. It was conceived as pure propaganda, almost in the Brechtian manner, for republic, revolution, rebellion. In the first sketch the hero's implied scruples have no dramatic function but to increase the suspense and excitement:

such things were done by both Shakespeare and Schiller, not to
mention the anti-dramatists of today. But it gradually changes
into a *psychological* play, because Ibsen takes his hero steadily
more seriously and tries to get to the bottom of his dissension
with himself. His final fall is not brought about as revolutionary
ideas would dictate: he is not the victim of evil authority, but of
his own inner weakness, as a logical consequence of his past and
his own split nature, personified in the play's two women.
Catiline is thus more closely related to Ibsen's masterpieces than
several of his later plays, in which he consciously aimed at making
the plays 'take' on the stage by pandering to the tastes of the time.

What marks Ibsen out as the creator of a new epoch in drama
is that he resumes the *merciless logic* which is characteristic of
classical tragedy, but which for centuries had been largely cast
aside. He cultivates a form in which the external circumstances
perhaps set the action going, but thereafter the wheels of logic
roll on mercilessly towards the climax. There are no curses from
the gods or demi-gods who ruthlessly draw people towards them
and death, but a curse from their own past and character, which
with the same consistent psychological conformity decides their
destiny. In this direction *Catiline* shows clear indications of
Ibsen's future brilliance.

Of the play's relationship to the historic events it describes, he
himself writes in the foreword that they are only a pretext 'for
the ideas running through the play'.

Twenty-five years later, when he had become famous, he took
up his first work again and prepared a revised jubilee edition.
This may seem surprising, for at that distance of time and in the
light of his later development, the play must inevitably have
seemed both clumsy and incapable of being acted. But he had a
weakness for it. And he was right in his assessment:

'The content of the book in detail I had almost forgotten, but on
re-reading it I found that it still contained a good deal which I
could own to, particularly if one takes into consideration that it is
my first work. A great many things which my later writing has
revolved round—the contradiction between ability and aspira-

tions, between will and opportunity, humanity's and the individual's combined tragedy and comedy—appear already here in indistinct suggestions. . . .'

The jubilee foreword to *Catiline*, which tells of the play's creation and history, is one of the most open-hearted and amusing autobiographical notes that exists from Ibsen's hand. Amongst other things he says that many people of Grimstad:

'. . . found it extremely peculiar that a young person in my subordinate position could occupy himself with discussion of things which not even they themselves dared have any opinions on. I owe it to the truth to add that my behaviour, in various circumstances, did not justify particularly much hope that in me society might count on any increase in bourgeois virtues, as with both epigrams and caricature drawings I had offended many people who deserved better of me, and whose friendship I basically appreciated.'

The atmosphere of those last happy years in Grimstad comes through these lines, as, from a distance of twenty-six years at a time of renewed growth, progress and triumphs, he looks back and sees in perspective the only earlier period which was filled with confidence and optimism.

So *Catiline* was finished in the spring of 1849. The triumvirate, who, though they may seem touchingly naïve to us today, were really alert, intelligent and full of fire, rightly sensed that something great had happened: the oppressed and famished little apprentice had gone for good and one of the world's greatest writers was on his way.

It is not to be wondered at that Christopher Due and Ole Schulerud were caught up in Ibsen's own creative excitement and lost in uncritical enthusiasm for the work and the man. This was not the time to criticize details or bring up doubts and afterthoughts. Now the world must have a share in it as quickly as possible.

It is characteristic of this hectic, explosive, youthful epoch that Ibsen, who was later to spend months polishing his plays, word by word, dashed off the manuscript in such a careless hand that Due, whose office experience had made him a fine writer, set to and copied it all out, so that it would be legible for publishers and theatres. In the foreword to the second edition in 1875, Ibsen, after smiling a little at the fact that the play was written at night and therefore is played out almost wholly at night-time, says:

'First and foremost it was now to be rewritten, under a pseudonym, to be submitted to the theatre in Kristiania, and then it was to be made public by printing. One of my faithful confidants undertook to deliver a clear and fine copy of my roughly written sketch, a task which he carried out to a degree of conscientiousness that he did not forget a single one of the innumerable dashes, which in the heat of creation I had put in all over the place, when the right expression did not at that moment occur to me.'

The plan was now that Schulerud should take Due's copy with him when he returned to Kristiania to study in the autumn of 1849, and there deliver it to the Christiania Theatre, which the triumvirate assumed would want to put it on at once. As a pseudonym to hide behind he had chosen the poetic name of Brynjulf Bjarme.

Meanwhile Ibsen struggled on with various forms of writing— a one-act play entitled *The Norsemen* and a sketch for a play about Olav Trygvason was ready to be shown to his friends before Schulerud left. He also wrote several poems during 1849, but they are more romantically conventional than glowing with inner fervour.

The summer of 1849 came and went. Schulerud returned to the capital and Ibsen waited in uncertainty and excitement. In this state he must have written an uncontrolled and stupid letter to his faithful friend, as in the next letter he begs Schulerud to forgive him and asks him to burn the offending letter, which Schulerud must loyally have done. For meanwhile two things happened. Ibsen, as has been said before, had experienced the joy of seeing his first poem in the paper, but on the other hand he had received a polite but negative reply from the management of the theatre, and it was about this that Schulerud had written.

We are now in January, 1850. In letter number two, Ibsen

accepts unconditionally Schulerud's alternative plan of trying to get *Catiline* published so that at least it could be read if the theatre was right in saying that it could not be staged. By this time Schulerud must already have suggested that if they could not find a publisher, they could together pay for the printing, thus keeping any profits themselves. Ibsen had no money, of course, so he warned them strongly against going into anything so risky. But Schulerud's enthusiasm was not be be quenched. After every conceivable publisher had refused the play, he himself, with a small legacy, paid for the printing of 250 copies. Ibsen quotes him as saying—partly out of genuine enthusiasm, partly in jest:

'. . . that with this promising outlook for the future, he was thinking of giving up his studies completely, to be able to devote himself to the publishing of my works, two or three plays a year, and as a result of the calculation of probabilities he had made, he had come to the conclusion that on the profits, we would shortly be able to undertake the journey through Europe and the Orient so often agreed upon and discussed between the three of us.'

Schulerud's 250 copies came out in the spring of 1850. About forty were sold. Most of the remainder, unbound, were later sold by Ibsen and Schulerud as wrapping paper when one day they found themselves penniless in Kristiania.

That exciting winter of 1849–50 Ibsen continued various kinds of literary experiment. But it seems that after the triumvirate dispersed Due ceased to be an active source of inspiration, though he continued to be a stimulating reading-forum. In letters to Schulerud, Ibsen says that he is working over the two plays that had been planned before his friend left, and that he has found new material of which perhaps something may come. There is in existence the rough draft of the beginning of a play, *The Prisoner at Agerhuus*, dealing with the Lofthus rising in Lillesand in the 1780s, a fund of dramatic material, which no one has since made use of. We do not know if the first scenes of a play entitled *The Ptarmigan of Justedal* were already written before Schulerud left Grimstad; but it is probable, for when Ibsen first went to Kristiania, he had enough to struggle with for a time.

It has not been established how he managed to finance his reckless attempt to acquire an academic education, beginning by going through Heltberg's 'student-factory' in Kristiania, and going on studying with his matriculation as a basis. He himself had no money. He was probably given a few dalers by his kindly employer Nielsen when he left his service. Due has said that Ibsen was very pleased about this settlement, but it cannot possibly have been enough to pay for his keep in Kristiania and his school fees. Knud Ibsen was presumably not at this time in a position to help Henrik at all, but it is conceivable that a Paus uncle promised him money, and even gave him some.

However that may be, he left Grimstad in April, 1850, and stayed for a few weeks in his native town of Skien before going on to Kristiania. He had been undecided about the detour from Brevik, where the regular steamer called, for he was not certain whether his father wanted him to come home. Several reasons have been suggested for this odd state of affairs, among others that his father, despite everything, had been involved in scraping together the money he needed to take a matriculation course, and that Henrik did not want to put him to the extra expense of paying for the journey. It is more likely that the relationship between Henrik and his father had already reached a kind of breach during the holiday which Henrik had spent in his native town in 1848, about which we know nothing. Also, Henrik knew that life at home was extremely disturbed and inharmonious and he must have had a natural reluctance to view these difficulties at close quarters.

A letter from Hedvig or his mother made him change his mind; but his reception must have been terribly depressing and disappointing, for he never again set foot in his native town—not even after his parents were dead, when his town wanted to honour its world-famous son.

Perhaps a contributory reason for this trip to Skien may have been the hope that he would be able to raise some more capital in order to continue his studies after matriculation; for some of his father's half-brothers and sisters were well off. But if he did ask, he was refused. It is much more likely that what the lonely young man secretly hoped for and expected was some affection from his mother and sister, somewhere in the world where he, too, could feel at home. He had had to do without this at Grimstad—and even long before he left home at fifteen—but being still very young, no doubt he could not help hoping against hope that there was still something left of warmth and security there in his childhood's secret loft.

But he did not find it. No financial help; no personal contact of significance with his father or mother. Only with his sister Hedvig was he on speaking terms. The years of separation had turned the gulf into an insuperable chasm. He himself had found his vocation as a writer, after struggling through his lonely youthful years. He had laboriously built up a perception of life which was not Christian, and in most fields was diametrically opposed to the conventional ideas of the time. His family had gone a completely different way, to shield themselves from life's slings and arrows. His younger brothers and sisters, his mother also to some extent, had been seized by the religious fervour inspired by Lammers the priest, which all that winter had been setting men's minds alight in southern Telemark. Headed by his sister Hedvig, the family had been converted and put their trust in a stern God who would be their Saviour. Not his fifty-three-year-old father, for this fervour had not bitten deeply into him, but the rest of the family were strengthened by an active faith.

Henrik made some fumbling attempts to get his sister Hedvig to see matters from his point of view; and Hedvig also made energetic attempts to convert Henrik. Neither of them had any luck. But it at least brought them on speaking terms and he did not wholly lose contact with her, though she is said to have caused him irritation later on by letters begging him to be converted.

Hedvig has told of a trip up to Bratsberg, where Henrik told her all the great things he was going to do with his life. 'And when you have got there, what will you do then?' she asked. 'Then I'll die,' he replied. The violent collision of opinions of two young people, both inarticulate and rigid, is charged with enough drama to deserve a place in his later writings.

Many years later he wrote to Bjørnson, 'I have all my life drawn away from my own parents, from my whole family, because I could not remain in a state of semi-understanding.' So when, on April 27th, he boarded the steamer *Prince Carl* in Brevik to travel on to Kristiania, he may well have had great expectations of the future, but behind him life was dark.

4

Student Days in Kristiania

Catiline came out the day before Ibsen left the apothecary's so he must have had a copy either sent there beforehand, or posted on to him at Skien for he would hardly have had the patience to wait for weeks before seeing his first book. If he had it when he was at Skien, it can only have added to the disappointment of the visit, as Lammers' followers disapproved of literature, and therefore might have looked on the newly published masterpiece as something sinful and improper.

When on April 28 he stepped ashore at Kristiania, *Catiline* had at least been reviewed—only in the Norwegian Student Union's handwritten paper *Union News*, but the criticism was very appreciative and written by the paper's editor, Paul Botten-Hansen, who later became a close friend and ally of Ibsen's, until his death in 1869 at the early age of forty-five.

Early in May Ibsen started work at Heltberg's crammer, that remarkable school from which so many intellectual leaders of the time benefited as a short cut to matriculation. Both Jonas Lie and Bjørnson later paid sonorous homage to 'Old Heltberg' (he was then a man in his middle forties), and Bjørnson's poem about the school, apart from mentioning Vinje, Jonas Lie and Henrik Ibsen by name, also conveys atmosphere and describes Heltberg himself. He speaks of 'Massive bearded men sitting beside youths of seventeen', 'powerful seamen whose adventurous minds had sent them out into the world', and who have come back to the school bench, and 'bankrupt merchants who, hidden behind their desks, have wooed their books' and are now studying on loans. And he says of Heltberg, tormented by gout and asthma, 'he threw out strong thoughts and he did not throw low'.

H-16319 7

Even if time has made Bjørnson seem to over-dramatize a little and amongst other things to exaggerate Ibsen's pallor in order to find a rhyme, the poem does give a vivid picture of the inspiring milieu in which he and Ibsen found themselves, first at Heltberg's and, for those who passed the examination, later on in the Norwegian Student Union.

People who were virtually beginners in the art of reading had to reckon with two years at Heltberg's, but Ibsen had chosen the shortest course of all, which lasted only three months. Presumably his money would not suffice for more, but he must have been a compulsive optimist to calculate that such a short time would be needed to perfect himself in subjects he had been unable to learn on his own or for which he could not get coaching in Grimstad. He especially lacked Greek and Latin, and when he took his matriculation examination at the end of August, 1850, the results were not good.

He passed the examination in fact, with the lowest possible marks, but he failed in both Greek and arithmetic, with a six in each subject, and thus he was not able to matriculate into the university until he had taken these two subjects again. He must have felt especially bitter at getting only a three, or just 'good', for his mother tongue.

He did not retake the subjects he had failed in and so never entered for the university. The fact that he later received his degree as honorary doctor—and insisted on always being addressed as Doctor—is quite another story. In 1850 he had no chance to support himself and study at the same time, but nevertheless the examination was very important to him. He could call himself 'Student Ibsen', which at that time and in that remote country gave rise to considerable respect. But it was even more important to him that through the examination he could become a member of the Student Union, for it was still there that the intellectual élite of the youth of the day met together and struggled through their days of 'Sturm und Drang'. It was there that a young writer with intense interest in the problems of the day had something to learn and something to give. He did not neglect opportunities in either of these directions.

WEST GEORGIA REGIONAL LIBRARY
HEADQUARTERS

He had not in fact concentrated entirely on his studies during the summer course at Heltberg's. As soon as he arrived in Kristiania he threw himself with great enthusiasm into several things in which he was interested, one of them, of course, being his writing, to which we shall return later. He soon moved in with his friend Schulerud, who then lodged in the house of Mother Saether, at the time a well known and respected 'wise woman', though now she would perhaps be called a quack; and Ibsen's pharmaceutical knowledge and Mother Saether's activities as a healer must have provided mutual interests. He was no doubt allowed to share Ole Schulerud's rooms in the attic very cheaply, in exchange for instructing her son. A painting by Ibsen which she is said to have owned was probably in lieu of part of the rent. She lived on the corner of two streets called Philosophy Way and Angle Street (apposite enough names for a home for Ibsen), in Vika, an area later demolished to make way for Oslo City Hall, which in the middle of last century was a very poor suburb of Kristiania. It is probable that Vika even at that time had a reputation for prostitution, bohemian life and jugglers, for which it later came to be notorious. The neighbouring area was sheer slum, known as the 'Robber States of Algiers and Tunis', and was demolished a couple of decades later by a rich Consul-General who was ashamed because it would have been from just *this* particular sight that the Swedish–Norwegian monarch, King Oscar II, would get his first impression of the capital on his arrival. So he bought the whole area and built the towering Victoria Terrace of large grand apartments, where, incidentally, Ibsen also was to live for four whole years after he had become famous, at the time of his triumphant return home after twenty-seven years abroad.

But back to Vika. There were cheap lodgings to be found there for poor immigrants and students such as Schulerud and Ibsen. Another student, Theodor Abildgaard, who was reading law, lived at the same place and Ibsen must soon have made friends with him. Abildgaard was to mean a great deal to him a year later, for through him, Ibsen was thrust headlong into the rising political storm.

A month after he had come to the town, he went to his first

political meeting, in Klingensberg Hall, a few hundred yards from his lodgings. The meeting was being held in protest against the expulsion of a socialist 'agitator' called Harro Harring, who originally came from Holstein, but had since been a political emigrant, speaker and journalist in many countries. Now Harring had come to Norway to make contact with the Thranite Movement, which was then in full swing, but he had been expelled as a danger to the community. The meeting passed an indignant protest, with 146 signatures, among them Ibsen's, Vinje's and Bjørnson's, and the protest was taken to the Minister of Justice by a procession of demonstrators. Protest demonstrations of today have the best of prototypes. It is clear that it was Abildgaard who had brought Ibsen to the meeting, for Abildgaard was an enthusiast for the movement and the following year took a leading position in it, which eventually cost him many years in prison.

An epoch in Norway's history was created in those years through this political movement, which grew so swiftly that it frightened the life out of the King, the government, the judiciary and the bourgeoisie, as if it were a crass revolutionary rebellion. Later it was looked upon as an almost touchingly romantic and idealistic attempt, for the first time in the New Norway, to organize the Fourth Estate, the workers, into defending their most elementary human rights. It was ruthlessly crushed, and not until thirty years later were new attempts made, and then the snowball did not allow itself to be stopped.

As has been mentioned before, in 1848 the February Revolution had raged over France, and had been crushed. It was for that revolution that Marx and Engels wrote their famous communist manifesto, and during that year it was translated into a great number of languages. When in December, 1848, Marcus Thrane began to form workers' unions, he was not aware of it, but he did know of other socialist literature of the time.

Thrane was considered a talented young writer when in the autumn of 1848 he was appointed as editor of *Drammens Adresse*. He had no doubt always held radical opinions, but the clever printer who published the paper considered him harmless. Thrane became anything but harmless, for the reality which he found in

Drammens Valley and Buskerud made his idealistic social opinions flare up into fury.

There were crises all around him: there was a great deal of unemployment in the new industrial Norway, and even those who had work were so wretchedly paid that they lived on the verge of starvation. Marcus Thrane rolled up his sleeves and set about producing increasingly challenging articles. Cancellations of subscriptions rained down round the ears of the printer and by the New Year of 1849 Thrane had been given the sack. But by then he was busy organizing the workers into unions and publishing his own weekly paper, the *Workers' Union News*. Grimstad was also among the places where he started a union, so Ibsen must have known of his activities before he came to Kristiania.

Ibsen never allied himself completely with the Thranite Movement, or any other collective movement, but he had great sympathy for it and was in agreement with many of its views. Both he and his friend Vinje became contributors to the *Workers' Union News* and when in the winter of 1850–51 Abildgaard began a 'Sunday school' for workers, both Vinje and Ibsen became teachers in it.

However, yet another great event, on September 26, 1850, occurred shortly after his matriculation exam. That day Brynhulf Bjarme, alias Henrik Ibsen, had his first play performed on the stage. This was the one-act play *The Norsemen* which he had written in Grimstad, but for the completion of which after his arrival in Kristiania he must have stolen several hours from his studies. The assertion that he did this during his brief Whitsun holiday in the middle of May cannot possibly be right; he could hardly have worked at that speed, even in his early youth. But it must have been done quickly, for the play was submitted to the Christiania Theatre in the summer, accepted and then performed, under the name of *The Warrior's Barrow*.

It had been with ecstasy that Ibsen had seen his first poem in print. But it was with both anxiety and terror that he now looked forward to his first meeting with that horribly many-headed monster, the audience, which all through his life he partly woos, partly challenges, although he wins greater victories over it than any other writer of drama of his century in the world. 'It was terrible, I hid myself away in the darkest corner of the theatre.' The play was performed three times, which at the time did not mean a fiasco, but anyhow it was not a success. Sheer fiascos were performed only once, plays which perhaps had a chance twice, occasionally three times. Even a play as attractive and popular as Molière's *Scapino*, which was on the boards of the same theatre four years later, was not performed more than three times.

There is nothing much to say about *The Warrior's Barrow*. It was in the Oehlenschläger style and is about the heathen Viking Gandolf, who avenges his father who has fallen in an expedition against Christian Valland. Today it seems almost a parody, but it shows Ibsen approaching a period in which he learned to master verse lines and the conventional lyrical form favoured by the times, a process which he had to undergo before he could proceed further.

The play was praised both in the *Christiana Post* and in the *Cruiser*, but Ibsen did not include it in his collected works. It is relevant that it was Schulerud again this time who went from publisher to publisher and finally had a bite. Here is Henrik Ibsen's first publisher's contract *in extenso*:

'I, the undersigned Bookseller Steensballe, herewith admit to concluding an agreement with Herr Student Schulerud, with reference to the purchase of Brynjolf Bjarme's manuscript *The Warrior's Barrow*, dramatic poem in one act, and *The Golden Harp*, epic poem, on the following conditions:
1) Steensballe shall have the right to print 1, one, edition of 4–5000 copies.
2) Steensballe shall pay for the right to this 1st Edition, 25, twenty-five speciedalers, whereof 10, ten speciedalers are paid immediately, the rest when 250, two hundred and fifty, copies are sold.
Xania 19th December 1850.   Ole Schulerud
I have received from Herr Steensballe 10, ten, spd, as payment for the above.
                                        Ole Schulerud.'

Steensballe had had the best of intentions, but came no further than the setting of the first page, and then failed. The play was first published in a revised edition in *Bergen News* in 1854, after Ibsen had used it as his 'annual play' at the theatre there, for the anniversary of the theatre's foundation on January 2.

But even if *The Warrior's Barrow* did not become a great theatrical success, it meant a great deal in prestige to Ibsen. The town was not, and is not today, large enough for the successful first performance of a new Norwegian play on the town's biggest stage to pass unnoticed.

Kristiania has rightly always been considered an inhospitable, closed and hostile town to the young men who come from all corners of the country, expecting to be made welcome and to be asked indoors. No one has described this better than Knut Hamsum in his first novel, *Hunger*, which begins like this:

'It was at the time when I went round starving in Kristiania, that singular city which no one forsakes until he has been marked by it. . . .'

Such in 1850 was the situation of Schulerud, Ibsen and their friends, a turbulent but in its own way very proud little circle. They had at all costs to keep up the outward appearance of being academics, young gentlemen of the upper classes, on the right side of the razor's edge between the upper class and the common people. But financially they were in a worse position than most of the common people.

After a while, Schulerud and Ibsen moved away from Mother Saether and got a small 'apartment' in another but less obscure suburb, Hammersborg, consisting of one room, a kitchen and an alcove. When they had earned a little money, they engaged a servant, who did not cost them much. He must have seen through them; but helped them where it pinched, acquiring credit for them at the shops, for what that was worth. Occasionally he went on a spree and was away, but he undoubtedly got his small wage when they had anything to give him. This lasted, however, only a short time, and then they could no longer afford him.

They took dinner with their landlady, Miss Holt, but when they had no money for dinner, a frequent occurrence, they put on their best clothes and 'went out to dine'. Then they did not come home again until the presumed restaurant visit was over, having meanwhile bought a little bread, butter, Dutch cheese and beer, and eaten it in secret.

Often they had not enough money even for that. It was in a situation such as this that they sold the large number of remainders of *Catiline* as wrapping paper to the chandler on the corner. If only he had known that if he had hidden that paper up in his loft instead, his descendants today could have made a fortune from it! Copies of first editions of *Catiline* today fetch between 5,000 and 10,000 crowns and the price is rising almost as swiftly as that of paintings by Cézanne and Rembrandt. In such ways these students, secretly both proud and shy, hid their poverty, for poverty was then a great disgrace. Their position was common among peasant-students and other impoverished students in Norway's capital until the middle of the present century.

Nevertheless, in that inhospitable climate, then as later on, small, significant intellectual circles came into being. Round Ibsen grew an atmosphere in which Schulerud and Abildgaard gradually fell into the background, one on account of his law studies, the other swallowed up by his ambitious political interests. There remained three main figures, of the same social background and so firmly united that at the turn of the year 1850–51 they started up their own weekly paper, their first vigorous frontal attack on the wretched society in which they lived.

Apart from Ibsen, this circle consisted of Aasmund Olavsson Vinje, ten years older, a peasant boy who had overcome even greater difficulties than Ibsen, with an intelligence and intellect on a level with his, and with much the same temperament. They had what is called in simplified Norwegian 'twin sight'—both were split between enthusiasm and scepticism, between belief in all the new things in the offing, and deep doubts. Both were financial and social outsiders, both possessing an often regal self-confidence and scorn in face of what they had perceived as worthless. Neither of them could entirely ally himself to anyone or anything, and they totally lacked the capacity to acquire allies of their own—in short, they were both exactly the opposite of the confident young enthusiast, Bjørnson, who was just about to spread his wings in full flight.

There was another thing which bound these two impoverished but aggressive young men together in their first student year and that was that they were both a trifle overawed by the academic milieu in which they were to move. But that was *not* true of the third of this newly formed circle of friends, Paul Botten-Hansen. He was six years younger than Vinje and four years older than Ibsen, but it was he who had a general view of what was going on at the time, both in Scandinavia and in the rest of Europe, and who was the most mature and knowledgeable of the three.

Opinions are divided on Botten-Hansen and especially on the circle of friends who gathered round him through the years and became known as the 'Dutchmen'. He never really became a creative person of any stature, but as an orderly pathfinder in a confused world he had great influence on both Ibsen's and Vinje's early student years.

What Ibsen lived on during this first year in Kristiania will no doubt continue to remain an unsolved mystery. His industrious writing activities cannot have sufficed to keep him on the right side of starvation. During the autumn and the following spring, he wrote anonymously in the Thranite Movement's weekly paper, *Workers' Union News*, which may have brought him a few riks-dalers, for at that time the paper had by Norwegian standards a wide circulation. (It could also have earned him a prison sentence, as we shall later see.)

But from the beginning of 1851 until the following autumn when Ibsen went to Bergen, the three friends published their own paper. Ibsen wrote a good deal for it, but the paper never had more than about a hundred subscribers, so it cannot have brought in enough to live on. It came out weekly and for the first six months had no title, but the front page was decorated with a drawing of a sceptical-looking man, so the paper came to be known as *The Man*. In the summer of 1851 a title-competition was announced and the paper's three editors, who were also the judges of the competition, gave themselves the first prize for the title *Andhrimner*. This was the name of the cook in Valhalla, who every evening killed the same pig, Saehrimnir, and served it to the gods, who meanwhile had been out and killed each other in battle; so the title was appropriate enough.

In *The Man*, later *Andhrimner*, Ibsen wrote a number of poems which have survived and are still part of Norwegian literature. Apart from these, he wrote theatre reviews—after the performance of *The Warrior's Barrow* he had received the rare privilege of free tickets to the theatre—but his reviews are far from kind. In addition he wrote satirical articles on political and social matters. The articles are radical, wide awake and essentially youthful. Ibsen was also a contributor to the Student Union's paper, *Union News*, and he even took on the task of writing the glorious history of the Union, but he never got further than a short introduction.

So these three friends had plenty to talk about, both in their work and in their discussions on life, fired as they were by Thrane's struggle for the working people, and at the same time stirred by national romanticism, conscious of the brotherhood of all Norwegians. Among their great models at this time were Heinrich Heine and the great Danish writer, Goldschmidt; and perhaps it was these two great minds, fire and ice combined, that saved the two young writers from identifying themselves completely with any of the movements round them in this great period of fermentation.

And this was good for both Ibsen and Vinje—both were meant to be revolutionaries, but not in the rôle of active politicians. But their friend, Theodor Abildgaard, was. He plunged headlong into the growing workers' movement, tried to out-manœuvre the founder, Marcus Thrane, and became its leader, and succeeded so well that eventually, together with Thrane himself, he became a victim of one of the most savage judicial murders in the recent history of Norway.

It is understandable that the Thranite Movement aroused anxiety and fear in all good citizens, and especially in the authorities, for it was like a prairie fire, not to be stopped with wise words and admonitions. Its followers were unversed in the accepted methods of political conflict. They were simply working men, desperate and full of hatred, who saw their women and children starving and wanted to put an end to it. In the new workers' unions many fiery speeches incited men to get arms and use them.

At a distance of more than a hundred years, we can record dispassionately that in such circumstances the government was forced to make arrests and crush the movement; and in fact it did. On July 7, 1851, the movement was smashed by the imprisonment of all the leaders. Ibsen was fortunate not to be arrested too. That he had been a teacher in Abildgaard's Sunday school was not in itself a reason for having him arrested; but in addition to this, and far worse, he had been an anonymous contributor to the movement's paper. When the printing works which printed the paper was searched, there were several manuscripts by Ibsen lying about, but the manager was a resourceful man and swept all the manuscripts, including Ibsen's, on to the floor, so the police thought they were waste paper and did not look at them.

As we know from the rest of Ibsen's life story, he was no hero; and he must have been extremely worried and anxious for several days. When the Sunday school was about to reopen after Abildgaard's arrest, it had to advertise for new teachers, because Ibsen could no longer spare the time. In view of what happened to the idealistic socialist leaders, it must be said that Ibsen had good grounds for his fears. Thrane and Abildgaard and many others had been in prison for three long years when the Higher Court finally sentenced these two men to four years' hard labour —four years in addition to the time they had already been in prison. The sentence, three years after the movement had been smashed to pieces, was a cool act of revenge on the part of the Higher Court, and was carried out without remission or pardon.

In the autumn of 1851, however, something happened which took Ibsen out of this little academic world in Kristiania and gave him five whole years' grounding in the world of the theatre which was to be his for ever.

5

Formative Years in Bergen

IT was Ole Bull, the world-famous violin virtuoso, who caused
Ibsen's life to take a new turn, at a time when the young writer
must have been somewhat at a loss and standing at a crossroads
in his life. We have come now to the autumn of 1851 when
Ibsen had been in Kristiania for a stormy year and a half. He had
broken completely with his home, his family, his native town
and the pharmaceutical profession. He had tried in vain to obtain
the means to continue his studies at the University, though he
had at least acquired the status title of 'Student'. By the skin of his
teeth he had succeeded in the difficult task of living by his pen
within the small academic circle of the capital. But on that front
too, the outlook was gloomy.

Then too, that somewhat uneven trio, the publishers of
Andhrimner, had continued a rather more cautious opposition to
society throughout the autumn of 1851; but that project died by
starvation, for Norway was going through a phase of comfort-
able conservatism in which all attacks on accepted norms suffered
long periods of repression.

But during this short time, Ibsen had acquired a position which
should not be underestimated, and that in three different fields.
First as a dramatist, with two plays published, of which one had
been performed—a fact that did not pass unnoticed in a very
'Norwegian' period, hungering for its own drama. Second in
polemics, anonymous or under a pseudonym (though in such a
small town, pseudonyms were seen through almost at once).
Reading his polemical writings of that time and bearing in mind
the fire which he displayed later on, in quarrels with theatre
managements in Bergen and Kristiania, in articles and records in

Rome(for quarrels were never carried on face to face, always in writing) we can see that here is the raw material for a first-class political journalist, a masterly fencer, logical, vehement and intelligent.

But it was a third talent that he had cultivated during this time which had received such recognition that he was included among the intellectual élite chosen to represent Norway. This was his poetry. It has been truly said that compared with Bjørnson's great lyrical vein, which shortly began to pour forth its incredible wealth of fantasy and inspiration, Ibsen's poetry is conventional and academic, not the product of a truly poetic disposition. Ibsen's lyric poetry is the outcome of deep thinking and patiently acquired technical skill. His mastery of the art made an explosive break-through in *Brand* and *Peer Gynt*, in which he embodies his thought and vision in images and phrases so vivid and concise that quotations from these works have become part of the Norwegian language and are still alive today, the universal currency of ideas common to the whole of the Norwegian people. But already in his first student year he had written poetry, published in *Andhrimner* in editions of only a few hundred, which placed him high in the intellectual life of Norway.

We now come to the autumn of 1851, a time of defeat for all those who wished for something new in Norway. It was now that Ole Bull came to Kristiania. In order to fill in the background of this portrait of Henrik Ibsen we must now digress for a little to say something about Ole Bull and the remarkable circumstances of the association between the two men.

Practising artists, whether musicians or actors, are unfortunately often forgotten, for man's memory is short. A few survive as legends, artists such as Sarah Bernhardt, Garrick, Paganini—and Ole Bull. It is not too much to say that when Ole Bull came home to his native town of Bergen in the summer of 1849, he had had both Europe and America at his feet. He came home to a town which was marked with profound pessimism, after cholera had taken nearly 700 lives during the winter. Nevertheless his arrival was of course celebrated, in true Bergen fashion, in honour of the first Norwegian artist of world fame.

It was during these celebrations that he began to think of setting up a Norwegian theatre in Bergen. Bergeners are proud of their town, and Ole Bull was no exception. But during the course of his travels, he had also become increasingly patriotic towards Norway, and he felt it an insult that the only permanent professional theatre in the country was in Kristiania and employed only Danish actors. At the same time, he remembered the great artistic achievements of the Dramatic Society in Bergen in his childhood—with amateurs it is true, but on the borders of professionalism and with talents far greater than those of most amateur societies. Now this dramatic society was lying dormant and the society theatre was used only by Danish touring companies during part of the year.

Ole Bull had the ability not only to become enthusiastic himself but also to inspire enthusiasm in others. He did not doubt for one moment that Bergen was full of acting talent. It was simply a matter of digging it out and giving it a little artistic and professional polish, then they would all have a theatre. And he was right.

In the summer of 1849, he simply rented the theatre for a year and put an advertisement in a Bergen paper which stated that ladies and gentlemen who wished to sing, play instruments, act or do national dances would be considered for engagement. With that arose the Norwegian Theatre in Bergen. There were many applications, mostly from young people. They followed a variety of crafts and professions, but they had one thing in common: all of them wanted to play the buffoon and act and sing.

Ole Bull himself, as usual, was to go on tour again, but he had managed to persuade his friend Fritz Jensen, theologian and landscape painter, to undertake the instruction of these young people, a task which must have seemed like the toil of Sisyphus.

Among those who applied were young domestic helps who had been employed in educated families and had learnt to 'carry themselves' well, a former house-decorator, a lithograph-apprentice, Johannes Brun, who was known as a great joker and played polite pranks while paying court to Louise Gulbrandsen, whose parents ran a taproom. She also applied. Seamen and young people, who had learnt their national dances in their home towns, also came. Most of them were quite young and totally unschooled. Nevertheless, the 'drama school' which Fritz Jensen started became the breeding ground for Norwegian theatrical talent in the years to come. From this atmosphere Norwegian theatre was created, and it received a great following in the next generations.

They had little time, for it was a matter of urgency to start performing as soon as possible. They had a little money: for Ole Bull could probably still easily afford the project, but his resources were not unlimited and he was a restless and impatient man. In addition, a sour scepticism had begun to spread round the town over the great musician's foolish undertaking. Ole Bull was a sensitive man and to change the atmosphere he allowed his pupils to give a trial performance on November 21, 1849, of Holberg's *Henrik and Pernilla*. And the miracle occurred. It was a huge success.

Then The Norwegian Theatre started off in all seriousness on January 2, 1850, with Holberg's *The Fickle One*. It was naturally richly reinforced by Ole Bull's own splendid number, which would have filled the house anywhere in the world. But even when he had left and was not present as an attraction, the theatre was astonishingly successful. During the first season there were performances on twenty-seven evenings, of sixteen different plays. By April 1850, the theatre's opponents, the 'Danophiles' were already definitely vanquished. At a general meeting of the Dramatic Society, which owned the building, there were thirty-five votes to thirty-four, a majority of one, in favour of transferring the building free of charge to Ole Bull, on condition that he did not take out any further mortgages on it and that it should be used as a theatre, and that the actors should be Norwegian. So Bergen has every right to claim that she is the cradle of Norwegian theatre.

From early in 1850, Ole Bull was touring round the world again. He had lodged a draft and some bonds as security for the management of the theatre, but the managers he had chosen were not only patriots and theatre-enthusiasts but also good Bergen merchants, and in the course of a year, Ole Bull received nearly the whole of his investment back, for the theatre's income was good and salaries very low. The ten members of the first-ever company in Norwegian theatre received only fifteen to twenty riksdalers a month. Today this tells us little, as we have no idea what a riksdaler was then worth, and it is no use comparing prices at that time with those of today. But it can be said that at that time many a working man managed on less, a good craftsman earned about the same sum or a little more, but anyone with any pretensions to 'bourgeois living standards' had a poor time on such a salary and would have to hide his poverty.

It was Fritz Jensen, then Ole Boye and later Fritz Jensen again, who directed the 1850–51 season, during which performances were given on sixty-nine evenings of no less than thirty-eight plays, with average audiences of 400.

In the autumn of 1851 Ole Bull went into action again to secure the future of the theatre, by asking for State aid. In a long and detailed letter to Parliament, dated September 2, 1851, he applies for the very modest sum of 2,000 riksdalers, emphasizing that to have Parliament's approval of the social value of the theatre to the community was of far greater importance than the actual sum of money. It is hardly necessary to add that Parliament, both then and later, refused the application.

But the theatre debate in Parliament had strong repercussions in the press throughout the country, in polemics within the pro-Norwegian and pro-Danish factions, and the Norwegian Student Union also took active sides in the battle by arranging an evening entertainment in Logen's large hall in aid of The Norwegian Theatre in Bergen. This took place on October 15 and Ole Bull played, so the house was packed, with a net haul of 300 riksdalers. The prologue for the evening was written by a student called Henrik Ibsen.

The story of The Norwegian Theatre in Bergen now ceases to be a digression and becomes part of Henrik Ibsen's life during the next six years. Both while Ole Bull had been planning the theatre and later when he was managing it from a distance, he had felt the lack of a Norwegian dramatist of their own. He now found in Kristiania a young writer of twenty-three who had already written two plays for the theatre, and so might be interested in having the security of being the theatre's own writer, both for plays and for prologues. Ole Bull immediately offered Ibsen permanent employment as the theatre's playwright.

Ibsen agreed. He was free to do so, for *Andhrimner* had published its last edition at the end of September and he was not tied to any other paper. When Ole Bull returned to Bergen at the end of October, he brought Ibsen with him.

This was something of a surprise for the theatre management in Bergen, who had long been uncertain who would be at their head. Fritz Jensen had borne the main brunt but he had not received the remuneration he considered necessary, and in addition he wished to become a priest. (He did become a parish priest in 1854.) The management had appointed Herman Laading as director from October, 1851. In his memoirs written fifty years afterwards Peter Blytt, a merchant, who shortly after took on the task of chairman of the management of the theatre, has given a brilliantly clear picture of Laading and of Ibsen—as Bergen saw these two men who were now to work together for five years.

Of Laading, who was fifteen years older than Ibsen, Blytt writes that he was a very well-educated man with elegant manners and an encyclopaedic mind. Professional studies were not his line and in Kristiania he had taken a cursory look at law, medicine and theology, not to mention aesthetics and biology. In addition, he was an able joiner and a skilful fencer and pistol shot. To crown everything he was: '. . . a handsome, stately man, a great conversationalist, a masterly talker with exceptional narrative skill. He spoke vividly and knew how to captivate his audience.'

Such a director must have been in every way the ideal teacher for each new brood of aspiring actors. He must also have been the exact opposite to Henrik Ibsen in every respect. We shall return to Blytt's characterization of Ibsen a little later. In passing it is enough to say that the theatre management naturally did not grumble at the agreement Ole Bull had come to with Ibsen, and the contract was signed on November 6, 1851. Ibsen was to receive payment of twenty riksdalers a month, back-dated to October 1. Basically he was to act as resident writer, and write at least one play a year for performance on the anniversary of the theatre's foundation. It was clear that he could not have a play ready in the course of the first few weeks, but he made his debut as writer of prologues when the theatre, thanks to the Student Union's stimulus, gave a special performance in aid of the Union's building fund. He also wrote a prologue for the anniversary of the foundation of the theatre on January 2, 1852.

Meanwhile Ole Bull was off again, and this time for a very long time. By the following summer Bull was deeply involved in another idealistic plan for the founding of a Norwegian colony in America—Oleana—an undertaking which brought him great disappointment and considerable financial troubles.

The theatre management was left with the problem of Henrik Ibsen. They had not asked to have him and now what could they possibly do with him? It was too pointless to let him just sit there writing, even though his controversial articles were probably good publicity for the theatre. (There was in particular one extremely arrogant critic whom he reduced to silence, and that was Paul Stub—ironically enough the same Stub from whom Ibsen had learnt to write Norwegian by correspondence during his Grimstad years. Ibsen now pronounced Stub quite unqualified to be a drama critic.)

So it became a matter of using Henrik Ibsen in practical theatre work now that he was there. He had had no experience of the theatre so the management found that they had to educate him, and gave him a grant so that he could go away and learn. At the same time they gave grants to the two most gifted young players in the theatre, Johannes Brun and his wife Louise—the Louise Guldbrandsen whom Johannes had courted whilst he was still a lithographer.

The condition attached to Ibsen's grant of 200 riksdalers was that he should tie himself to the theatre for a period of five years, with a salary of 300 riksdalers a year, and learn the profession by travelling abroad to foreign theatres, particularly Copenhagen,

Berlin, Dresden and Hamburg, so as to be able to take over the position of stage-manager and producer.

It is necessary here, before Ibsen and the Brun couple go off to Copenhagen, to give some account of what a theatre production in Bergen in those days was like, and what the task of stage-manager involved.

From January, 1850, until the summer of 1851, the theatre put into rehearsal no less than fifty-four different plays, with about two performances of each play. That is to say there was on an average one première per week, whereas, as we know, the professional theatre now reckons on a trial period of at least six to eight weeks. The performances were therefore also quite different from those of today. It is obviously impossible for an actor to learn by heart a long or even average part for a week only, let alone familiarize himself with it. The theatre company was so small that most of the members had parts in every play. So what the actors and actresses had to do was first to acquire a swift preview of the part's setting and character, of the play's content and ideas. Then, after reading the play several times, they had to have instructions on how the scenes were to be 'arranged', so that they could manage three things: to be placed so that they could hear the words from the prompter and then repeat them aloud, word for word; to be placed so that to the audience it looked as if they were talking to the actors they should have been talking to; to be turned towards the audience so that the spectators could clearly hear what they were saying.

It was thought quite usual at that time to have two stage-managers for the same play. First a stage-manager who went through the text and explained it, then another who was responsible for the stage directions, the action, costumes and 'props', and who went round borrowing furniture and other properties. The whole thing had to be set up within a week, in the daytime and on any evening when there was no performance. It was for this job of stage-manager-cum-property-manager that Ibsen was to train, the literary and intellectual instruction being undertaken by the older, and in every way superior and more knowledgeable, Laading himself.

On April 15, 1852, an ambitious little company consisting of Ibsen, Johannes Brun and his wife, left Bergen, via Hamburg, with Copenhagen as their first goal. Among other duties Ibsen had undertaken was to obtain for the Bruns some instruction in Copenhagen in plastic art and dancing, and also to try to find a dancing teacher for the company in Bergen, which must undoubtedly have been sorely needed when young maid-servants and craftsmen were to appear as grand ladies and gentlemen in vaudeville. Ibsen was also to buy notes and books with illustrations of costumes of different periods, mostly old editions in bookshops in Copenhagen.

Ibsen was better received in Denmark than a young man totally inexperienced in the theatre world could possibly have expected. He and the Bruns were given free tickets to the Royal Theatre and were thus able to watch a number of the finest performances in the theatre's repertoire in one of its most brilliant periods—a great experience for a twenty-four-year-old provincial writer. Ibsen also received good advice from the theatre's stage-manager and resident writer, Overskou, a very experienced theatre man who showed great generosity in giving a kind of lightning-course of instruction to this greenhorn of a Norwegian colleague. In addition he was invited to a grand dinner with Johan Ludvig Heiberg, then Denmark's reigning authority in the field of aesthetics and director of the theatre, as well as a State Counsellor. The dinner was a great disappointment for not a single pearl fell from the great man's lips, except on the subject of food.

But Ibsen was also received with friendliness by several of Denmark's great men, including the greatest of them all, Hans Christian Andersen, who gave him good advice on the next steps to take. The reports Ibsen wrote to the theatre management in Bergen during this time deal mostly with facts, and have been called arid letters, but a vigorous and confident tone is apparent in his attempts to get the management to see that he must have more riksdalers if he is to carry out the tasks they have set him. He mentions in passing, apparently quite unimpressed, the names of the great men with whom he has become acquainted, and reports on technical theatrical matters with a confidence that ought to have made it quite clear to the merchants at home in Bergen that a real professional was being trained for the benefit of the town.

This was true up to a point. He did his work very thoroughly and became in time a very useful, dutiful and valuable assistant to Laading. He also managed to get some financial reinforcements to enable him to stay in Copenhagen a few days after the theatre season was over, and thus travelled on at the beginning of June to Berlin and Dresden. Hans Christian Andersen had strongly advised him to go to Vienna too, where theatrical life was said to be especially interesting, but this did not materialize. At Dresden he had to turn back, returning to Bergen via Hamburg at the end of June. Now his new life was to begin—with a contract which virtually bound him to stage-management for five whole years, at a monthly salary of twenty-five riksdalers.

It was anything but an ambitious conquering hero who now set to work. One's thoughts involuntarily go to another young Norwegian writer's reception in the same town, at the same theatre, five years later, several months after Ibsen had left. This was Bjørnstjerne Bjørnson who sailed in when only about the same age as Ibsen was in 1852, but as director, in triumph. In a short time he had the whole town seething, throwing himself into politics, editing articles, deciding nominations of those who should represent Bergen in Parliament, a raging storm the like of which Bergen had never seen before.

When Ibsen began, he aroused little attention. Let us now turn to the sketch of him in Peter Blytt's memoirs, remembering that they were written long after Ibsen had become famous, by a man who had the greatest admiration for him as a writer:

'There was nothing special about him to indicate the brilliant creative power he later showed. This still, quiet, not very impressive, but modest young man, his eyes usually veiled, seldom and then only briefly lighting up, largely gave the impression of being of an extremely withdrawn and timid nature. It was known that he possessed an easy and fluent poetic vein. He had written some poems which were thought-provoking and full of atmosphere. He had written dramatic works such as *Catiline*, the originality of which had aroused considerable attention in limited circles, but no one would guess that behind this pale bearded face, with its tightly closed mouth, was hidden a brain that would be able to grapple with and draw out with inconceivable mastery the deepest problems of the human mind and heart.

'He moved quietly, almost silently, between the wings at rehearsals. He was not used to the theatre at first, or rather the stage. He sometimes seemed somewhat helpless and was embarrassed when he had to approach one of the actors directly, or especially the actresses, with a reprimand or even only a correction. Producing was entrusted to him and the books were carried by him without his being in the true meaning of the word the producer. Subordinate work was carried out by another official appointed for the purpose. Everything Ibsen wrote in his producer's books was precise, neat and almost pedantic. The contemplative side of his nature was clear to anyone who at that time came in touch with him, so naturally he found his many practical tasks as stage-manager, and all that that involved, very tiresome.

'It happened repeatedly that the financial calculations and estimates which were inseparable from his position proved to be considerably beyond his scope. But no one doubted his good will. Unpretentious and retiring, in the emotional and somewhat passionate theatre world, he aroused no one's ill will, though it could perhaps be that a certain indolence was occasionally noticed, possibly the consequence of his quietly "fermenting" inner life.

'People soon noticed in him a personality which was quite outside the ordinary. He was regarded with a certain shy veneration and as he silently made his way, or as people of the time said, "padded" round back-stage in his strange, capacious and somewhat worn top-coat, he was respected, but he did not arouse sympathy.

'He made hardly any real friends and he himself perhaps lacked any capacity for affection, but neither did he make any enemies.'

Despite the deference for Ibsen's genius, this somewhat crushing description is obviously genuine. (With regard to the reference to the top-coat it should perhaps be added that for the sake of economy the theatre was almost wholly unheated except during performances.) And the glimpses of depths of thought Blytt believes he has seen are sheer hindsight. The truth is probably that Ibsen was scarcely noticed, while Laading, as artistic director, wholly and obviously dominated the scene.

We know of only one quiet friendship from these first years in Bergen, and that was with Mrs Helene Sontum, in whose house he lived when he came to the town and with whom he continued to take his meals after he moved in 1853 into two rooms in the theatre building itself. Otherwise he closed up like an oyster, just as he had done as a boy in Skien when his father's business failed, and later in the service of Reimann the apothecary in Grimstad, just as he consciously shut himself away behind the Ibsen-mask after he had made his break-through.

The first two closed periods in his life are easy to explain: he was very poor, unhappy over his fall in society, lonely and bitter. But why did he shut himself away for the third time, after his rich extrovert spell in Grimstad with Schulerud and Due, where he discovered the talents he then came to spend the rest of his life perfecting, and after his time in Kristiania which, despite his poverty, was a time of rich development, outward-looking interests, growing to maturity and, between failures, achieving recognition? In addition to this he had travelled abroad for the first time.

The explanation must be that from his first moment in Bergen, he felt as if he were back with Reimann the apothecary in Grimstad. The charming, vain Ole Bull had bought him, but he had not won his heart. Ibsen's opinion of the great master was always cool, critical, almost hostile. And then Bull had almost at once deserted him and gone abroad again, after which the theatre management in Bergen had treated their problem child as the undesired phenomenon he was, a whim left behind by Bull. If he had hoped to enter into some kind of intellectual milieu in Bergen, then he must have been immediately disappointed.

So, reluctantly, he became a drudge under Laading at a theatre

where he made no contacts, in a closed town with a large merchant society from which he was excluded. The whole world
should be grateful for the drudgery he was forced to endure. But
at the time he felt as spiritually exiled as it was possible to be.
He kept himself to himself; closed up and said nothing. Even
when an actress in her enthusiasm and under Laading's directions
declaimed her lines in such a way that Ibsen choked, he preferred
to ask one of the other actresses to correct her.

In the meantime he was also supposed to be writing plays,
which was what he had originally come for. But in that capacity
too he had become uncertain of himself. He had been gripped by
revolutionary movements which had been brutally crushed in
every country. He had gone through several periods of patriotic
enthusiasm for Norway, and seen through them. At the same time
he had received a constant stream of new material for his nationalism. During these years there appeared in Norway an almost
confusing surge of knowledge of the Norway which had been
hidden under Danish supremacy: fairy-tales, folk-songs, the
whole cultural treasure was revealed. Ibsen was taken by it, but
saw how it had been misused in hollow oratory and romanticism.

Ibsen's double nature is shown most strongly in the bad play
he wrote as his first under contract, *St John's Night*, which was
performed on the day his contract demanded, January 2, 1853.
The play was never printed with Ibsen's approval. It appeared
first in a posthumous collection after his death, when it was felt
necessary to preserve, publish and comment on everything the
genius had ever written.

The author himself describes *St John's Night* as a 'miserable
product', and there is only one point on which one can disagree.
This concerns the description of the play's young poet, chatterbox
and oratorical hero, Julian Paulsen, a satire which is executed with
both humour and malice. But otherwise the play falls between all
stools. Ibsen himself perhaps sensed that it was not going to be
much of a success, for he introduced the performance with a
prologue begging for indulgence.

Modesty did not help him. There was a full house on the first
night but when the performance was over it was both hissed and

booed. The play was put on once more and after that abandoned. So the management must have shaken their heads once again and asked themselves what on earth they were going to do with this Ibsen.

In the late spring and early summer of 1853 he had his first brief period of happiness in Bergen. Every Ibsen biographer has retold the story of his love for Rikke Holst, an immature little girl, but it cannot be omitted. He worshipped her with great ardour, wrote her poems and letters, went out with her, and finally proposed. Her father, a master mariner, would not hear of it—she was not even confirmed—but they became secretly engaged, tied their rings together to a key-ring and threw them into the sea. We also know that the enraged father once caught them and the bold suitor fled, running away as fast as he could.

Their brief exchange of words many years later is also too famous to be ignored: Ibsen met her in 1885, when she was Mrs Tresselt. He asked: 'Why did nothing ever really come of things between us?' Mrs Tresselt smiled and replied: 'But my dear Ibsen, don't you remember that you ran away?' 'Yes, yes', said Ibsen then. 'Face to face, I never was a very brave man.'

Perhaps it was because of his love for Rikke Holst that Ibsen returned to and rewrote his romantic love story *The Warrior's Barrow*. In Kristiania it had been performed with some success, but at a special performance in Bergen in 1854 its reception had been so cool that it was abandoned after the first night.

These two major failures had had a strong effect on the shy and withdrawn Ibsen and he was feeling uncertain and anxious when he set about his next play, though he cannot have doubted that the subject would be right for the Norwegian theatregoer. The idea he obviously got from C. Paludan-Müller's recent book in which is an account of how Mrs Ingerd Ottisdotter Rømer of Austråt— one of the last members of the Norwegian aristocracy—attempted to start a Norwegian rebellion against King Christian II between 1527 and 1528.

It is well known that the real Mrs Ingerd was not as she became in Ibsen's play, but that in itself is of no importance: in his portrayal of others, too, Ibsen has the power to transcend reality.

What mattered was that here was a theme with an appeal to contemporary Norwegian romanticism, and a plot which shows that Ibsen had profited from working on the production of so many contemporary comedy intrigues. Here are exciting confusions and murky designs, violent love and dramatic rebellion.

Nevertheless Peter Blytt says Ibsen was visibly nervous when he submitted the manuscript, pretending that he was offering a successful play by a friend in Kristiania because he himself had not been able to finish anything for the next anniversary. Blytt says that *Lady Inger of Østeraad* made an immediate appeal to him and he persuaded the management to accept it. Just before the performance, Ibsen abandoned his anonymity and allowed it to be put on under his own name. This did not do him any good, however, for the performance was not a success and after one more the play was set aside.

Now, more than a hundred years later, it seems strange that this powerful, living drama was such a flop and remained in virtual obscurity until the time of Ibsen's European fame, when theatres all over the world were interested in his earlier plays. In this century the play has been performed on a number of stages in the world and is the only one of the author's youthful works which the passing of time has not made unplayable.

Ibsen had now made three different experiments since his arrival in Bergen and failed each time: first with a semi-lyrical, semi-satirical 'folk-tale comedy', with a contemporary background, but with hobgoblins and the underworld in the plot; next a romantic drama from Viking times; and finally a grand drama of the days when the last relics of Norway's freedom were lost in the years of the reformation. He had tried three times to woo the audience by following the fashionable trends of the time, but always without success.

Peter Blytt and other eye-witnesses—writing much later— claim to have seen all along that these were, for Ibsen, the years of germination; and indeed Ibsen himself has confirmed this, adding that he had difficulty in adapting himself or attaching himself to anyone. But these 'fermenting-years' were not a time of inactivity. He had taken part in the production of a couple of hundred plays, and in the course of his duties must have read several hundred which were not performed. The preparation for the plays he wrote must also have meant extensive reading in many fields.

These three or four first years in Bergen demonstrate one thing very clearly: he was not a born dramatist. It had been almost a matter of chance that in his youth he had chosen the drama-form for *Catiline* for his enthusiastic little audience in Grimstad. He continued, with his left hand so to speak, to write the first version of *The Warrior's Barrow* while he was studying for his matriculation exam in Kristiania.

It seems as if he developed very slowly, heavily and laboriously working on the techniques of drama, philosophizing somewhat fruitlessly over what lends itself to dramatic material and how the action should be employed. The people of Bergen had given him overwhelming proof that, from their point of view, he had failed. He had not become the inspiring stage-manager they had hoped for, nor the skilful administrator they needed, nor even an intellectual power-house. On the contrary, he worked himself up by degrees into such a state of querulousness and aggression towards other people that the few people who did invite him home considered him an unpleasant guest—even the good-natured Peter Blytt.

The cause was clear enough: he could not help agreeing with the people of Bergen. Nothing succeeded for him. He had never found himself, never given expression to what was really in his heart. He undoubtedly dreamed of appearing as the figure he later became—the great castigator, the prophet who could hold a mirror up to his day and show it all the filth which lay behind the complacency. But to tackle such a task would have been foolish in the small town he was stuck in, impoverished and dependent.

The year 1855 must have been in some ways the most difficult of all. But in the course of that year he immersed himself in a type of literature which appealed very much to the lyric writer in him—folk-songs, with their concise, laconic humanity, their dramatic simplicity and basic poetry. His fourth duty-play for the theatre in Bergen was built on a folk-song motif; it was written in a mixture of prose and verse, interspersed with songs.

Today *The Feast at Solhaug* reads like a mild parody, but many of the verses are pithy and alight with the fire of rebellion. The proud Margit loved her poor kinsman Gudmund, but he has left the country, so she has married the rich, foolish Bengt. But Gudmund comes back and now it is on Margit's younger sister, Signe, that his eyes light. And then come the intrigues with the poisoned flask and axe-blows and armed men fighting. At the end of the feast the next morning, Margit has become a widow and retreats to a nunnery, while Gudmund gets his Signe and, from being hunted by the King's men, has suddenly become the King's favourite.

So much for the plot, but the play has one really good part, that of the designing but passionate Margit, who suffers all the agonies of love.

The Feast at Solhaug became Ibsen's break-through in Bergen, in more ways than one. It is perhaps best to allow him to tell of the great evening himself:

'It received an excellent and unusually warm performance. It was done with pleasure and abandon and was received in the same way—"Bergen lyric poetry" swelling loudly that theatre evening into the packed house. The performance ended with continuous calls for the author and the players. Later on in the evening the orchestra, accompanied by a large part of the audience, played a serenade outside my windows. I think I almost allowed myself to be carried away into making a kind of speech to the gathering. Anyhow, I know that I felt very happy.'

The Feast at Solhaug was put on six times, which in the Bergen of the time was a sensational success. But more than that, the Christiania Theatre performed it that same spring and there it also ran for six performances. A year later it was performed at the Royal Dramatic Theatre in Stockholm, on Union Day, November 4, only one other Norwegian play having ever gained this honour before. The play also came out in book form.

But this success was of great significance to him in another way too. He came to know the Thoresen family. Thoresen was the parish priest at Korskirken in Bergen. When he had been

widowed for the second time and was priest at Herøy in Sunn-
møre, he had engaged a young Danish lady, Magdalene Krag, to
teach his many children, and then he had married her in 1843,
when she was twenty-four and he forty-three. Mrs Magdalene
was extremely interested in literature and art. She had, amongst
other things, already translated plays for the theatre and herself
had had several plays performed, though under the strictest
anonymity. The priest's home was a kind of salon for several of
the leading intellectuals of the town.

It is evidence of how completely the young writer and producer had been ignored by the good citizens of Bergen that during
his first four years there he was never once invited into the
Thoresen family's hospitable house, despite their keen interest in
theatre and the arts. It was not until she was on her way home
from this unexpected and tremendous success on January 2,
1856, that Mrs Thoresen—with the applause still ringing in her
ears—had the excellent idea of suggesting to her husband that they
should invite this young man home to their house.

Five days later Ibsen visited the family for the first time.
Already that evening he began to show considerably greater
interest in one of the young daughters of Thoresen's first marriage
than in his much-fêted hostess.

Mrs Magdalene's real opinion of the man who became her
son-in-law she expressed many years later:

'When Ibsen came to Bergen he was like a shy little marmot.
There was something funny, but not pleasant, almost clumsy and
anxious in his behaviour. He was afraid of becoming the subject
of laughter, of disgracing himself, and he had not yet learnt to
despise his fellow human beings, so his behaviour lacked cer-
tainty, and in addition he possessed a certain implicit deference
for finer things, for he felt that in the fine, more prosperous
world there was no unrest and lack of ease as in himself, but that
there all was beauty—he felt himself a forsaken, harried, despised
creature, who carried on an existence outside society.'

This description probably fits, even if it includes quite a strong
portion of malice, and very likely jealousy—for it was not

Magdalene, but her step-daughter, Suzannah Daae Thoresen, nineteen years old, to whom Ibsen was paying attention. It must have been mutual attraction from the first moment. He soon met her again in January, at a ball where they did not dance, but talked the more. Then he went home and proposed to her in a poem 'To the only one'.

Suzannah accepted immediately, but their engagement was not announced until the spring and they were not able to get married until the summer of 1858, amongst other things because he could not possibly support a family on his salary in Bergen.

What was she like, this young woman with whom he fell in love so swiftly and violently and who later stayed at his side for half a century? So far as we know, he had had only two fleeting affairs before, his remote youthful affair in Grimstad and his short swift one with Rikke Holst. What has been said about his life and conduct in Bergen indicates that he was anxious and reserved, and that he had few opportunities and little experience of mixing with young ladies.

But at the same time it is quite clear that it was not just a long-felt need which this time gave his love a depth and warmth which put all else in the shade. It could hardly have been her looks, although even Magdalene Thoresen's rather malicious portrait— to which we shall shortly return—cannot conceal the fact that Suzannah must have had a charm of her own which made the few people who had eyes for it consider her even very beautiful. Neither can it have been any pronounced intellect, as from what several people say, including Ibsen himself, she could be both illogical and shallow.

Ibsen himself, in poetry and letters and dedications, has revealed what won his lasting love. The briefest sketch is to be found in the letter written to Peter Hansen in 1870, from which we have already quoted: 'Not until I married did my life contain anything of importance [then he goes on to mention *Love's Comedy*]. . . . The only one to approve of the book this time was my wife. She has qualities which I particularly need—illogical, but with a strong poetic instinct, with a broad-minded way of thinking and an almost violent hatred of all pettiness.' Note the words '*broad-*

minded way of thinking and hatred of pettiness'. He has accentuated these qualities by comparing her to several of the strongest and most uncompromising female characters in his earlier dramas. Her loyal comradeship through Ibsen's years of oppression has proved how strongly she must have hated all the pettiness by which he was held in check.

By her 'poetic instinct' he probably meant simply this: *she believed in him*. It seems pretty certain that the first spark ignited on that first evening. So it must have been then that she told him that she admired the play nearly everyone else had despised, but which he himself obstinately, and rightly, considered to be the best he had yet written: *Lady Inger*. This led to the 'marmot' becoming expansive and confident, seeking the trust he had so bitterly lacked, and finding it, for she had 'poetic instinct', human warmth and understanding.

We cannot know what would have happened to him if he had not been sustained in life by this firm handclasp, but it is quite certain that this first meeting in January, 1856, really was of literary significance.

What did she look like then? Ibsen himself has said nothing on this subject, but the closest witness, Magdalene Thoresen, has indeed done so, though not until as late as 1901, when her son-in-law's fame led her into gross errors of memory when it came to *him*. At the time she was eighty-two years old, but much quicker and more mobile than her stepdaughter, who was already crippled with rheumatism and in poor health. In the Danish Christmas booklet, *Christmas Roses*, she writes an article on *Henrik Ibsen and His Wife* telling how the rising young writer had the world at his feet: she remembers among other things that he had written several plays—which he in fact wrote later—and that he was always surrounded by women, but that he managed to keep them at a distance until he finally laid eyes on Suzannah.

Her description of Suzannah, however, bears the definite stamp of authenticity, and demonstrates how remote this extrovert and youthful stepmother was from her grown-up stepdaughter, and presumably from her many other stepchildren too. On Ibsen she concludes with these not altogether truthful words:

'. . . so he had managed to dip his pen in the heart's blood of the nation, and at once he was a man of the people. It was at this stage that Henrik Ibsen made his entrance into our house, and became engaged to my second stepdaughter. . . . The engagement took place very quietly—it seemed more like a personal agreement, which in fact it was: when the two were in agreement, the matter was clear!' [He could not support her, so there were no celebrations.]

'Whilst he was thus acclaimed by all as a rising writer, not least by young women, she kept herself quietly in the background, constantly keeping him company with every beat of her heart.

'Suzannah Daae was a strong and unusual personality, who had hitherto lived among us as an enigma. Thus it had never occurred to any of us that she was beautiful. She had deep lively eyes, and she also had what was called "wide vision", that is to say, when she opened her eyes it was apparent that she had an unusually wide field of vision. She also had lovely hair, and her full lips could shape themselves into a charming smile—almost a simple childish smile. But there was a certain formlessness about her face which did not allow these lovely features to stand in the right relationship to each other. But momentarily a flush disguising hidden fire would gather her features into a radiant countenance—and then she was beautiful.

'Usually this exuberance was kept beneath an even, gentle surface, and few words were let fall to indicate an active mind. But they who knew her from childhood knew that it was there. Ever since she had been able to read she had filled her mind with sagas and stories which almost made her alien to earthly life.'

There seems to be a good deal of malice and antipathy packed into this description. Mrs Magdalene had been Suzannah's stepmother for no less than thirteen years, without discovering more than what is quoted here; that she had pretty hair, large eyes, thick lips, and was quite good looking. An unremarkable nonentity in the family.

In March 1856 the theatre company went to Trondheim for a

lengthy guest tour, with Ibsen as leader. His reports back to the theatre management give quite a good insight into what theatre-tours were like in those days, and here there is no lack of accurate factual information. But already, after a few weeks' stay in Trondheim, he asks to be relieved. It is not difficult to discern what brought him back to Bergen so quickly that he missed the final success of the performance of The Feast at Solhaug at the end of May, at which the applause was great and the company—which had then heard about Ibsen's engagement—drank a toast to him after the performance—on the house.

That summer went down in the annals of Bergen as 'the princely summer', for no less than three royal highnesses visited the town. The scenes that are said to have been played out in private over who was and who was not to be invited to what, were of such violence that they became a legend for a hundred years and caused lifelong friction between good friends. Ibsen, however, was involved in only one of the royal festivities. This was when Prince Napoleon—popularly known as 'Plon-plon'—came to the town at the end of August and a performance was hastily arranged in his honour. The Feast at Solhaug was put on again and during the performance on August 24, the Prince was gracious enough to take a drink with the performers during the interval. Ibsen presented him with a copy of the play bound in red morocco, and the Prince personally promised that he would see to it that the play was translated into French and put on at Napoleon III's Imperial Theatre in St Cloud. This was greatly to the taste of the ambitious young Norwegian writer. The Prince did not keep his promise, as is often the way of princes, but that Ibsen could not be expected to know.

But now the critics began to attack Ibsen's work in real earnest. The Feast at Solhaug, his break-through play, had been successful with audiences in Kristiania too, and all seemed to be going well. But then came the Kristiania critics and they were devastating. The only person to defend the play was Bjørnstjerne Bjørnson, but he did so on premises which in Ibsen's eyes were pure insult—that Ibsen quite simply was not a dramatist, the play was a lyric, and not until that was clear could its real value be appreciated.

The blow was almost annihilating for Ibsen, for it was the capital which decided the country's intellectual life and a failure there devastated all prospects for the future. How deeply this criticism affected him becomes clear when one reads the foreword he wrote for the play when he published it again twenty-seven years later. He does mention Bjørnson's article, but puts it in its place with the words:

'It was not really a review or a criticism, but more of a spirited free fantasy, poetically improvised over the play and the performance.' He goes on, 'But then came the real criticism, written by the real critics.

'How did one become a real literary critic at that time—I mean the years between 1850 and about 1860—and especially a dramatic critic in Kristiania?'

Then follows a scathing massacre of the critics' qualifications, after which he continues:

'And then the critics in the capital of Norway of the time had one particular peculiarity, the origins of which I could not understand for a long time. Our critics took care, every time a new writer published a book or had a small play performed, to behave as if through the publication of the book or the performance of the play a dreadful insult had been inflicted upon both themselves and the papers they wrote in. As I say, I brooded over this singularity for a long time. . . .'

The intense bitterness in these lines, written in 1883, at a time when he was victorious all along the line, shows how strongly he had felt his failure in 1856, just when he at last believed that he had won through.

As an excuse to get permission to leave the company as early as the beginning of April, he had referred to work he had to do in Bergen, the writing of the fifth consecutive annual 'duty play'. This summer, however, instead of concentrating on a particular dramatic story, he and Suzannah resolved to widen their scope. In view of the audience's reactions to *The Feast at Solhaug*, the obvious course was to continue in the vein of folk-song, and a walking tour through Hardanger and over Voss, with the whole of Vestlandet's magnificently dramatic countryside, caused Ibsen to take up again an earlier play which he had never finished. This was *The Ptarmigan of Justedal*, begun during his first autumn in Kristiania, after his début on the stage with *The Warrior's Barrow*. He rightly considered that he knew much more about these matters now, almost seven years later. Not only had Lanstad's collections of folk-songs come out, but he had also become acquainted with the old Icelandic sagas, and had at the same time worked his way through layer after layer of nationalistic and national-romantic views of how this ancient cultural heritage could—and could not—be used as inspiration for the new Norwegian literature which was now emerging.

He got the title and the germ of the story from the folk-song about Olaf Liljekrans, who was 'taken by the mountains'. But again there is nothing much to the folk-song or the old saga of this young girl, the only person said to have survived the Black Death in Jostedalen, the Jostedal Ptarmigan.

There are divided opinions on the play's worth. Some scholars call it Ibsen's most confused play from the point of view of style, others find in it indications of his later psychological dramas. With the success of his previous play in mind, the theatre management had for the first time offered him a fee of 100 riksdalers for writing the play, and had great expectations of repeating the previous year's success. But it was a complete fiasco when it was produced in Bergen on January 2 and 4. It was never performed on the stage again as a spoken play, never published in Ibsen's lifetime, and from the point of view of the general reader, we need say no more about it, except that Arne Eggen, the composer, set the text to music and the opera was performed in the National Theatre in Oslo in the summer of 1940.

The spring of 1857 must have been a critical time for Ibsen. His optimism after his success in Bergen with *The Feast at Solhaug* boosted his self-confidence enough for him to go courting, and his life with Suzannah had also carried him through his loss of prestige in Kristiania, but the fiasco with Olaf Liljekrans not only damaged his prestige, it also threatened his whole future, the very foundations of his existence. After the fiasco his stock was at its lowest just when he was considering founding a family. He had already been engaged for a year.

When Magdalene Thoresen says that he felt himself 'looked down on' in Bergen, this is a devastating truth. It was not only his progress that was affected, but also his financial position. During these years he was obliged to live on twenty-five riksdalers a month, with perhaps a little extra revenue occasionally, and right up to the 1860s he also had to pay the humiliating paternity maintenance for his son in Froland. It became impossible for him to make ends meet, even with his very modest needs.

In his excellent work on Henrik Ibsen published in 1916, Gerhard Gran as usual hits the nail right on the head;

'Ibsen, who had left Kristiania in 1852 [in fact it was 1851] as naked as the day, returned in 1857 even more naked, his only achievement during those years a not particularly impressive but anyhow more than adequate burden of debt. And his reputation was in no better state than his finances.'

Gerhard Gran, who was a Bergener, born shortly after Ibsen had left the town, understands how painful it must have been for Ibsen, so jealous of his honour, to have to run the gauntlet from one lender to the next. Every speciedaler he borrowed to pay off a loan was a favour which humiliated the borrower and exalted the lender, for he was not the smart type who could impress merchants and make them believe they were investing their capital in something which would pay.

Many Ibsen scholars linger over the spiritual, poetic and intellectual debts which he repaid a thousandfold. In his private life, they prefer to concentrate on his personal relationships. After only the most cursory mention of his poverty, they hasten back to the effects of different phases of national romanticism on Ibsen's youthful works.

It can probably be said that Ibsen's 'fermenting time' in Bergen was not only a period of maturing, and slowly and painfully devoting himself to a profession which did not come easily to him, but also that the bitter substance which caused the fermentation and determined the consequences was financial rather than spiritual need. He felt banished to an outpost, a place of exile. He could not get away and had nothing new to go to. Had he lived in the capital, he would have had a milieu, a circle of his own to protect and inspire him. In the spring of 1857 he committed himself to spending one more year in Bergen for the same wretched salary, but he knew only too well that he would have to earn more than double this before Mrs Magdalene and her priestly consort would allow him to marry his betrothed.

An unexpected opportunity arose in the spring. It came from the Norwegian Theatre in Kristiania, and reached Ibsen by a somewhat indirect route.

Inspired by Ole Bull's attempt to create a *Norwegian* theatre in Bergen, bold 'Norwegian-enthusiasts' in Kristiania had thought of trying the same thing in the capital. One might rightly call them romantics, romantic nationalists; but they were realists too. They had discovered how quickly Norwegian was ousting the Danish official language and they were intent on carrying this further, so that ancient Norwegian culture from the regions and new Norwegian writing could flourish. They were downright 'anti-Danish', as they wanted Norway to be herself and not continue to be a Danish province from an artistic point of view. But they had less luck than the company inaugurated by Ole Bull. They had so many things against them. First, there was an established professional theatre, Christiania Theatre, with Danish players, patronized by the whole of the capital's compact Civil Service. Secondly, Kristiania did not have the amateur traditions which in Bergen had survived from the late rococo period, and which to a great extent had retained the patronage of the town's upper class. Thirdly, there were no people in Kristiania of the quality of Fritz Jensen and Laading, who could shape a group of amateurs into a professional theatrical corps.

Kristiania Norwegian Theatre began in 1852, as a kind of national–political school for theatrical amateurs, but first took shape as a regular theatre with a building of its own in Møllergaten in 1854. It was led by a small number of men who were more enthusiastic about the linguistic than the artistic side. It limped along, but mostly with popular entertainment on a some-what low level; and the enterprise lost money, so it became in-creasingly difficult to get people to join the management and to obtain financial support.

In the spring of 1857 the theatre was just about to close, but it was decided that it should carry on and if possible reorganize. The artistic director had hitherto been, ironically enough, a Danish actor called Jens Cronberg. Now it was decided that he should be removed and a new Norwegian director found. An obvious place to look for the right man was the theatre in Bergen, which had been the spearhead of the nationalist movement for seven years.

It was one of the actors in Bergen, Georg Herman Krohn, who, in the spring of 1857, received the first feeler. Naturally enough, Krohn went to Ibsen, as it was more or less unthinkable that Laading might accept and Ibsen was the only possible alternative. Ibsen let it be known through Krohn that if the terms were acceptable, and if the theatre management in Bergen would release him from his recently renewed contract, he might be willing to come. He then received a definite offer and at once went to Kristiania to negotiate further. In the meantime he said nothing to his own theatre managers, and his departure from Bergen on July 18 passed unnoticed. Neither then nor a few weeks later, when he embarked for good with the small number of possessions he must have accumulated over the years, was there even as much as the usual report in the papers, which in those days conscientiously reported on every commercial traveller who entered or left the town.

6

Early Struggles in Kristiania

IT is understandable that Ibsen had not said a word to his theatre management about his desire to leave Bergen. He considered perhaps that he owed them nothing more than a few speciedalers, and no deep loyalty or trust. But when in the letter which he had to send them immediately after his arrival in Kristiania, he maintains that a definite offer was made to him the same day he left Bergen, he is hardly being truthful. It must have taken him a few days to scrape up the money for such an expensive trip—his first journey to Kristiania for six years. Leaving in such haste can mean only one thing: that he had already decided. The offer from Kristiania was six hundred speciedalers a year, plus a percentage of any eventual profits—a guaranteed minimum double that he had earned in Bergen. With such a salary he would be acceptable to the Thoresen family as a bridegroom.

The day before his departure he writes to Botten-Hansen and asks him to find lodgings for him, and his temporary address was, as one might imagine, 'c/o Advocate Schulerud, Kjøbm. Hassels Gaard, Torvet'. But he stayed at the Hotel du Nord.

By the time he had reached Kristiania by coastal steamer, the news of his appointment to the Kristiania Norwegian Theatre was in the newspapers; so the first thing he had to do on his arrival was to write to Bergen and ask to be released from his contract. He does this in a letter dated July 23, a letter which throws a clear light on the working conditions under which he had lived. After first apologizing for his secrecy somewhat elaborately and not entirely truthfully, he writes:

'The advantages to me of living in the capital, I need not emphasize, for they are overwhelming, and whatever harm it may do me to forsake Bergen and Bergen Theatre, I am in no doubt that it will not be inexcusable of me to refuse this opportunity which has now arisen to accept a reasonably remunerative post. I mention salary and advantages here, but truthfully I am neither egoistic nor ungrateful. What I owe Bergen Theatre I shall never forget, but I also have duties to myself, and the conditions at Bergen Theatre have long oppressed me; every direction in which I could have made an impression has been barred to me; I have never had a free hand and I have therefore daily felt myself oppressed by the thought of having to work without making any effect.'

This letter carries the stamp of being anything but a hastily improvised note. It is extremely courteous and well-considered in tone, but firm in its reasoning. It is a free man who at last speaks out and tells these grand gentlemen that neither financially nor from a work point of view has he had endurable conditions, and that now he is to have both. The theatre management consented at once, and without sorrow disclaimed their problem child. The chairman, Peter Blytt, who had undoubtedly been one of Ibsen's greatest supporters, some years later became his friend and boon companion as well. Personally as well as financially the relationship between them through the ensuing years continued to be to their mutual satisfaction.

Ibsen's contract with Kristiania Norwegian Theatre stated that he should have 7½ per cent of the gross takings, and in any event not less than fifty speciedalers a month. If all went well, this would be enough to enable him to pay off the worst of his debts in the course of a year and thus lay the foundations for his marriage to Suzannah. When he left Bergen in the autumn and took over the direction of the theatre in Kristiania on September 3, he took with him a manuscript of which he himself had great expectations—*The Vikings at Helgeland*, which he submitted to Kristiania Theatre, fully aware that his own theatre in Møller-gaten had not the resources to perform it.

The season at Kristiania Norwegian Theatre was then in full

swing. In the invitation to take out a subscription that the theatre sent out at the beginning of August, it is clear that with the appointment of Henrik Ibsen a new epoch had begun:

'Neither should it be forgotten that the theatre may now be considered to have taken another step forward towards its essential aim, in that it has now a Norwegian as its Artistic Director.'

For the opening of the season on August 27th with H. Ø. Blom's musical play *Tordenskjold*, Professor Monrad wrote a prologue which must have been poorly performed as the newspaper *Morgenbladet* gives this as grounds for printing it. Here Monrad states the theatre's great aims:

'A stage where the life of the people can be enacted and the true quality of the language heard.'

The first performance for which Ibsen himself was responsible was a combination of two Norwegian 'classics': Bjerregaard's *Mountain Adventure* and Wergeland's *Sequel to Mountain Adventure*, a great success which ran for seventeen performances. And Ibsen himself received praise: '. . . the stage management bore witness to much care and was thus a good omen for Mr Ibsen's activities in the theatre'.

But he soon found that this success was a flash in the pan and that the theatre in Møllergaten had neither personnel nor audience for anything more than the simplest entertainment. The players were from various parts of the country and had not even any common dialect to make into a stage language, and the audience was drawn from the lower middle class and artisans who came for light entertainment and farces. Such were the tastes of the day at the Christiania Theatre too to some extent, and in Møllergaten Ibsen submitted and tried to use his theatre routine to make the entertainment as good as possible.

On the whole, the 1857–58 season showed good results, with takings of 9,000 speciedalers, which was enough to balance the books, an event that had not occurred the previous year.

In the spring of 1858, apart from his theatre work, Ibsen was much occupied with something else, namely a very violent and lengthy controversy in the papers. His antagonist was none other than the director of the rival Kristiania Theatre, the Danish theatrical personality Carl Borgaard; the subject Ibsen's own play *The Vikings at Helgeland*. Kristiania was small enough at that time for the director of one of the town's two theatres not only to review performances at the other theatre, but also to submit his own play to his rival and attack him violently when he refused to put it on.

The battle in the press over *The Vikings at Helgeland* during the spring of 1858 must be difficult for anyone but Norwegians to understand. Here we return to the almost explosive transformation of the spoken language in Norwegian towns throughout the nineteenth century, which was also the basic reason why Ole Bull started a Norwegian theatre in Bergen.

The youthful Norwegian literature had begun to be both conscious of itself and vociferous. But the diminishing civil service, concentrated in the capital, defended its ramparts. One of its ramparts was Christiania Theatre, to which one went not only to see but also to be seen—especially after the theatre had put in a new chandelier. The director was Danish, and most of the actors Danish—although Johannes Brun and his wife had already been brought from Bergen.

Ibsen had submitted *The Vikings at Helgeland* to Christiania Theatre because the play, inspired as it was by the companionship of Suzannah, was the apple of his eye, and it could not be performed in the music-hall he himself was to direct. He submitted it in the autumn of 1857, and waited for an answer until the New Year of 1858. When he sent a reminder, it appeared that Borgaard, the director of the theatre, who had received it 'by some means', had not even read it, and had no particular desire to put it on. A little later Borgaard received support from the high priest of good taste in Scandinavia, J. L. Heiberg in Copenhagen, who rejected it in very contemptuous terms.

But Ibsen and his Norwegian-minded friends used this to start a definitive attack on the 'Danophiles'. In contrast to *Lady Inger*, *The Vikings* now belongs to literature—and Norwegian culture. It is seldom performed, but it presages the claws of the lion; and to a greater extent than *Lady Inger* it indicates the renewal of Greek tragedy in modern dress.

Since his first visit to Kristiania, Ibsen had been searching for his own cultural roots. This is evident not only in the plays he wrote in Bergen: like so many others of that generation, he had tried in articles and lectures to define what made them Norwegians and not just borrowers from a Danish-German-European common culture. Such endeavours, for that matter, were not confined to Norway, for the Danes themselves had rediscovered their past and its special qualities, and through Grundtvig, Oehlenschläger and others had sought for their sources back in history.

Historical themes were much admired. Fairy-tales, folk songs and sagas were becoming very popular in many parts of Europe. Ibsen's approach to this material had hitherto been considered influenced by Oehlenschläger's poetry and J. L. Heiberg's thirst for aesthetics, then characteristic of Europe as a whole. This is the main reason why his juvenile plays appear to be 'apprentice-work', steadily improving in construction, but conforming to accepted norms so unlike those of today that they died with their time—notwithstanding that in their dramatic content there are hints of the explosive future.

He had long shied away from the sagas, finding them unsuitable material for drama, in that they are such completely stripped poetry, so naked in their finely polished form; and indeed he should have perceived all along that the sagas, with their stark brutal simplicity, would disturb theatre audiences who preferred charm to truth, perfume to sweat.

But Ibsen, under a new influence, had achieved new confidence. He had met a girl who gave him courage to aim at a massive simplicity, to sacrifice finesse to strength and clarity of design. For many people, *The Vikings* is an infatuated, almost frightening, play about Hjørdis—Suzannah. Once more the form is taken direct from the saga itself.

It is not easy to say how it happened that the ageing, good-natured Borgaard, as director of Christiania Theatre, gave his young colleague at the people's theatre in Møllergaten some kind of promise to put on the play. But anyhow Ibsen waited nearly six months for a reply, and finally received the following rejection, which he must have thought both cowardly and hypocritical:

'. . . as the theatre's financial state and the outlook for takings in the near future do not allow the theatre's funds to pay an honorarium for original work, the play *The Vikings at Helgeland*, submitted by Mr Ibsen cannot be staged during the present season.'

This was a signal for Ibsen's bitterest feud hitherto, for the rejection was directed not only at his own play but against all Norwegian drama. He dashed into the fray in the evening paper *Aftenbladet* on March 10th with an article, since called *The Ibsen Manifesto*; and those who believe that the cultural debate of the old days was on a high academic and tolerant plane from which it has since declined, may find some of it diverting reading.

The *Manifesto* itself is both clever and amusing, for example the following passage:

'First Christiania Theatre defended itself against emergent Norwegian art with the argument that our language, our inborn lack of lightness, etc., put insuperable obstacles in the way of scenic performance. . . . But it is a good thing that this statement has been made. Peace in our dramatic world must and shall now be shattered. The public must take sides *for* or against, as the present neutral position is untenable.'

The theatre management chose to ignore the challenge, but four days later Botten-Hansen came out on Ibsen's side with a powerful salvo in his weekly paper *Illustrated News*; some weeks later he published *The Vikings* as a supplement for his thirteen to fourteen hundred subscribers, a select clientele including most Norwegian intellectuals.

The theatre management, however, soon acquired a defender, one of the most rabid Danophiles of the day, of ill repute in all Norwegian-minded circles; one Richard Petersen, a lawyer. He poured scorn on this boundlessly vain man Ibsen, who considered himself significant as an author, and who had the temerity to 'identify himself with the whole country's dramatic literature'.

'Mr Ibsen is a great nonentity as a dramatist, round whom the
nation cannot with any warmth plant a protective hedge. *The
Feast at Solhaug* is too devoid of the freshness of originality to
hold out any hope for the future; and his next dramatic work,
Lady Inger of Østråt reveals an astonishing lack of idealism and
poetry. Every character in this play is marked with the stamp of
baseness. . . . Nationalist sentiment which allows itself to be fed on
domestic weeds is not worthy.'

He concludes by characterizing Ibsen's attack on the theatre as 'A
strident outburst in the trashy Norwegian tongue. . . .' (Incidentally, it can be added that Petersen found his true bent and became
a prison governor.)

Ibsen was by no means at a loss for an answer. In the next two
articles the abuse is not spared:

'In truth one has to be turned by years of insult into some spiritual
galley-slave before one can disregard the simplest demands of a
sense of honour and to that extent forget official decorum which
forbids an honest person to use dirty means to help a good cause,
rather than say an unclean thing! . . . There is a platitude which
all kinds of intellectual parrots use continually, when they are
really demanding the attention of the public eye. I mean the
platitude about European culture, how this may not be shut out,
etc., etc. This constant tirade repeated to a loathsome degree, my
opponents have naturally not disdained.'

And then the final salvo—italics by Ibsen: '. . . have taken refuge
in *stupidity, dishonesty and obvious falsehood*'.

The battle over *The Vikings* echoed throughout the Norwegian
press during the following weeks and caused the new Norwegian
drama to make considerable strides. Bjørnson himself, who was
then artistic director in Bergen, chimed in, despite the fact that he
could not claim that *The Vikings* was a play. Ibsen was in his eyes
no playwright, but a useful lyric poet, and here there was not even
poetry, only echoes of the sagas. But the rejection of the play was

an insult to the whole of the new Norwegian literature. '. . . truly there is a sense of decency in the country—there must be an end to this sort of treatment of the country's authors, and most of all when one drags them in the mud simply to maintain by their ruin a Danish theatre.'

Of the later fortunes of the play, all there is to say is that Ibsen ventured to have his own extremely inadequate company perform it in the November of that year. He spared neither pains nor money in the production and he received very important favourable reviews. And Bjørnson also produced it later in Bergen, despite the fact that he disliked it. He wrote to Clemens Petersen, the powerful Danish critic, in March, 1859:

'I hope one day to get him back to himself and away from all this damned imitation. The day Ibsen admits that *he is small*, he will at once be a rather endearing writer. I have said this to him quite clearly, but I fear he is *jealous*. He has annoyed me several times, and still does. It has offended him that I have not taken *The Vikings* into my repertoire, but I really cannot oblige in this. Now one of the actors has chosen it for his benefit performance, to get a full house, and I have been working on it so much that today I am tired. I have completely changed *the play*.'

In the same letter is this comment on Ibsen: 'To this must be added that in stature he is quite a small little fellow, without backside or chest. . . .'

It must have been a strange performance.

The irony of fate struck Christiania Theatre three years later. *The Vikings* was then performed there, with the theatre's young tragedienne, Laura Svendsen—later to become the most famous Norwegian actress of the century, under the name of Laura Gundersen—in the part of Hjørdis, and was a success, so much so that the part remained one of Mrs Gundersen's favourite rôles for the rest of her life. She performed it a hundred times altogether, the last time when she was in her sixties. Halvdan Koht was among those who saw her on that occasion, and in the 1956 edition of his great biography of Ibsen still recalls the performance as dreadful.

7

Towards Defeat

IBSEN'S first year as director of the theatre in Kristiania, after much toil and struggle, had been a good year for both the theatre and himself; for the theatre in that it had enlarged its audiences and also to some extent trained its company. It also probably had to increase expenditure, so the increased receipts were not sufficient to pay off old debts, but the progress made gave cause for optimism.

And Ibsen himself had, or rather thought he had, found a foothold in the capital again, achieving the position of a man of the theatre, finding allies and emerging into the limelight within the cultural life of the town. But more than that; his income, for the first and last time until he was over thirty-eight, must have been greater than his expenditure, so he was able to pay off a little of his burden of debt, although his correspondence shows that it must have been slow going.

Anyhow he could now take the plunge and he married Suzannah in the summer of 1858, after an engagement lasting two and a half years. The wedding took place in Bergen in June, 1858, very quietly and simply, as Suzannah's father had died only a few days earlier. Then the two young people returned to Kristiania and with great optimism Ibsen began his second season at Kristiania Norwegian Theatre. Soon, however, in fact by that very autumn and winter, a slow and merciless stagnation began. There is nothing to indicate that there was anything wrong with his marriage at this time; perhaps that happened later. But the crisis that began that winter seems to have been at the time a conflict between his boundless ambition and the little he could achieve.

He did not really fail in his theatre work during that second season. He receives praise in the press for being industrious and conscientious, but at the end of the season we can read between the lines of his annual report that he is beginning to become extremely tired of the obligations of stage-management, in the struggle against inertia, lack of talent and indifference. He had probably hoped that at the drop of a hat he would be able to create a national Norwegian theatre, forming a focal point in intellectual life, and now he discovered that he was fundamentally wrong.

It cannot have surprised him that the town's 'good audience', the secure little nucleus of officials included, continued to associate themselves with Kristiania Theatre, where Thursdays were especially favoured by the best people. But he must have been disappointed that the champions of the Norwegian theatre who had brought him from Bergen proved to be so few and so uninterested. Kristiania Norwegian Theatre was forced to go on building on the extremely ordinary and mixed audience, who preferred fun to intellectual life, who applauded loudly when the actors overplayed to the gallery. Most of the players with talent were in the rival theatre, and those who were left were unruly because they knew far better than the stage-manager what a not always entirely sober audience expected of them. And purely linguistically, because of Knud Knudsen's much too impatient and somewhat uncertain efforts on behalf of national language reform, they were forced to use unnatural speech, which did not improve matters. Approximately every Wednesday a new show had to be set up. Ten years later when he was well out of it all, Ibsen wrote the following heartfelt cry to Bjørnson: 'Theatre work for a writer is a daily criminal abortion. The laws of our society punish such things. I do not know whether Our Lord is more broadminded. Think on that, my dear Bjørnson! Talent is no right, it is a duty.'

But his fatigue at having to perform unavoidable abortions to give the audience in Møllergaten popular entertainment was by no means the only reason for the approaching crisis. He was growing steadily more confused within himself, both about

D

what he wanted to do in his writing, and what form he should give it.

When he had come back from Bergen, naturally enough he had rejoined his old friend Paul Botten-Hansen, who had now become the central figure in another small inner circle of the intellectual élite. Botten-Hansen's weekly paper was one of the most important cultural organs in the country, and the circle round him formed a kind of discussion-group which gathered in his 'den' or in the taverns, where they discussed the cultural lassitude of the time. This circle was feared for their sharp tongues and their scorn of all humbug—and not only against official conservative hypocrisy, but also against everything they found of this kind on the left. They went under the name of 'The Dutchmen' and it was clear that they did not take their cocksure political discussions completely seriously, but regarded themselves as a *collegium politicum* which criticized all and sundry.

It is clear that Ibsen at first felt at home in this circle. He shared most of its antipathies, and it was at this time that he received the name of 'Gert Westphaler', after the vociferous barber in Holberg's comedy. The difference between this circle and himself was simply that his antipathies went so much deeper than the superficial criticism which was in question here, and also that he was very uncertain of his own sympathies.

The work became steadily more of a burden to him. Friends of the theatre also began to complain, calling the repertoire 'worthless trash', and writing: 'It is incomprehensible that in untroubled jollity and light, the whole theatre is allowed to wander its way along the Danish rut—and under the leadership of a *Norwegian* writer.' This crisis became more acute during the ensuing years, because the theatre management, encouraged by success, entered into the hazardous undertaking of buying the theatre building itself so that they could keep it, thus incurring a considerable debt.

At the turn of the year 1858–59, Ibsen tried to defend himself: 'At a theatre one learns to be practical. One gets used to conceding to the forces of circumstance and temporarily giving up higher demands when this must be so.' The resignation in this heartfelt statement shows how far he had gone.

But things were sliding rapidly in other directions too. As a lyric poet he had been acknowledged by all, and at first he never stopped writing prologues and festive songs to order. But after a year or so, this too began to fade, he could no longer bring himself to write them and when later on he published his poems, he firmly excluded nearly all those written at this time. Only one or two poems, which must have involved a great deal of work, survived and are included among his best work.

Things were no better with his dramatic writing. He tried to rewrite Olaf Liljekrans as an opera libretto, he brooded over ideas for *Love's Comedy* and for what later became *The Pretenders*, but neither gave birth to nor aborted any of them. And linguistically he also found himself in an uncertain period of experiment, wavering between urbane festal-songs and sudden violent attempts to Norwegianize his language, almost to the lengths of the 'national language' which Ivar Aasen had created with his dictionary a year or so earlier.

It is evident that the company of the 'Dutchmen', which at first tended to stimulate and develop his critical understanding, had a negative effect upon him in the long run. So it was with obvious delight that Ibsen welcomed Bjørnson when he returned from Bergen in 1859, after having turned that town upside-down for two years. Now Bjørnson had bought a half share in the evening paper, *Aftenbladet*, which he was to edit in order to conquer the capital too, a conquest which took him very many years. Ibsen lived then in a small apartment in Maltheby—the three-storey block on the corner of Akersgaten and Teatergaten, which still stands today—and Bjørnson and his Karoline, a childhood friend of Suzannah's, lived in the same block for a while. Bjørnson also mixed with the 'learned Dutchmen' a great deal at first, but soon became a target for their wit and later came to regard them as deadly enemies.

In the autumn of 1859, however, relations between Ibsen and Bjørnson were very good, and it was Ibsen who urged Bjørnson to start a Norwegian Society, for the promotion of 'Norwegianism'. At the same time Ibsen renewed his friendship with Aasmund Olavson, who had now adopted his Telemark dialect

in his writing and developed into a serious writer. He was thus at
the time under the influence of no fewer than three strong and
fundamentally different schools of thought.

In the New Year something happened to which Ibsen's bio-
graphers have paid no attention, beyond noting it in records.
Suzannah had given birth to a son on Christmas Eve, 1859. He
was christened Sigurd after the hero in *The Vikings*, and Bjørnson
stood godfather. But no sooner had she arrived home than she
declared that she did not want any more children. Indeed, she
said so with such emphasis that it echoed all over Maltheby, and
became something of a scandal in the town. This is her only
known flagrant breach of the loyal silence of a life time: perhaps
her famous strong temperament got the better of her; perhaps a
specially painful and difficult birth provoked a cry of agony.

Anyhow, it is a fact that she did not have any more children,
which, though the reasons may well have been physiological
(perhaps including post-natal complications), *could* also mean that
with the strength of mind of which everyone knew this quiet
woman to be capable, she became from that moment his faithful
but platonic friend. We do not know. Ibsen, reserved and closed
in childhood, youth and young manhood, remained so to the end
of his days and was successful in guarding the secrets of his private
life—apart from the implications of this violent outburst of
Suzannah's and one or two spells of illness, called 'nerve-fever' by
his daughter-in-law in her memoirs, *The Three*. But if after
Sigurd's birth Suzannah did cease to have sexual relations with
her husband, that would be another and very human reason for
the depression which troubled him during the ensuing years.

He wrote only two really great poems during these years, the
philosophical poem 'In the Mountain Wilderness' and 'Terje
Vigen', two poems as different as night and day. 'Terje Vigen' has
become folk-lore. Every child in Norway knows it to this day:
indeed, its resonance, rhythm and dramatic force are such that one
can get long sections of it by heart after only a few readings, and
then one ceases to consider what it really means. The other poem,
'In the Mountain Wilderness' is regarded by Ibsen scholars as the
beginning of his release from aesthetics, from everything that had

hitherto bound him, and of his journey towards a 'higher vision'.

It has been called obscure. I must confess that I see it in a slightly different light. The poem is about a young man who goes up into the mountains. On the way up to his lonely destination, he meets and loves a young woman; she becomes his, but then he resumes his climb. And always, later on, when he longs to return to the valley, to everyday family life, he is pierced by a mysterious inner voice which questions his motives and counsels: 'You should be alone.' Then from the mountain slope he sees his mother's house burning, and his love becoming another's bride, but still he has to choose life in the wilderness.

First, the story is obviously the precursor of both *Brand* and *Peer Gynt*. Brand goes to the mountains in order to *find* himself, Peer to *flee* from himself; the one in an almost perverse lack of belief in himself, the other betraying himself.

Secondly, if Suzannah had indeed chosen to follow the writer rather than the husband, then on the personal level we have a sermon by Ibsen himself, about the need to be free from everything down 'in the valley', free from Botten-Hansen, Bjørnson, theatre troubles, consideration, debt and caution—even from the ties of love.

But in the meantime things went badly for him for several years. The intellectuals of Kristiania industriously noted in their diaries that he grew more and more unkempt, he neglected his work, he failed to go to management meetings. It happened that the aloof gentlemen in the management came to hear that Ibsen was sitting drunk in some tavern or other while he should have been giving an account of himself at a management meeting. So they picked up their hats and silver-topped sticks and went to the tavern and took him to task, as he sat there alone in the coat 'he lived in', his soft broad-brimmed hat on his head, being reprimanded by his betters. Usually it was in the back room of the Café l'Orsa in Prinsensgaten. For a long time he went about dressed in a so-called poncho, a large woollen rug with a hole to put your head through and belted round the waist, such as shepherds wear in many southern countries.

And he was ill too. At the time several names were given to his illness, usually nerve-fever, but anyhow depression, crushing depression, was what it was. It has also been related that he ran amok in the streets, and that his Suzannah had to fetch him back home and nurse him. All the witnesses agree that in *that* respect, she never let him down.

Much fun has been made of Ibsen's later vanity and his weakness for honours. He was probably just as vain at this time too, just as keen to avenge the humiliations of his childhood years. But who was he now? A public scandal, in debt and tied hand and foot, degraded and lonely, and just when his two literary contemporaries looked like succeeding. His place in the intellectual world in the spring of 1860 is indicated when Bjørnson, Ibsen and Vinje applied for travel grants. Bjørnson asked for a thousand riksdalers, Vinje for five hundred, to travel to England, and Ibsen contented himself with applying for four hundred riksdalers for a study-journey to the theatres in London and Paris. The University, which had now glimpsed what was inside Vinje, accepted him, and the government, which had not been able to avoid noticing Bjørnson's success, accepted him too. Bjørnson received five hundred riksdalers, Vinje two hundred and fifty, and Ibsen nothing.

Things did not become any easier for Ibsen when Bjørnson and Vinje went their own ways, leaving him alone among the 'Dutchmen'. As relations between Ibsen and Bjørnson have already been mentioned and a couple of flippant comments by Bjørnson about Ibsen have been quoted, it is perhaps relevant here to put in their true perspective the ill-considered sarcasms Bjørnson permitted himself in a private letter, in irritation over having had to work hard all day on a play he detested, certainly never dreaming that his words would be preserved for posterity. The relationship between Norway's two greatest writers is in fact quite a complex one, and if one takes them too literally, the picture will be distorted, for both of them were irascible when they first put their indignation down on paper and their recriminations were expressions of anger rather than genuine opinions. It is therefore no digression, but necessary to a true portrait of Ibsen to try to separate bagatelles from main issues.

Ibsen's career was a complete contrast to that of Bjørnson, the other Norwegian writer of his century to become world famous. Ibsen came to dominate the drama of the world for generations. He therefore also came to mean indirectly an enormous amount to his own country. He carved his words in stone, and they have endured. Bjørnson's nature and character were quite different. Four years younger than Ibsen, he conquered, seduced and enchanted his own country's cultural life long before the older Ibsen's influence was felt. His writing sprang from the heart. He not only became the country's greatest lyric poet, releasing all its pent-up creative powers, but he also became a vigorous playwright, and a politician deeply concerned with culture and human values, who as speaker, writer and agitator compelled the attention of the whole world, from Russia in the East to America in the West, on an equal footing with all the greatest men of his time.

All this is hindsight, and it is easy to see that Bjørnson did not always carve his words in stone. He poured out his life-giving force upon the world for direct use, and much of it was used up in his time and is played out and obsolete for readers of today. But his contribution to Norway and the whole of Europe cannot be denigrated on those grounds.

Was it then just the primitive jealousy of two cocks on the same dunghill which made them become alternately close friends and bitter enemies? Well, no doubt there was some of that on both sides. Even if Ibsen was by nature quieter and more withdrawn than his younger friend and enemy, Bjørnson's success must necessarily have rankled a little. That Bjørnson for his part underestimated Ibsen for a number of years, must also be attributed to the fundamental differences of temperament. They moved in two different worlds, and Ibsen's real capabilities first appeared above the surface of the earth after Bjørnson had laid it at his feet. But that Bjørnson was a good friend to Ibsen during these years and that he wholeheartedly wished him well, there is no doubt.

It was not Botten-Hansen, the faithful ally, who came to Ibsen's aid when things were at their worst, for he had no influence which would have helped straighten things out then. It was Bjørnson, who from his immense breadth of mind saved Ibsen from ultimate ruin, applied himself to getting grants for him, collected money for him, helped and supported him. Had Bjørnson not done this, it is hard to say what would have happened to Ibsen's potentialities as a writer of immortal plays. Later we shall take a look at the letters Ibsen wrote to Bjørnson after he had departed, largely through Bjørnson's help, from his humiliating fatherland and was able to breathe freely. They were the warmest letters Ibsen ever wrote, and Bjørnson deserved them.

Later on a breach occurred between them, then ambivalent reunion and breach, and then relationship by marriage, and both grew older and neither of them liked what the other wrote. That was natural enough, considering their different temperaments. But certainly Ibsen lost a much needed friend when Bjørnson went away on his travel grants, and Bjørnson was the saving of Ibsen when he returned.

Bjørnson left and Ibsen went round Kristiania frittering away his life, doubting his future aims, doubting almost everything. At the end of what turned out to be the last year but one of theatre rivalry, he excuses himself, in August, 1861, by saying that many external circumstances have gone against the theatre. The rebuilding has cost money, the flight of the best actors from the theatre has made proper planning impossible and everything has been insuperably difficult. And although the theatre's takings that year were the highest they had ever been, they were nowhere near enough to cover the large new debt. He ends his revealing annual report with the following lines:

'If one weighs up these figures and takes into due consideration what I have mentioned above in reference to the internal circumstances of the theatre, then it is to be hoped that it will at once be acknowledged what weight can be given to the criticisms which have been brought against my leadership of the theatre during the past season.'

The following season found the theatre facing dissolution. Who was to blame is hard to say, as everyone blamed everyone

else. The purchase of the building had not been carefully considered, the rebuilding had been poorly administered, the theatre
director had been slack and indulgent and the takings were again
on the downward slope. In these circumstances, the management
of the Kristiania Norwegian Theatre attempted to arrange a
merger with Christiania Theatre. This failed, however, as Christiania Theatre could not manage to take over the quite considerable
debt of twenty-eight thousand riksdalers by which the theatre in
Møllergaten had finally been broken.

The growing bitterness of the men who had fetched Ibsen
from Bergen five years before receives its clearest expression in
Knud Knudsen's memoirs. He relates how he shrank for as long as
possible from dismissing Ibsen and did not do so:

'1. Because we had no one else available.
2. Because we always expected that the pressure exerted from the
   management would eventually have an effect.
3. Because he undoubtedly *understood* the job better than anyone
   else we could find.
4. Because we hesitated to let a man otherwise so deserving
   become destitute.'

A final attempt was made to keep the theatre going by the
players hiring it for the 1862–63 season at a rent of eighteen
hundred speciedalers, to be paid off at the rate of eighteen speciedalers after each of the first hundred performances; later this rent
was lowered. In the course of the season, the theatre question was
settled, after much controversy: the theatre in Møllergaten was
declared bankrupt, while because of the bad times Christiania
Theatre was on the brink of ruin too; and as there had been for
several reasons a good deal of criticism of both theatres, the plan
for a merger of the two theatre companies into one, which would
perform in the theatre in Bankplasse, was abandoned.

Meanwhile, however, Ibsen had received a much-needed
breathing space in the summer of 1862. He had applied for one
hundred and twenty riksdalers from the University to enable him
to take a walking tour over the mountains to Vestland in search
of folk-lore, legends and fairy-tales, and he had in fact received a

grant, if only of one hundred and ten dalers—as Koht bitingly remarks: 'in accordance with the firm Norwegian tradition of never giving quite as much as has been applied for'.

He set off at midsummer in 1862, first by train to Eidsvoll, on Norway's first railway-line, and then by paddle-steamer to Lillehammer and on up through Gudbrandsdalen. For the first part of the tour he was accompanied by the actor Andreas Isachsen, whose acquaintance he had made earlier in his Grimstad days, and who had later co-operated with him both at the theatre in Bergen and in Kristiania. Many years later Isachsen related a story which again tells us a little of Henrik Ibsen's ambivalent relations to the concept of clothing. A few miles north of Lillehammer they stopped overnight at an old post-inn, together with Yngvar Nielsen, later Professor Nielsen, and his father. Ibsen noticed that the Nielsens were both wearing knee-breeches, as they were so practical. Yngvar Nielsen was a pioneer of what later became tourism. As Ibsen and Isachsen walked on up through Gudbrands valley, Ibsen speculated a great deal over those knee-breeches, especially when during their wanderings his own long trousers became more and more frayed at the bottom. Then he made a swift decision and cut his trouser-legs off at the knee.

From Gudbrandsdalen, he went on westwards, now in the company of a strict Catholic priest and a young Norwegian lawyer, who was at the time very much in love, and the journey over Sognefjellet and Fanaråken has in every way made its mark upon his writing: the powerful and dramatic impressions of his native Norwegian mountains haunt him for ever, and he uses them over and over again in his writing; and the strict priest and the lovesick lawyer are not hard to find again.

From Sogn he went northwards to Møre. He collected a great deal of folk-lore, but much of the material was lost when his possessions were sold by auction after he had abandoned Norway. So this enterprise too remained uncompleted; he was still fumbling, experimenting and letting things lie.

In the autumn of 1862, however, he collected himself for the great effort of finishing his next play, the one for which he had for years been trying in vain to find a form. Originally it was to have been called after the saga princess, Svanhild—alias Suzannah—but it was now given the title *Love's Comedy* and published as a New Year supplement to the *Illustrated News* at the turn of the year 1862–63—the paper was now in the hands of the writer, Jonas Lie.

Love's Comedy is unique in Ibsen's work. Drawn from his situation in life, it is at the same time confusing and explanatory, burlesque and serious.

It is very easy to show that it is influenced by Søren Kierkegaard, and that it is an important step on the way towards the great clash in *Brand*. For *theatre people* of today it is rather uninteresting, as it is written in such an emphatic verse form that it cannot be modernized and is so bound to its own day in much of its dialogue that if it is performed nowadays it is only as a respectful gesture towards its author.

But as a cultural phenomenon it stands alone. For the first time since *St John's Night*, Ibsen chooses a theme and environment from his own time; Kristiania in 1862. One would have thought that such realism would have made him choose prose, but finally he chose verse—and what verse! Lavish, satirical, humorous verse, which in its rhymes often makes fun of itself, and deliberately stumbles over its own feet, but which is a cascade of witty epigrams on all tepid intimacy miscalled love.

The treatment is pure farce, the characters caricatures, and when the writer Falk thinks to expose the weaknesses of these wretches, their fears are quite unreal, because none of them for one moment can have believed that he was dangerous. But in this tremendous display of scornful fireworks, there is a corroding bitterness which makes the play rewarding reading even today, a sort of parodoxical toast, 'Hurrah for friendship, tea, love and females!'

But behind all the farcical jokes—about the priest Straamand (Strawman) and his twelve children, Miss Skjaere who yearns for her clerk Styver, the slightly infatuated merchant and all the women—lurk the signs of tragedy, in the relations between two individuals, Falk and Svanhild. The writer Falk, despite his biting chastisement of all the lies which stifle the air, is himself also pretty much of a hypocrite. Underneath the lyrical pathos Ibsen has deliberately smuggled in so much hypocrisy and hot air that the end of the whole comedy is logical enough. When Falk has finally persuaded the honourable, fearless and genuine Svanhild to promise that she will follow him in total rebellion against all the conventions, the merchant Guldstad punctures the whole idealistic enterprise by the simple expedient of offering them money to make the rebellion reality. Then Falk does not dare, and Svanhild resigns herself. But in another way there is also a good balance in the comedy, because Ibsen lets the wretched Straamand of the first two acts be transformed in the final scene of the third act into a wise and humane defender of his own resignation.

In short Ibsen had written a farcical comedy about his own time and his own wretched life. He later stated that his wife was the only person to approve of the play when it came out; a fact which seemed to suggest that to a far greater extent than in any of the other plays, she had been involved in working out the problems inherent in it—sharing his scorn, but sharing his self-irony as well.

Love's Comedy naturally attracted attention when it came out, with its ridicule of the respectable, its deliberate denunciation of contemporary top people, its scorn for the society that Henrik Ibsen lived in and all its institutions. It is remarkable on the whole that he dared send it in at this, the poorest period of life. All his earlier plays had in different ways bowed to the tastes of the audience, had tried to express what was of current interest. By contrast, this one was pure challenge, a battle-cry. Did he think that its easy form, its glowing elegant humour, its aphorisms and paradoxes, would make people laugh at themselves without knowing what they were laughing at? Or is it depression and the humour of depression which *had* to be aired?

People did not laugh. They slaughtered him as emphatically as they could have done. *Love's Comedy* was received enthusiastically nowhere. Jonas Lie wrote to Bjørnson that as the publisher of the book, he naturally would not profit from Professor Monrad criticizing it too strongly, 'but I cannot see my way to defend it'.

Monrad's conclusion was that the end of the play involved 'a break with ideas, which upset human emotions'. Ditmar Meidell called it 'an appalling product of literary amateurism', a member of the Academic Collegium is said to have stated that whoever wrote such comedy should be thrashed and not receive the grant he was seeking, and Botten-Hansen himself, Ibsen's close friend, declared that the writer of *Love's Comedy* 'unfortunately was entirely lacking in ideals and convictions'.

The verdict was sometimes that 'the devil was stupid and had not reckoned with his audience', sometimes that the play was desperate hysterical laughter. Either way it caused him even more wretchedness.

What did Ibsen live on at this time, apart from the hundred riksdalers Jonas Lie had given him as author's honorarium? He had been dismissed from the directorship of the theatre. It must have been a wretched time for him, even if he did earn a little by long articles in *Morgenbladet* throughout the autumn on the current struggle of the two theatres to achieve a merger, and as a critic (he unashamedly wrote a glowing review of his stepmother-in-law's latest collection of stories). His reviewing activities came to an end at the beginning of 1863, when he became tied to the Christiania Theatre as literary consultant at a salary a little less than half what had hitherto been his lowest subsistence level. He was to have twenty-five riksdalers a month, and that only if the theatre did not do too badly—which, in the ensuing months, it did. In addition, Koht is undoubtedly right when he says that *Morgenbladet* would not have wanted him to continue as a reviewer after the fiasco of *Love's Comedy*. But he was at least able to return to his earlier activities as a diligent writer of commemorative verse, for in *this* particular line everyone knew he reigned supreme.

In February, 1863, the government put forward a motion to the effect that Bjørnstjerne Bjørnson should receive a literary stipend of four hundred riksdalers a year. He was not the first, as the much older Andreas Munch had a similar grant three years earlier. While the matter was making its way through a parliamentary committee and to Parliament, Ibsen sent in an application for a literary stipend too. First he gives an account of his career, and then he turns to his financial situation:

'My appointment at the Kristiania Norwegian Theatre amounted to an average annual income of about six hundred speciedalers! but the theatre's bankruptcy caused me a loss of one hundred and fifty speciedalers and simultaneously left me without definite employment. At the Christiania Theatre I was paid a nominal salary of twenty-five speciedalers monthly, but the payment of the full sum presupposed larger takings at the theatre than it has been able to achieve during the current winter.'

He continues in this vein, saying that in Norway it is impossible to live as a free-lance writer, and that he plans to emigrate to Denmark if he is refused. How can he have thought that he would be able to support himself better there than in Norway?

That the government did not wish to recommend his application was clear, but its report to Parliament was not entirely negative and it was implied that there was a possibility of his at least reciving a travel grant the following year of the same type that Vinje and Bjørnson had received in 1860.

In parliamentary circles things were stormy. It was clear that the majority was against a literary grant to Ibsen, but there were also several people who were in sympathy with him, but thought it tactically unwise of him to apply just then, as this could also put the literary grant to Bjørnson in jeopardy. During the debate in April, however, Rolf Olsen, a Member of Parliament, proposed a grant to Ibsen. The proposal failed, but there were only forty-nine votes against, to forty in favour.

This large minority, together with the possibility of a reasonable travel grant the following year, must have been very encouraging to Ibsen. He had already applied for and received a hundred dalers to continue with his collection of folk-lore—a stipend he just used and never accounted for. But now he applied for the *large* travel grant—no less than six hundred riksdalers 'to stay in Rome and Paris for a year to study art, history of art and literature'. He says at the end of his application: 'I am venturing to observe that travel grants of this kind have already been offered to all

Norwegian writers, with the exception of myself, who have made literary activity their exclusive occupation, and it is therefore that I herewith humbly . . . .', etc.

But that spring and summer gave Ibsen other encouragement which indicated that his wretched years of wandering in the wilderness would soon be over. The students asked him to be their guest at a choral festival they were to hold in Bergen. One would have thought that he would obviously be included. Ibsen had written more songs and prologues for students than anyone else and was now about to write some more. As a poet he was acknowledged everywhere. At the student gathering in Sweden the year before, he had probably written the songs, though he had not been present himself. But Ibsen was so starved of praise that he regarded this as an honour, and he no doubt also thought that the Bergeners had been in part responsible for the invitation. This was not the case. On the contrary, the small town of Bergen knew all about the gossip that had been circulating in the small town of Kristiania, and was fully aware of Ibsen's very dubious reputation. So there was some difficulty in finding anyone who would give him lodgings—both he and the students were to be accommodated privately.

The coastal steamer arrived at Bergen from Kristiania on June 14, 1863. Naturally enough, Bjørnson was there to add glitter and festivity to the occasion, and festive it was in every respect. Ibsen afterwards remembered this trip as one of his happiest experiences. No doubt he owed much to the fact that Bjørnson, the central figure, embraced him and honoured him in every way; but anyhow Ibsen saw in his reception a sign that the Bergeners had at last taken him to their hearts. And certainly they soon discovered that at least he neither behaved badly nor got drunk. His former chairman, Peter Blytt, who during his Bergen years had been indulgent and friendly, as well as standing surety for his debts, now became his close companion and friend for the rest of his life.

But it was first and foremost Bjørnson's company which meant so much to him. Bjørnson was at one of the many peaks of his career and was naturally the cynosure, the students' god, and he had just received Parliament's greatest honour for life. Ibsen, on the other hand, had gone from failure to failure. Bjørnson knew this as well as Ibsen himself and realized that he *needed* encouragement and praise; so, generous and impulsive as always, he did everything to push him into the limelight. In the conversations between them he managed to melt Ibsen's frozen heart and fire him to new achievements.

Ibsen returned home from this trip happily intoxicated by his localized success and with renewed courage to return to the attack. This time he went back to historical material, but used it in quite a different way. And when he had once got started, he went on writing until he had finished. This time it was not to be any kind of imitation saga, illuminating the sources of Norwegian culture, but simply a psychological play, set in a historical framework which would make it clear to all.

Only six months earlier he had come out strongly in defence of Bjørnson's *Sigurd Slembe*, and the end of that review might well stand as a justification of his own new play, *The Pretenders*.

'That the language is not that of the saga, and neither should it be, will be clear from the above, but in case anyone should regard this as some kind of reproach, then he should consider that a definite historical language would have been wrong where the writer, as here, has set himself the task of portraying a mental struggle that will be valid and comprehensible for all times. Writing with these foundations has nothing to do with time and contemporaneity.'

By this statement, to a certain extent Ibsen admits Bjørnson's objections to *The Vikings*, for in *The Vikings* Ibsen had not only set himself a psychological task, but also a cultural one, for he had attempted to approach the saga's own prose style.

This new play was the first purely psychological drama that Ibsen had attempted since *Catiline*, though once again he chose a historical framework, this time with material from Håkon Håkonsson, who in the thirteenth century managed to put an end to civil war in Norway and unite the country. Certainly he did not manage to fulfil the promise of the battle-cry which Ibsen put into his mouth: 'Norway is a kingdom; she shall become a people'; but the slogan endured and was repeated over and over again in Norwegian politics throughout the rest of last century.

It has been implied that Ibsen borrowed the material from Bjørnson's great festival speech during the choral festival in Bergen in June, in which he named Håkon Håkonsson as Norway's greatest king. But this is probably not true. It is very probable that the two friends during their conversations in Bergen had discussed themes from sagas and history, which they had both used a great deal, and when Bjørnson calls King Håkon the great unifying symbol, this is more likely a result of these conversations than a sudden notion which Ibsen then immediately made use of.

The characters, anyhow, were created by Ibsen himself, out of problems he had brooded over during the past few years: the conflict between the demands of ideals, the call he knew he had to follow, belief in himself on the one side, and on the other gnawing vacillation, doubt, the little daily betrayal. That he had also found inspiration in the powerful rays of Bjørnson's confidence is more than likely, but this inspiration he was also able to draw from many other sources in Europe at this time. He had worked on the problem himself both in his writing and in his own difficult life.

Some people have thought that the two contrasting characters, the confident Håkon and the doubting Duke Skule, are Ibsen's portraits of Bjørnson and himself, but it is more probable that both these two main characters, and for that matter Bishop Nikolas too, are different aspects of Ibsen himself, contrasted one with another.

In his letter of 1870 to the Danish Peter Hansen, from which we have already quoted, Ibsen describes this period after the failure of *Love's Comedy* as a time when he was excommunicated and everyone turned against him. He goes on: 'This matter of everyone being against me—this obsession that I no longer had anyone outside, of whom I could say that he believed in me, must, as you can well imagine, have created an atmosphere which found release in *The Pretenders*. Enough of that.' As we can see, this is only partially true. Bjørnson had already proved his belief in him, and was to prove it still further. But it must be remembered that this letter was written during a period of Ibsen's life when he wanted to forget the former close friendship between himself and Bjørnson.

As history, *The Pretenders* is a somewhat free fantasy. It does not give a true picture of the cunning and wily politician Håkon, who successfully carried out his great idea, but not without betrayal and villainy. Among other things, he had Snorre Sturlason assassinated: if he had not, if Snorre had been allowed to bring his royal chronicles of Norway up to date, perhaps Ibsen would have had more subtle and varied material for his portrait of Håkon Håkonsson. But dramatically, *The Pretenders* is so firmly constructed, so clear and tense in its conflict, so clean cut in its spontaneity and so psychologically lucid, that it is still performed from time to time round the world today. It has literary scope and is effective theatre. And Duke Skule is not only the best psychological study Ibsen had yet done, but also an outstanding part for a great actor.

The story goes that when Ibsen had finished the play at the beginning of September, after only two months' serious work, and was on his way to the theatre with the manuscript under his arm, he met in the street Johan Dahl, the bookseller and publisher, who in his time had been publisher to Wergeland, amongst others. Dahl had made a contract with Ibsen to publish the folk-lore which he had collected during his study-trip the year before, but the book had never materialized, and now Dahl took *The Pretenders* instead. The honorarium came to all of one hundred and fifty riksdalers, a large sum for those days; but perhaps an advance which had already been paid on the folk-lore collection had been cancelled as a bad debt. The book came out at the end of October. At first the reviews were somewhat confused, for now this mad writer had changed his style yet again. But three long and very favourable articles by Professor Monrad in *Morgenbladet* in January put matters into perspective and no doubt saved Ibsen from the more or less senseless criticism to which he had so often been subjected before. In Denmark, on the other hand, it was almost universally regarded as a crude bit of saga-bragging; the critics did not even notice the psychological content. In January,

1864, it had its première at the Christiania Theatre, with Ibsen's own stage-instructions: the players' performances are said not to have been especially good, but the production was a success and was put on eleven times that winter.

Now, one would think that the worst crisis in Ibsen's life should have been over. He had held out through poverty and ignominy, he had earned a decisive victory on his own home front with *The Pretenders*, and he had finally—as the last of the new Norwegian writers—received a grant to travel abroad. Not the six hundred riksdalers he had applied for, but anyhow four hundred, which ought to have made it possible to travel abroad and there study in peace and quiet.

As luck would have it, however, Ibsen in his great penury had already in October 1863 received an advance of a hundred riksdalers of his grant to send Suzannah and their son ahead to Copenhagen: presumably Magdalene Thoresen was already living there. No more than three weeks later, before the end of October, he asks the department for the rest, as he is planning during the 'course of the next few weeks to leave by steamer for Hamburg'. It appears from later correspondence, however, that the department was not trusting enough to give him the money, for long after he has settled in Rome, he reckons that there must still be some money to be claimed. But Koht is undoubtedly right in saying that at least half of this grant, together with the honorarium for *The Pretenders*, had been spent on living in Kristiania and completing the staging of the play. And the interest on his debts must not be forgotten either, for all this time Ibsen had had to borrow from moneylenders, against good securities at very high rates. When he was finally supposed to be leaving in the winter of 1864, things looked absolutely black for him. Penniless as never before, he had come to the end of his resources. All his hopes were crushed. Again it was Bjørnson who saved him, and this time it was a matter of life and death.

Bjørnson had moved back to Kristiania in the autumn of 1863 and the two men were at that time close and loyal friends—a friendship which both of them later tried to forget. Bjørnson threw himself whole-heartedly into the task of saving Ibsen and, relying heavily on the success of *The Pretender* he managed to charm well-to-do people—and others—into signing a regular subscription list to replace the grant which had been used up. He obtained promises of no less than seven hundred riksdalers— more than Ibsen had originally applied for, and enough money to keep him just above starvation level for at least a year abroad. He could leave now, but he would have to be careful. Bjørnson had been obliged to promise subscribers that payment would be made under the responsible trusteeship of Dunker, the lawyer, so that Ibsen should only receive what was absolutely necessary, and that by instalments, not in a lump sum. After his arrival in Copenhagen, Ibsen writes a letter thanking Dunker for one such instalment and in a letter to Bjørnson in the autumn of 1864 from Rome he says of Dunker: 'Each time he has sent me money he has added a few kindly words and I shall always remember with gratitude his pure and human feeling, which, although I owe him so much, has never allowed him so much as one word either to imply that he regards me as his property on the journey or in any respect to give me detailed instructions.' Even on this decisive trip abroad, Ibsen was afraid of becoming a kind of serf, and is happy that the mortgage-holder allows him to feel free.

8

Towards Inner Clarity

THE 'Dutchmen' held their farewell party about April, 1864; the exact date is unknown and anyway it is not important. These bohemian, sceptical, critical lookers-on were just beginning to find their true rôles. One of them, Birkeland, became State Archivist; Botten-Hansen, the king-pin, had just found his right niche in life as University Librarian, while Ibsen was on his way out into the world to follow his chosen vocation. A chapter was closing and the party was to be a combined celebration of Botten-Hansen's appointment and Ibsen's journey abroad. Ludvig Daae had written a tribute in Latin, and Ibsen received many good wishes to speed him on his way. The following day, together with Botten-Hansen, he boarded the steamer for Copenhagen.

What was his condition on leaving his native land, not to return at all for ten years, not to settle there again for twenty-seven? Was he an oppressed refugee who had to get away at any cost? To some extent he was. He had striven to devote himself to his calling; but his small victories had always led to new battles. He felt shipwrecked; he could hardly breathe in the stifling air of Kristiania's spiritual life; he had become embittered by the pettiness, tepidness and hypocrisy. He hated the town, and he had to get away.

But may he not have felt something more positive—like the falcon who is at last able to spread his wings in flight, at last escape the stings of the surrounding insects? Well, perhaps. But perhaps this thirty-six-year-old passenger on the steamer to Denmark felt more like the stormy petrel he described in a poem written at that time: 'Too heavy for the air, too light for the waves, poet-bird, poet-bird, you see the consequences.'

But had he found firm spiritual ground beneath his feet? Did he know what he was going to write now? How was he going to use his hard-earned exile? He had fought his way through both social and spiritual uncertainty, through faith and ambivalence and faith and doubt again. In *The Pretenders* he maintains that what is desolating is not doubt or belief, but doubting one's own doubt. This he had in all truth experienced himself. He had gone half way or farther towards joining several spiritual movements of the day. He had been in the national-romantic and Thranite movements, had worked for 'Norwegianism' and at the same time as the sceptical and vociferous 'Gert Westphaler', all the time doubting even his own doubts, for behind the negativism and scorn and his attempts to adapt himself—the sort of thing we today sweepingly dismiss as an 'inferiority complex'—he had nevertheless maintained with incredible fortitude a defiance, an inner self-assertion. One might well call it a prophet complex, to use another well-worn term. It had smouldered since childhood, when he had held the other children at a distance, through his first years in Grimstad, and can be traced in much of what he wrote later, for example in the character of Falk in *Love's Comedy*, the man who makes demands but dares not take the consequences.

Only eight years later, when Ibsen had at last found his place as a castigator and prophet, he himself gave an unambiguous account of his feelings on leaving his native land. On the tenth centenary of the Battle of Hafrsfjord, which completed Norway's first unification and was to be celebrated in Haugesund in 1872 with the unveiling of the Harald Monument, Ibsen was asked to write a festive poem. He did, and the result was masterly; but he could not resist including in the first verse a biting comment on his complacent fatherland.

There are no half measures here. He is like a prophet from the Old Testament reading the scriptures to his people. For him it is as if he had been standing on the edge of his grave when he finally escaped; he had borne a killing burden of grief when he was forced into exile. But the most striking image is 'the swift soles of anxiety'—which have been thin and cold, not only from a literary point of view. Just as his friends in Grimstad had noticed that he

wore no socks, so the waiters at the tavern L'Orsa in Prinsensgate
remembered, a generation after he had emigrated, that he had
no shoes, only rubber galoshes, which force the wearer into a
swift pace in winter-time in Kristiania, not only from anxiety,
but also from cold. But inside this 'bundle of grief', he had nevertheless had something of value which he had to rescue undamaged.
The poem was not read at the celebrations, a point I shall return to
later.

His impressions of the journey south, however, were so strong
that he had little time for brooding over his own condition, and
even less inducement to complete the half-dead embryo of a new
historical drama about Magnus Heineson which he had brought
with him.

He arrived in Copenhagen at the beginning of April and was
there during the most critical weeks in Scandinavian history for
fifty years. While he was there, the fortress of Dybbøl fell,
completing Denmark's defeat and putting an end to Scandinavianism, which during the previous six months, had gone from
fiasco to fiasco. Scandinavianism was the last 'movement' of all
that Ibsen ever associated himself with, but he had set great store
by it. Denmark had long been threatened by Prussia. In 1849,
Prussia was unsuccessful in wringing from Denmark the German-
inhabited Holstein, but now things were serious—a prelude to
the great German unification and expansion, with the reconquest
of Alsace-Lorraine and the seeds of two world wars ahead.

Denmark became the first victim of this expansion, and she had
long been aware of the threatening danger. To improve her
position, she had sought help in two directions; diplomatic
support from the Great Powers in the west, of which nothing
came except platitudes, and at the same time help from the
monarchy of Sweden-Norway, whose reaction had been very
positive, not only within the very vociferous Scandinavian movement of the students, whose real political influence was naturally
minimal, but also at the highest level, from King Carl and his
Foreign Minister. Denmark hoped that in the long run Prussia
would hesitate to go to war against a united Scandinavia. But
Prussia, supported by Austria, was not to be stopped, and when it

came to the point, King Carl was forced by the Swedish and Norwegian houses of parliament into an abject diplomatic retreat.

The only help Denmark received was a great many pretty platitudes and a modest band of Norwegian and Swedish volunteers, so few in number that they made no impression whatsoever on the military result. With the fall of Dybbøl, the Germans had taken the last entrenchment of any importance and were able to dictate the peace terms: the cession not only of Holstein, but also of Schleswig, at that time a region with a German minority and Danish majority.

Ibsen's grief and rage were boundless, and they did not lessen when at the end of April, travelling via Lubeck to Berlin, he was obliged to witness the triumphal entry of German troops into the city. He gives vent to his griefs and anxieties in a letter to Bjørnson from Rome and adds:

'I regret having poured out all this bitterness to you, instead of giving you cheerful accounts of all the wonders you have enabled me to be elevated and ennobled by down here. But I cannot escape from my sad thoughts on the circumstances at home, nor have I been able to during the whole of my journey. Had I stayed longer in Berlin, where I saw the entry in April and the crowds surging among the trophies from Dybbøl, saw them ride on the gun-carriages and spit into the guns—into the same guns which had received no help and which even so had fired on until they were shattered—then I don't know how long I could have retained my reason.'

So he went on to Vienna and thence in stages by rail southwards through Austria and Italy to Rome, where he arrived in June. A happy period followed, in which he explored and revelled, first in Rome, then in Genzano, where the summer weather was better and the danger of malaria less. The local inhabitants nicknamed him 'Capellone'—the big hat. His closest companions out there, apart from the art historian, Lorentz Dietrichson, and the Finnish sculptor, Walter Runeberg, son of the great Finnish writer, were Mrs Lina Bruun, and her son and consumptive daughter; the Bruun family were waiting for Mrs Lina's other son, the theologian Christopher Bruun. As Christopher Bruun has been singled out as a model or source of inspiration for *Brand*, it should be mentioned that he was a Scandinavianist through and through. He had agitated at the Student Union in Kristiania for volunteers to sign on during the same evening that Ibsen was at his farewell party with the 'Dutchmen'. And he himself volunteered, but after a few weeks' participation in the war he was disappointed to find that the Danish soldiers were not particularly patriotic and were simply serving out of duty, wanting more than anything else to go home to their wives and 'toddlers'. Then he walked through Europe to his family.

An interesting and lively first-hand account of Ibsen's life and travels during the first summer in Italy is given by Lorentz Dietrichson in *Vanished Times*. His memoirs were written almost fifty years later and as an art historian of the old school Dietrichson allowed his memories to retain their patina, but it may be of interest to repeat a few of them:

Early one Sunday morning—June 19th—the doorbell rang at the Scandianavian Society, where Dietrichson was acting as librarian in exchange for free accommodation and a little pay. Outside, the voice of the genial Danish Consul, Bravo, could be heard, announcing that he had with him a good friend of Dietrichson's. It was Ibsen. It was a beautiful day, and they took a 'proper round tour', looked at a large part of the Tiber district, including Forum Romanum and Janiculum, went to high mass in St Peter's and in the evening ended up at a small tavern in Trastevere which they had 'discovered' together. They were overflowing with new impressions, and together they pictured 'a rich and beautiful period before us, which we would be able to enjoy together. Naturally none of us imagined how rich this day was to be as far as he was concerned; he was like a different person from the closed and bitter man whom three years earlier I had left in Kristiania'.

A few days later the Scandinavians who had not yet left Rome for the summer gathered together for a farewell party at an open-air restaurant.

'It was the first evening for a long time that Ibsen had spent in the company of Scandinavians, and he began telling them about the painful and disturbing impressions of the last few stages of the war which he had received on his journey. But gradually and almost imperceptibly his tale began to take on the character of an improvised speech, all his long suppressed bitterness, all the fiery indignation and love for the Scandinavian cause, which he had so long kept pent up in his heart, he now set free: iron came into his voice and in the dim evening light one saw only his glowing eyes, and when he stopped speaking, no one cried Bravo, no one touched his glass, but I think we all had the impression that it was the Marseillaise of Scandinavia that our little company had heard that evening, ringing out into the Roman night air. . . .'

Then on his summer sojourn: 'Together with my family I had taken Villegiatur in Genzano by Lake Nemis and Ibsen decided to settle down at the same place.' Together with Walter Runeberg, he went there and stayed at the town's *caffetiere*, in a room beyond the billiard room. Dietrichson also relates a story about the first time Ibsen rode on a donkey. The two of them wanted to go to Castel Gandolfo, where Pope Pius IX had his summer residence and was to make his entry. When they finally arrived safely on their donkeys, the whole population had lined the route to receive the Pope's blessing, and the two Norwegians had to run the gauntlet between lines of people laughing at them. At this the donkeys set off at a gallop; great jubilation, but just then the Pope appeared, so both the donkeys and the two Scandinavians were quickly hustled to one side.

It is clear that at this time, and also after he had brought his wife and child to Rome, Ibsen was cheerful, happy and argumentative. This story of Dietrichson's is typical:

'A legend used to be recounted of that unhappy young Englishman, Chatterton, who at eighteen years of age took poison after having starved for three days, that after his death his landlord looked in vain for the door-key which Chatterton had had, and finally found it in his gullet; he had devoured it from hunger. As soon as this point was reached, the argument always became lively, for there were always one or two worthy types who thought that there must have been some other means by which he could support himself, that instead of insisting on writing for his living, he could, for instance, have gone and worked as a clerk in a commercial office. Then Ibsen was in his element, asserting that the only right thing to do was to swallow the key rather than become a business man, and this he did in the most paradoxical form, inviting contradictions and argument.'

Dietrichson goes on to show that Ibsen used the same technique in analysing the models for his later plays.

A great deal has been written about what Ibsen did between the spring of 1864 and the late autumn of 1865, when he sent off the last instalment of *Brand*. This is to be expected; for *Brand* was not only a great writer's explosive break-through, but also a milestone in cultural history. We are still not finished with it, and it is acted on the stage in many countries and in many tongues—and in many different ways.

Ibsen arrived in Italy with mixed feelings. Immeasurable relief, almost boyish confidence, were combined with great resentment over the Norwegian-Swedish betrayal and brutal German power politics. On the one hand he seemed to see wretchedness and hypocrisy all around him. It is also possible that he may have had a slight qualm of conscience over not volunteering for war service himself, but this is not very likely. His self-realization must have made him face the fact that he would be of little use as a soldier, and that is not cowardice. But apart from indignation, his strongest emotion was probably an immense joy over at last feeling himself to be free and experiencing the overwhelming richness of new impressions of nature, people and, not least, Italian works of art.

He was idle all through that summer. Apart from his long walking tour in 1862, his struggle to earn a living had prevented him from taking a proper holiday for many years. He probably had with him the notes for a drama about the pirate Magnus Heineson, an agitator and warrior who was beheaded in Denmark, but received restitution after his death: but this material must have summoned up unwelcome ghosts of the oppressive days

in Kristiania. Instead—relates Dietrichson—early in the autumn
he felt the desire to write about the Emperor Julian Apostate,
who from a psychological point of view had been one of the
most interesting of the Roman Emperors, and a man with precisely
that division of mind that must have caught Ibsen's imagination.

At the end of the autumn of 1864, Ibsen brought Suzannah and
Sigurd down to Rome; and later, after Dietrichson had left, he
also took over his position as secretary of the Scandinavian
Society, which carried with it free living-quarters. Then we have
nothing from Ibsen's hand for nearly a whole year except the two
long, warm letters to Bjørnson—a third was lost in the post. They
are impulsive, optimistic letters in which he tells of his own situation. In connection with Bjørnson's rather dubious reaction to the
idea of taking part in the current theatre controversy in Kristiania,
he says a few words about himself which are worthy of note:

'I know I lack the art of being able to become intimate with the
people with whom it is demanded that one be quite open, and in
this way I have something in common with the poet in *The
Pretenders*. I can never quite bring myself to disrobe completely,
and I have a feeling that I have at my command in personal
relationships only a false expression of that which I carry right
inside me, and which is really myself, so I prefer to shut it in, and
so it happens that we have occasionally stood as if observing one
another at a distance. But you yourself must have realized this, or
anyhow something similar; anything else is impossible, for otherwise you would not have been able to preserve such a rich and
warm friendship for me.'

It is rare for Ibsen to express himself in such an open-hearted
way.

In his next letter, in which money troubles are already beginning to take up quite a large place, he still feels this warm gratitude for everything that Bjørnson has done and is still happy to be
doing for him. And so he should have done, for Bjørnson went on
begging on his behalf and it was through his efforts that the Ibsen
family was kept alive throughout the whole of 1865.

It looks as if Ibsen abandoned the thought of a drama on the

Emperor Julian as early as the beginning of the autumn of 1864; and it was ten years before he made something of the material. Instead, he started with what after a year's toil became *Brand*. It is not new material that Ibsen handles here, but the whole manner in which he attacks it is new for him. The sources of his inspiration are manifold. When—as not infrequently happens—he denies having been influenced by this or that writer or thinker, adding that he has not read much of their work, it should always be taken with a pinch of salt. It is true that Ibsen was not a particularly well-read or learned man, but rather an extremely industrious newspaper-reader. He must, however, have read much more than he cares to admit and he was well orientated in the intellectual currents of the time.

Søren Kierkegaard was undoubtedly one of the godparents of the fundamental ideas behind *Brand*. It is also possible that Ibsen's meeting with Christopher Bruun may have brought its theme to life. Christopher Bruun—who later came to make a great contribution to the folk-high-school movement—was at the time a young theologian with uncompromising opinions which caused him to have scruples about seeking office in the State Church; a man masterful and strong, ascetic and very aggressive by nature. He had himself volunteered in the war on the Danish side.

Bruun certainly fitted well into the pattern Ibsen was in the process of setting up. The revivalist priest, Lammers, of Ibsen's early childhood, must have also haunted his mind. Literary prototypes are also easy to find.

Brand became the great drama on vocation and responsibility, on being wholly oneself, in contrast to everyday half-measures.

At first it was conceived as a great epic-poetic cycle—the rough draft has been preserved. When Ibsen moved to Germany in 1868, he deposited various manuscripts with the Scandinavian Society in Rome, and when he returned again in 1878 they had been mislaid. A Danish collector found them at the end of the century and instead of sending them immediately to the owner, he kept them, as is the way of collectors. After Ibsen's death he produced them, thus creating a sensation.

The Brand epic begins with an introductory poem, called 'To the accomplices', which was undoubtedly not written first. Here, somewhat grandiloquently, but in torrents of powerful verse, Ibsen flays both himself and his people, emphasizing that he has lost his trust in both their future and their past, but nevertheless devoting a few lines to the peaks behind the glittering ridges and ending with an admonition to look for the poem hidden within the poem, for 'he who grasps that grasps the song'.

It may well be that Ibsen himself was not satisfied with 'the Brand epic'. His long-suppressed desire to become the castigating prophet of his time demanded also a new form, quite different from those he had hitherto used. He was tired, for the time being, of working for the theatre—that art which he had so painfully acquired, and he may even have temporarily lost his faith in it as a medium. So he made an attempt at the poem-cycle form, for he knew that in his poetic medium he had no rival in all Norway. Nevertheless here too his competent craftsmanship was apt to get the better of him. His own dexterity was so temptingly great that it was not always possible to stop where his idea stopped.

When he had finished what we now know as 'the Brand epic', he must have been almost irresistibly tempted to send it to Frederik Hegel in Copenhagen, the director of the House of Gyldendal with whom a contract had been obtained for him (this again was Bjørnson's doing). For having got so far, he again had cause to walk 'with anxiety's swift soles', to borrow wherever he was able. But he withstood the temptation.

Like all genuine prophets, Ibsen had had his vision, his revelation. He had experienced it in St Peter's, Rome, and one can think of worse places for inspiration. He himself tells about it in the third and last but one of the long, intimate letters he wrote to Bjørnson at this time. We have now come to September 12, 1865, and he is living out in Ariccia. He has completed almost a year's intensive work on *Brand*. His financial resources are strained to the utmost, and yet he has the strength to begin all over again. After recounting how things have gone badly with the work, he continues:

'So one day I went to St Peter's—I was on an errand in Rome—

and there suddenly occurred to me a strong and clear form for what I had to say. Now I have thrown overboard what I have spent a year working on without making any headway, and in the middle of July, I began on something new. It progressed as nothing has ever done for me before. It is new in the sense that I then began to write, but the theme and atmosphere have rested like a nightmare over me ever since the many horrible incidents at home made me look inside myself and our life here, and think about matters which had before gone heedlessly over my head, which I have anyhow not taken seriously before. It is a dramatic poem, material from the present day, serious content, five acts in rhymed verse (no *Love's Comedy*). The fourth act will soon be complete and the fifth I think I can write in eight days. I work both in the morning and the afternoon, which I have never been able to do before.'

After a few observations about how he has finally driven 'aestheticism' out of himself, aesthetics being as great a curse on poetry as theology is on religion, he exclaims: 'Is it not an indescribable gift to be able to write? But it is a great responsibility too, and I am now serious enough to sense it and be hard on myself.'

Then comes the famous story about the aesthete he had met in Copenhagen, who had designated Christ as 'an interesting phenomenon', exactly like a gourmet enjoying the sight of an oyster. Ibsen never became such a mollusc:

'. . . but what kind of spiritual ass could have been made out of me, if they had had me undisturbed, I do not know, and what has disturbed them, my dear Bjørnson, is precisely you. You have enough vision both for yourself and for me to see that my need coincides with what you have given and have wished to give. I seem to have an immense amount to tell you, but if I were to write down all of it, no postage would suffice, so over to business.'

It is unnecessary to reiterate the contents of *Brand* to those who know it, and useless for those who do not. It is not the external events that are important, but Ibsen's fantastically intense inner dialogue with himself, without thought of making either a book to please the public or a play capable of being acted at all. All the characters are fundamentally the voices of Ibsen. Brand, the priest, feels that the call of Our Lord demands everything of him and he demands that others shall likewise sacrifice everything which that God—i.e. what is within them—demands. That he brings misfortune and unhappiness to others, including those nearest him, his mother and his beloved as well as to himself, is of no account compared with the betrayal involved in hiding behind various excuses and refusing to follow the absolute demands which all men experience in the depths of their hearts.

Ibsen himself has sharply denied that the play is propaganda for Christian philosophy, and says in a letter to Brandes that he could equally well have given the preacher another profession. But it cannot be denied that it has been religious preachers— Christian and others—who have most often tried to inspire their fellow-men to rise above niggardly considerations. It is true philosophers and other thinkers have done so too, and of course he could have chosen a philosopher or a natural scientist, but by using a priest he was able to play on the whole of the cultural heritage of his time; the concepts of God and sermons were familiar to everyone and people were receptive to them; he reached contemporary readers on their home ground.

Ibsen maintained later on that the play was inspired by all the pettiness displayed during the events of 1864. In his mind he belonged to a people almost without a past, and anyhow with no future, a people who if they were attacked, for instance, by the Russians, would think it a misfortune for the State to be annihilated, but not for the people to be destroyed as a nation, as a people. On his travels through Denmark he had seen that the people there felt genuine grief over their defeat, so there was, despite everything, some hope for Denmark, but none for Sweden and Norway. The betrayal of which his own people had been guilty in 1864 was irretrievable, an outburst of the spirit of the time which denied Norway the right to call herself a nation. He gave expression to this in a poem, the only great one he sent home at that time, in which, trembling with indignation, he pours scorn on all the official hypocrisy surrounding the murder of Abraham Lincoln.

Yet seventy-five years after Ibsen's *Brand*, when Norway really was invaded by a foreign power, the people survived the ordeal and kept their identity as a people. We may well ask ourselves: What part did Ibsen's contribution to Norway's spiritual life, not least in *Brand*, play in forming that element in the national character which would not allow itself to be subdued? To what extent, for instance, did Ibsen's spirit influence the teachers who refused to yield, or the priests and others whose resistance was in the invisible realm of ideas? We do not know. But it is significant that when our great Bjørnson and Ibsen scholar, Francis Bull, during his long years as a prisoner at Grini, held meetings with his fellow-prisoners, it was his lectures on Ibsen which made the greatest impression, particularly the lecture on *Brand*.

Ibsen relates that while he was writing *Brand* he kept a living scorpion under glass on his desk. After a while it fell sick. When he put a piece of fruit in with it, it injected its poison into the fruit and recovered. He had felt the same way himself during this great castigation of himself and his countrymen. He went so far in his hatred for Norway that he thumped on café tables and declared aloud that one thing anyhow his son would never be and that was *Norwegian*. Unfortunately, to some extent he turned out to be right, for this restless man never really struck any roots in Norway, although with the help of his father and father-in-law he did become Norwegian Minister of State in Stockholm for a time.

But too much should not be made of the well-aimed attack upon Norway and the Norwegians. It must be re-emphasized that *Brand* is first and foremost Ibsen's settlement with himself. He had come out of a long dark tunnel, had burnt all his bridges behind him, and was writing powerful drama, his message to himself and the world.

The 'dramatic poem' was completed in November, 1865. The first pages he had already sent to Gyldendal, probably in the hope of receiving yet another advance. Now he sent the rest. After that, he could only wait. All round him were promissory notes and debts and squalor, but Hegel had hoped to have the book out by Christmas, and it should be possible to hang on till then. After that things would be different.

There followed several months of unbearable tension. His letter to Hegel of November 15, in which he enclosed the rest of the manuscript, is still business-like and without noticeable impatience. He gives Hegel a free hand when it comes to proof-reading and corrections. Time is short, so he has to 'depend on luck and Copenhagen's renownedly good proof-readers'. How Ibsen could have known that, as he had never had anything printed in Copenhagen before, remains a mystery.

Hegel's reply arrived on November 24 and he has obviously expressed strong misgivings over Ibsen's use of distinctively Norwegian words and orthography. Ibsen replies again, very agreeably, although he includes one or two mild objections on orthography. However, Hegel cannot have read the whole manuscript until some time later, and then his misgivings hardened. This was, after all, totally different from the play he had expected, both in content, form and proportions. He writes another letter to Ibsen in which he says that he cannot publish 1,250 copies of *Brand* but only 625, but that he still intends to publish the book by Christmas.

This was a serious matter for Ibsen, as it meant that he would receive no more royalties than the advance he had long since spent. But if *Brand* came out at Christmas, it would nevertheless support Bjørnson's present begging-round on his behalf, as well as the various applications for grants he had made, or was to make. So on December 2 Ibsen wrote agreeing to all Hegel's demands.

This letter to Hegel, however, must have been lost in the post. Ibsen wrote in December to both Magdalene Thoresen and Clemens Petersen, the critic on *The Fatherland*, and announced that the book was coming out at Christmas. And meanwhile Hegel was sitting waiting to hear from Ibsen whether he accepted the new conditions. For Hegel it would have been better to publish the book in the spring, and then the part of the edition to be distributed in Norway could have been sent up to Kristiania by the first boat after the ice had melted.

Christmas came and went. January came and went. The book did not come out. Finally, in March, Hegel decided to stick to the contract and publish the book. There is not a single letter or any other piece of writing in Ibsen's hand from the beginning of December to March. We know from a letter to Dunker of March 4 that he had meanwhile received some more money from the lawyer, which had reached him on New Year's Day. On March 4 too, there is a very long letter to Bjørnstjerne Bjørnson which begins with a cry of agony but ends on a cordial note. The cry of agony is caused by some murky loan-transactions which Ibsen has undertaken, and about which Bjørnson has justifiedly reproached him, with the result that Ibsen in his turn is very much annoyed.

On Hegel and *Brand* the letter runs:

'My book is presumably coming out sometime now. You call Hegel a noble man, and so does Mrs Thoresen, but to me his nobility is of a cowardly kind. He is considerate and careful not to give offence. I have had a thousand difficulties with him and gave way in all things in order to have my book out by Christmas, and then it did not come out after all. Among other things he said, long after the printing had been started, that you had described my poem to him as set in ancient times. Is this a misunderstanding? I remember quite distinctly that I once wrote to you that the material was taken from the present day, but that it was no *Love's Comedy*. That I have during all this neither demanded nor received any further advance from him, you will understand, and my present situation, waiting, consumed with anxiety and tension, in anticipation of the book, and with it perhaps all kinds of controversies and attacks, incapable in the middle of all this of setting about anything new, which however already lies complete within me,—well, I do not wish to write any more about that.

'My dear Bjørnson, it seems to me that by some eternal destiny I am separated from both God and Man; when I wrote my play I was despite all the pressure and distress, so indescribably happy, I felt a crusading jubilation within me; I do not know what thing I would lack the courage to oppose, but opposition is not so enervating and undermining as this desperate waiting. Well, perhaps it is a period of transition; I want and shall have a victory sometime. If I have been wished so much ill as to be brought into this world and made into what I am, then things must take their course.'

Sad words these. In *Brand* he has written a masterpiece, yet its fate still hangs in the balance.

A few days later, on March 7, Ibsen collects himself and writes a rousing letter to Hegel. He refers in it to his letter of December 2, which of course Hegel has not received, and to two other letters from Hegel, in the first of which he had said that February was a good time to publish, then that March was better, so that the book could come out at the same time in Norway. But now Ibsen has seen in the papers that the first steamer to Kristiania had already sailed on February 20 ... 'but I know nothing of my book; I go round here in anxiety and expectation which will shortly become unendurable. The publication of this book has in truth cost me a great deal; I do not wish to mention the reduced royalties, to which naturally I had to agree, as this proposal came so late that I had no choice if my book were to be published by Christmas, which for me was the main thing, and which you in the letter containing the proposal, still declared possible'. Then he added a desperate plea for another advance on his next book.

Ibsen never needed to plead in this way again. *Brand* came out on March 16 and in the course of a few months the whole of his life was changed. Now the wheel of destiny really began to turn. His great dramatic poem was brought out in the 1,250 copies of the contract, but only two months later Hegel had to have 550 more copies printed and in August, the third edition came out (574) and the fourth in December (774)—an almost unheard-of sales success. Meanwhile Ibsen had gambled on two other cards. Through Bjørnson he had applied for a travel grant and received one hundred riksdalers from the Royal Norwegian Academy of Arts and Science in Trondheim, and he had also applied for a writer's salary. The application for the writer's salary is dated April 15, 1866, a rather piteous letter addressed directly to the King. After giving an account of his career as a writer, he continues:

'The first fruits of my travels are now before the public through my dramatic poem *Brand*, recently published in Copenhagen, which now only a few weeks after publication has also attracted attention outside the boundaries of my home country: but I cannot live on expressions of gratitude received, and the author's royalties, under the circumstances abundant, are similarly insufficient to put me in a position to be able to continue my travels or on the whole to secure even the near future.

'It is after advice sent by telegraph from my friends in Kristiania that I hazard this unusual procedure of addressing my humble application directly to Your Majesty.

'We had earlier believed that within a year there would have been, through a Royal Bill, an opportunity to have my case brought before Parliament, but now it appears that this would mean waiting three years, and this I cannot.

'It is not for a carefree livelihood that I am struggling here, but for the calling which I believe unwaveringly that God has laid on me—this calling to do what I believe Norway needs most urgently of all, to awaken the people and make them think.

'The private bill, which I have been told several members of parliament wish to put forward, has no hope of being driven through; there is not time for an application to the government.

'My King is therefore my last and only hope.'

Ibsen's mention of a private bill is based on the fact that Bjørnson, who did not like *Brand*, but nevertheless was aware that the sensation round the book might open up new possibilities of a writer's award for Ibsen, had collected up twenty-eight signatures from members of parliament in favour of such a bill. But the result would probably be negative if the government went against the bill, and the indications were that the key man, Riddervold, Minister of Ecclesiastics, was not particularly keen to accept it. Fortunately Riddervold fell ill and Minister Frederik Stang stood locum for him. By immediate manœuvres and pressure, Ibsen's friends managed to get Stang to take up the bill and send it in to the cabinet in Stockholm. As it happened, Ibsen's appeal to the King had been unnecessary, but when Ibsen sent it he had no knowledge of the involved intrigues being played out in Kristiania.

As early as May 12, his writer's award was approved in Parliament with only four votes against. This ensured Ibsen a sum of four hundred riksdalers a year for life. This decision remains a record in Norway for speedy proceedings in cultural matters. On top of all this, the government gave him another grant on July 28 of 250 riksdalers.

The reason for all this haste was naturally not only that the case, as mentioned in Ibsen's application, would have entailed a three-year wait (the law concerning annual parliament was not carried through until 1869), but also primarily because of the stir that *Brand* had created.

Whereas earlier it had often taken weeks, even months, before an Ibsen play was given any special attention by the critics, the sensation this time was obvious after only a few days. It began in Copenhagen and the fact that the reaction there was swifter than in Kristiania was due to several causes; partly that the book came from the House of Gyldendal and thus had a stamp of quality which made the Danish critics read it with both immediacy and attention, and partly also because Ibsen was sufficiently unknown down there for the critics not to require any confused period of reflection to reorientate themselves in face of an Ibsen who was different from what he had been before. In addition, the soil was much better prepared in Søren Kierkegaard's country than in Norway for understanding the book's psychological problems. Georg Brandes, who at that time was twenty-four years old, but had gained a name as a critic, wrote in the Danish *Dagbladet* that the book made the reader feel that he was standing 'face to face with a strong and indignant genius, before whose penetrating eyes weakness was forced to turn its eyes away'. The whole of the Copenhagen press followed suit and newspaper correspondents in Copenhagen were able to write home about a sensational break-through of Norwegian literature.

Nevertheless, things moved somewhat more sluggishly in Norway, and the first reactions were rather negative. Vinje filled a whole issue of *Dølen* with a report on the book and a number of glowing words about Ibsen, primarily at the expense of Bjørnson, and—as always—with a great many digressions and diversions; but never had he heard Norwegian peasants talk or behave in this way. It is as if it had not really dawned on him what the book was about; and it is, for that matter, possible that it was not to the taste of this personification of Norwegian ambivalence. Bjørnson's reaction was very strongly and indignantly negative. It was so contrary to his own confident positivism that he was not able to read more than a page or two a day, and he wrote a caustic report on it in a letter to Clemens Petersen three weeks after publication, declaring categorically that the book would be dead within two months: he himself had not yet managed to get through it. Nevertheless is must be recorded that Bjørnson gradually changed his mind; and many years later, when he himself approached the problem of the power of belief, and wrote *On Eternity*, the greatness of the work was fully revealed to him, even if he for his part preferred to see the problem from a more human and sympathetic point of view.

Such was the reaction of Ibsen's two closest friends. They were backed up by Professor Monrad, who had indeed condemned *Love's Comedy*, but had approved of *The Pretenders*. Now he plunged in with four long articles in *Morgenbladet* showing with immensely detailed documentation that this dramatic poem sinned against every established law of literature and thought. But Monrad got as good as he gave in *Morgenbladet*, and all over Norway the controversy raged, becoming the subject of sermons from pulpits, as well as of social debate.

Ibsen in Rome was able to ignore Vinje, Bjørnson and Monrad. Not only did the praise from the Danish critics and congratulatory letters tell him that he was victorious, but also the heavy sales of the book showed him that at last—to use a present-day expression—he had broken the sound barrier. With his writer's award as financial security, and with the name he had acquired, he was now able to look the future in the face. The prophet had spoken and the people had listened. That so many misunderstood and misinterpreted him did not matter very much, for he had reached the first stage of his goal: to arouse people to thinking.

When *Brand* came to find its place in Norwegian literature and thought for generations to come, naturally this was not only because of the pathos and literary strength of the play, for there are great works of literature which have not succeeded until long after they were written. That it struck with such penetrating force was also because the time was ripe for it; as Koht so precisely puts it:

'If one wishes to understand the tremendous effect *Brand* had, then one must recall that the book came in the middle of the greatest break-through for individualism in society and cultural life. *Brand* made the individual into the pivot round which everything in the world must revolve—imprinting personal demands in the soul with a force which had never before been done, making individual conscience into the battleground where all problems would be settled.'

That is the crux of the matter. Since his childhood, under life's relentless bludgeoning, Ibsen had allowed himself to be hammered into the arch-individual himself, and now he had managed to write the gospel of individualism. It was open to many interpretations, like all gospels, but so deeply thought and sharply formulated that it remained a source of inspiration, and continued as a living part of our cultural heritage.

9

Successful Years in Italy

IT is perhaps not quite correct to say that Ibsen went round Rome
basking in his success. Rather, he stood upright for the first time
in his life, eventually assuming for good this stance which he had
always known to be natural to him.

The most obvious *external* change that came over him at this
time was noticed by several people, and is very significant. His
handwriting changes, from a style that seems to be made for
rapid temporary notes, to the calligraphically impeccable, stiff
fine style he used for the rest of his life—handwriting which
certainly does not lack self-confidence.

He altered his beard too. For the sake of a rhyme, Bjørnson,
in his poem on Heltberg's crammer, establishes him as having
a 'coal-black unkempt beard'; but in reality it was brown, though
it certainly was large, a fact noted in Grimstad, Bergen and
Kristiania. By his second Kristiania period it had probably
become stained with soup and beer. When he met Dietrichson in
Rome, he still had it, but by then it was shorter. Two years later,
when Dietrichson had become a professor in Stockholm, he
received a photograph from Ibsen and was surprised at the change
in his appearance; by now he had put on the Ibsen-mask, with
whiskers, for the first time revealing his strong, characterful jaw.

At the same time, his clothing changed. In Grimstad he had for
years worn his confirmation suit, as shiny as a tiled stove. In
Bergen, it was noticed he always wore his old greatcoat. In
Kristiania, it was said that 'Ibsen lived in his overcoat', and when
that was worn out, a rug with a hole in it for his head, a poncho,
was his winter garment. In Rome, after his success with *Brand*, he
wore a short dark velvet jacket, and soon started dressing in what

was at that time the correctest of wear, the long black double-breasted coat which became his uniform for the rest of his life.

But there is yet another change that is worth mentioning, and that is the altered tone of his letters. Earlier, he had not always been able to hide his anxieties and worries, although he always tried to remain formal. But from the summer of 1866, the tone of his correspondence with Hegel for instance, is friendly and correct, as to a business associate on an equal footing with himself, pecuniary matters being mere formalities.

One might deduce from these small changes that the success of *Brand* had suddenly made Ibsen vain, perhaps a little foolish. The truth is probably that this vanity—if one must choose such a word—had always been in him since his childhood years in Skien, a manifestation of a deep need to keep people away from his life. What had characterized his life until 1866 had been anything but distance from his fellow-human beings. On the contrary, he had been plagued by much too close a contact—the suppliant's necessary contact with creditors, money-lenders and superiors.

Now at last he could choose for himself his social conventions and attitudes, practise his individual demand for truth and wholeness, both in his life and his writing. This does not mean, however, that he became in any way invulnerable; it was the exact opposite. As the years went by, the Ibsen-mask probably gradually grew into an armour, on which neither pricks nor blows had any effect. But for many years after, he was extremely vulnerable and sensitive, and during the years 1866 and 1867 his state of mind was very unstable, shifting from cheerful openness to tremendous rage, from confident enthusiasm to almost petty vindictiveness, and then again to olympian indignation.

The richest source of information on Ibsen's life at this time is to be found in his letters, which are quite numerous and some of them long, informative and open-hearted. Among the eye-witnesses is the young Danish writer, Vilhelm Bergsøe, who spent much time with the Ibsen family, and who has thrown some amusing light on the writer's daily life, as well as on his character.

When Ibsen later wrote that after *Brand*, *Peer Gynt* almost came by itself, however, he is guilty of considerable contraction, for

after he sent in *Brand*, a whole year elapsed before he even began
to write the poem which was to be a complete contrast—a year in
which he matured richly but produced nothing.

In June, 1866, he spent the summer in Frascati in the Albany
mountains, and in a letter to Botten-Hansen he himself has
most vividly set the stage.

'We are living expecially well and naturally have forsaken Rome
during these hot summer months when the sirrocco blows pois-
onously over Campania. Out here in Frascati, up in the Albany
mountains, we now live in an old nobleman's palace, Palazzo
Gratiosi, marvellous and cheap. Frascati lies below the old
Tusculum, where, as you know, Cicero had his handsome villa
and from where he wrote his Tusculan letter. The ruins of the
villa are still standing, and his little theatre, presumably the same
building that he called his school and where he used to give
lectures to a chosen circle of guests, stands almost undamaged. To
sit up here of an evening is indescribably beautiful, 2,000 feet
above sea level, the view far out over the Mediterranean, Campania and Rome, all the beautiful Sabini country with the Appen-
ines to the east, and to the south the Volscian mountains rising
on the borders of Naples. From the windows of my work-room I
can see Mons Soracte in the far distance, isolated and beautiful,
rising out of the immense plain,—briefly, wherever you turn it is
as if you were looking over the battlefield on which the history
of the world has had its greatest encounter.—Now I shall start
writing seriously. I am still wrestling with the material, but I
know I shall soon have the beast subdued, and then the rest will
glide on of its own accord.'

In such surroundings a writer, who now knows his own significance, might well be able for the first time to breathe freely and
think independently.

He is grappling with several plans at this time, Magnus
Heineson and Julian Apostate again in his thoughts, but in the
meanwhile he has the excellent idea of asking Gyldendal to
publish *Love's Comedy* in a new edition. When the book came
out in Kristiania at the beginning of 1863, it had been slated by

all the Norwegian critics, but now there were possibilities of both praise and sales in Denmark. Ibsen writes on August 22nd to Hegel:

'At the moment I am doubtful whether my new work will be ready by the autumn. But I have a suggestion to make, and that is that you might be willing to publish *Love's Comedy* as a Christmas book. It was published as a New Year gift for the subscribers of the *Illustrated News* and is hardly known in Denmark. The book can be regarded as a forerunner of *Brand* and in Denmark it will find a public. The language must be purified, some alterations made, etc. . . .'

Naturally Hegel was willing to publish a play which was called a forerunner of the best-seller *Brand*, but he had to make sure that the remainders of the first edition were brought back from the bookshops, and Ibsen set about a frenzied campaign to bring this about. To Birkeland, he writes that he must do *everything* he can to achieve this: 'Take Bachke, Løkke, Botten-Hansen, Sars, Daae and so on, with you, go in procession to the person concerned and don't let him go until the matter is settled.' The person concerned was of course the great writer, Jonas Lie, who held the disputed rights, and relinquished them with a wry smile over Ibsen's aggressiveness.

It is at this moment, in the middle of his success, that Bjørnson at last brings himself to tell Ibsen that all his possessions, his rough drafts and papers included, had been sold by auction by his creditors almost ten years before. Bjørnson himself was quite without any guilt. Whether, on the other hand, Ibsen's 'guardian' in his needy years, the lawyer Dunker, could have avoided the auction, is a matter of argument, but at this information, Ibsen, naturally enough, lets out a cry of agony, and what had happened sharpened his intense hatred of Norway during these years.

In a letter to Bjørnson in October, 1866, he writes,

'. . . my ill humour was not directed at you. No, no, my dear Bjørnson—I know definitely that nothing will ever be able to come between us, which in truth would be able to separate my temper from you and what you are. But you can well imagine that it must have been to me an indescribably bitter message to receive. I have not complained over the loss of my furniture and such things, but to know that my private letters, papers, roughs and so on, were in just anyone's hands, that was to me an extremely aggravating thought, not to mention the loss of much that had another worth than the sum of the taxes.'

It is as if the long delayed news has made him break his last ties with his native country.

It was probably about this time that he finally abandoned his plans to write about Heineson the pirate. True, in a letter to Hegel as late as November 2 he speaks as if he were thinking of working on it, but he makes some provisos:

'From your letter I see that there is a slight misunderstanding over the possible work I wrote about. This will not be *about* Christian IV's youth, but the material is taken from that time. Whether this work will be the *first* I come to complete, I do not yet definitely know. I still have a couple of other subjects in my mind, but this very spreading of my interest shows that neither of them is yet sufficiently matured; nevertheless, I feel certain that this will soon happen and hope that by the spring I will be able to send you the finished manuscript.'

There seems no longer to be any doubt: he has made his muse pregnant with a child which was to overshadow even its predecessor and display itself audaciously and vigorously on the world's stages for the next hundred years—*Peer Gynt*. In another letter to Hegel at the beginning of January, he indicates the subject and hopes for a short gestation period, but it took him, nevertheless, nearly a year.

Both for the student of literary history and from the human, biographical viewpoint, the birth of *Peer Gynt* is perhaps the most exciting period of Henrik Ibsen's life. While *Brand* is the explosion of his anguished mind, the eternally fleeing writer who halts and hits back, *Peer Gynt* is the most lavish, vital work he has ever produced. It is as if he had shabbily awaited the sunlight of life until he approached forty years of age, bearing powerfully germinating seeds which he had protected against the cold in the heart of this 'bundle of grief'. Now he has received warmth and scatters these seeds inside himself, and round about himself, so that they sprout and grow in all directions.

And now his hatred and indignation are no longer impotent either; now he can allow himself to say what he thinks on both small and large issues, and this he does at the top of his voice, in *Peer Gynt*. What enables generation after generation to experience it as something new, using what is relevant to their time and eliminating what is not is that it really does present the conflicts of the times in which it was written, in such a way that though the issues, no less than the characters, have long been dead, the vigour of the images and ideas, the strength of the psychological backbone, make it valid for posterity.

Ibsen himself did not regard it as an important work. Not until it was proclaimed in Norway and had won through in other ways than those he himself had expected did he begin to popularize it and wish to have it played in theatres. By then he was far enough away from the work to think on these lines: 'Now that "Ola the Norwegian" has accepted this rogue as a mixture of a distortion of the Norwegian people's character and a folk hero, it is time to make the characters come alive on the stage too.' Not until then did he ask Edvard Grieg to romanticize the whole comedy; something which Grieg did very reluctantly, as we shall shortly see.

He found a name for, and a few features for the kind of character he now wanted to write about, in Asbjørnson's second collection of legends and folk-tales. But in Asbjørnson, there is only the story of Peer's meeting with the boyg, which was always invisible and meant that he always had to go roundabout, and of the mountain dairymaids who were visited by the Faith in Valfjellet. Otherwise all that is written about him is what Anders says: 'This Peer Gynt was a man apart. He really was a legend-maker and a story-teller you would have enjoyed; he always said that he himself had been in all the stories people said had happened in the old days.'

It is of course possible that Ibsen himself, during his long walks up through Gudbrand valley during the summer of 1862, also heard about this Peer, but it is hardly likely, and anyhow he has left us no note of anything of the kind. But he found some more material in his good friend Botten-Hansen's play, *The Mountain Wedding*.

So it is the catchwords *story-teller*, *legend-maker* and most of all, *go roundabout* which set Ibsen's imagination going. All the rest is free creative writing, but set in a milieu which is a mixture of features of Asbjørnson, his own collected folk-tales and the Norwegian countryside as he himself knew it; he uses geographical features as scenery superbly, without the slightest regard for topographical facts. This milieu and this geographical backgroung afford fertile soil for his genius to grow in and create the exact counterpart of the character of Brand—the liar, the boaster, but cowardly when it comes to the point, a caricature of the idea of individualism, the man who betrays everything and everyone, but mostly himself.

It is clear that this character has had a tremendous appeal to Ibsen's imagination. He says he has borrowed parts of it from impurities in his own mind, but he has included examples of everything that he did not like in his own countrymen. And the legendary distance makes it at the same time possible for him to see the fairy-tale-like, charming, almost disarming qualities in this man's strength of imagination. He is of course Askeladden (the Ash-lad) too.

It is evident not only from the literary sources, but from the poem itself, that it was written in three stages. First Ibsen laid the keel of the first three acts—the story of the boy who lets the farm decay, while he goes hunting or fighting and drinking. When drunk he carries off the bride from the wedding, but soon betrays her because he has fallen in love with the innocent daughter of a settler. Balked of his desire, an outcast, he roams the mountains, where he meets the trolls, the boyg and the milkmaids of the fairy tales. Then he is given the chance to possess the innocent girl he adores, but dares not take the responsibility; and in the end, on his way out into the world, he sees his mother's death-throes, and tries to lie away that experience too.

From the very beginning, it had been Ibsen's intention that the poem should also have a fourth act, about Peer's life away from his native land, and a fifth, the final reckoning. But both from the content and the method of work, it is clear that the next two acts had been only roughly sketched in his imagination, and had to remain so until the first acts were completed.

These first three acts are among Ibsen's most cheerful and imaginative work. They are written in rhyming but increasingly free verse, sparkling with ridicule and wisdom and tumbling easily between the world of fable and reality. In these three acts Ibsen also burlesques certain definite aspects of Norwegian life, chiefly in the scene in old man Dovre's hall—a scene which was later rewritten. In the first draft, the scene opens with the trolls singing the national-romantics' familiar festive song, 'For Norway, Birthplace of Warriors' to the melody he himself had always used when he wrote occasional songs to order, but this he later eliminated. Ibsen had come through his own period of national romanticism and now his main target was the smug advocates of national language reform. He had a considerable amount against them too and continued throughout his life to 'Norwegianize' his language. But he did not like New Norwegian either, least of all after Vinje had tried to make fun of Brand. Also, as head of the Norwegian Theatre in Møllergaten, he had been forced to carry out an often inartistic and cumbersome Norwegianization. The person who had got the theatre going and was the main personality behind it was of course Knud Knudsen, who throughout his long life fought indefatigably for the Norwegianization of the written language, and Ibsen had had to slave away under him with increasing reluctance and concealed vindictiveness.

In the scene with the trolls, Ibsen lets his countrymen, especially the national language reformers, unmistakably see themselves in caricature. One would think that this contemporary political satire would have been just the sort of thing to become unplayable and incomprehensible later on, but oddly enough, it seems to have retained its vivid dramatic power. Many a learned work has been written in foreign languages to explain who the trolls really are, but in the theatre, these remarkable creatures of Norwegian fairy tales have shown themselves to be dramatically comprehensible in all countries.

He began *Peer Gynt* at Christmas, 1866, and in March, 1867, he writes to Hegel:

'In my new dramatic poem I have now progressed to the middle of the second act (it will be five) and as far as I can calculate beforehand about 250 pages long. If you wish, I will send you the manuscript in July.'

But it did not go so quickly as that. In May, he writes to Hegel:

'It is my intention to go to Ischia in the middle of this month, to spend the summer there and complete my new work, of which two acts are now ready and the plan for the rest now quite clear and worked out. Here in Rome I am unlikely to write any more, for I feel the wanderlust in my blood and even more the need for greater solitude.'

Not until August 8th did he send the first three acts to Gyldendal; he had the fourth act finished in the middle of September, and the last was sent from Rome on October 18th.

The fourth and fifth acts are quite different from the first three, and the fourth act cannot possibly have been thought out before Ibsen reached it, although the preliminary sketch describes it as taking place in Africa. That Peer in the fifth act must be home again for the final settlement with himself and his betrayal, is evident enough. But in the meantime the fourth act is said to show what happens to him in his manhood, what the flight of imagination, his vacillation and his egoism make of him. Without being able to furnish any kind of watertight argument for it, I have nevertheless always thought that *originally* Ibsen did not want Peer to travel farther than to Kristiania, to show the Norwegian 'character' developing there, but that he abandoned the idea because *that* settlement would have broken every canon of the dramatic poem.

Anyhow, he turned this act into pure farce, a play on its own within the play. When *Peer Gynt* is now performed all over the world, the fourth act is often severely cut, not only because the play is too long for today's theatregoers, but also because the satirical farce is so overloaded with allusions and diatribes aimed at the state of world politics of his time that despite its fireworks it has little scenic strength.

In the fifth act, Ibsen is soon back in the subtle world of the fable which carries the first three acts. The dialogue sparkles with witticisms here too, such as the remark that one 'does not die in the middle of the fifth act', but soon subsides into the slightly melancholy, resigned mood in which Peer is driven back from entrenchment to entrenchment in his inner confrontation with himself. The act is full of 'caprices', as Ibsen calls them—but the writer lets his work flow into forgiveness for Peer, despite everything, not *only* because there have been women who have loved him, Solvejg and Mother Åse, but also because behind all his stone-cold egoism, he has nevertheless held fast to a visionary ideal of womankind.

Before we go on to the publication of the work and its consequences, it may be of interest to take a look at what the outside world thought of him at this time. We have several snapshots taken from different angles, but all agreeing that he was not exactly a pleasant man-about-town. He roamed about the Scandinavian Society in Rome, was very argumentative and easily offended, but at the same time obviously full of vitality.

The Danish writer, Vilhelm Bergsøe, has given the most lively account of life with Ibsen. Bergsøe was a few years younger, had lived in Rome before, but had been very ill and for a while had been blind. During his illness he finished writing, or perhaps dictated, in Copenhagen, one of the greatest novels of the day— *From Piazza del Popola*, which brought him fame, but which was at first slated by the critics, led by the feared and powerful Clemens Petersen.

At the beginning of 1867, he returned to Rome with his brother and sister, having recovered from his illness as well as his mauling by the critics, and he soon went to the Scandinavian Society in the hope of meeting friends, but

'instead of my usual fellow-countrymen, I saw only a dark-haired man unknown to me, sitting so absorbed in the papers that he simply did not notice my arrival. . . .

'When one sunny morning I was walking across Capo del Casa, I discovered that the dark-haired man from the Society was walking towards me. As he had not greeted me up there, I did not greet him either, but he came straight up to me and said in Norwegian:

' "I didn't greet you up there because I didn't know who you were, but now I hear you're Vilhelm Bergsøe, I greet you twice over."

'I stared in astonishment at the stranger. He was a stocky man of middle height, with black hair, large dark side-boards and sharp, penetrating eyes. He was wearing a short seaman's jacket, a coloured Roman scarf and all in all gave me the impression of being a seaman, but who he was I did not know.

' "Well, I'd better say who I am," he went on, "as I can see you do not know me. My name is Henrik Ibsen."

'I had never for a moment thought that he might be Henrik Ibsen and when I went on staring at him he said cheerfully:

' "Yes, I am what I am, and I suppose you are too. I've read your novel and see that it's written according to reality, and that is what we need nowadays—the time for seductive fictional heroes has passed."

' "Then you've probably read the criticism in *The Fatherland*?" I asked. "It wasn't favourable. I'm afraid it'll finish the book."

' "No, never," exclaimed Ibsen, with unusual liveliness. "When one writes such a long and violent review, it arouses attention, and then comes the opposition. Criticism can balk a good book for a time, but can never destroy it. I predict that some day you'll find out that what I say is true, but what have you done to Mr Petersen that his attack was so violent? You must have offended him in some way or other." '

It then appeared that Clemens Petersen had believed himself to be portrayed in Bergsøe's novel. It is hideous to think of the determining power a critic such as Clemens Petersen possessed during his short despotic reign. Ibsen himself flattered him with thanks for his mention of *Brand*, which had meant a great deal to the book. But a year later, Ibsen had come to look on him as the executioner in person.

But to return to Bergsøe. Ibsen and he became close friends and harking back to the jargon of the 'Dutchmen', Ibsen called him *Shoemaker Jakob* after a character in Holberg's comedies—no doubt because Ibsen liked to take a drink in his company when the long day's work was over. They spent the summer together in Ischia, the same summer during which Ibsen wrote his cheerful and uproarious farce, the fourth act of *Peer Gynt*. It was to Bergsøe that he directed his famous words: 'Yes, now I can work. I feel like a rearing stallion about to leap.'

Bergsøe's account of Ibsen that summer is a vivid portrait written by a writer about a writer, by a friend about a friend. It was written many years later, but with no veils of reverence for Ibsen's immense world-fame to spoil the impression of two friends at close quarters. Bergsøe tells of Ibsen's office-like methods of work, of his unapproachable distraction when they were walking together, when Ibsen in reality was just thinking, of how Suzannah and little Sigurd were banished from Ibsen's place of work during 'office hours', and also of cheerful excursions.

Ibsen often involuntarily let it be seen that he was very homesick, and Bergsøe once asked him why he did not go home. 'Then he straightened up and replied: "Home? Do you think I want to allow myself to be trampled to death by geese? *I* won't go back to Norway until Norway calls me." '

What Bergsøe says next should also be included: 'Generally speaking, Ibsen was very self-confident and often said that he was not working for his day, but for immortality, and when I replied that no writer could reach that far, that even the greatest spirits are forgotten when thousands of years have gone by, he rose up and said almost in fury: "Take your metaphysics away. If you rob me of immortality, then you rob me of everything." '

Finally, a complete account of one of their gay outings after a hard day's work. Bergsøe had just published his first collection of poems with Gyldendal, but Clemens Petersen had again slated the book, calling it dirty linen in a fusty bedroom. Ibsen eventually heard about this deadly slaughter, and asked if he could read it. Bergsøe replied that he would be permitted to, if he would accompany him up Epomeo, Ischia's highest volcano, about 2,400 feet above sea level. To Bergsøe's surprise, Ibsen agreed, and one day they started off at five o'clock in the morning to avoid having to climb in the worst heat.

'At first all went well, but gradually as the winding mountain paths grew steeper, the heat also grew more and more oppressive. The sun began to beat down mercilessly and Ibsen continually stopped to wipe the sweat from his face.

' "I'm not going to manage any farther," he said suddenly. "I've not eaten anything today and I'm both hungry and tired."

' "I know a vineyard-owner a little farther up," I replied. "We can probably buy some breakfast from him."

' "Let's go on up there then," said Ibsen, and so we climbed on.

'Eventually we arrived there, and the owner showed himself very willing to grant us our wish, and soon there appeared a steaming omelette on an upturned wine-press barrel, but unfortunately it was so strongly spiced with garlic that just the smell of it took our appetites away.

'From a cave in the mountain, our host then fetched a couple of fogliettes of local wine and we had hardly tasted it before we realized that this was a wine of the very best kind.

' "Your health, Jakob," said Ibsen. "Let us now hear what that bailiff [Clemens Petersen] says, but first we must have another couple of fogliettes—I've never tasted anything like this wine."

'Our host came out of the cave with the sparkling wine and I began to read, but every time I came to some bold assertion, Ibsen said:

' "Cheers, Jakob," and emptied his glass.

'Seldom has a review been read in such marvellous surroundings, seldom with such good humour, so that Mr Petersen would no doubt have been quite annoyed if he had witnessed this bucolic scene. When I stopped reading, Ibsen said:

' "I don't think he can write himself, but to tell others how something should be written, something he is not able to master himself, that he can always do. Give me that page and I'll show you how it should be used."

'I handed him the paper and suggested we went on up, but Ibsen wanted another fogliette, and when that was empty, we went on our way.

'Now something remarkable happened. The old volcano began to sway, and however much we tried, we were not in a state to walk straight along the road. It was as if we were walking on a bouncing floor.

' "What's happening?" said Ibsen. "I think it's an earthquake."

' "No, it's the wine. Perhaps we'd better go down again."

'Ibsen had nothing to say to this, and walked quickly ahead of me, with small, stiff, dancing-master steps, so that he was soon quite a distance in front of me.

' "Here's a short cut," he cried, and swung off to the right.

' "No, there's no other way but the one we're taking."

' "Yes, there's a path here. We'll miss out a whole bend."

'I hurried after him, but not until I arrived there did I discover that what he had thought was a path was just one of the many screes on Epomeo, which really consist of loose pumice and chunks of lava.

' "Stop, stop," I called. "You'll fall if you go any further. That's not a path, it's a scree."

' "No, it's a path," replied Ibsen stubbornly, and now there was nothing else to do but run after him and stop him. I caught hold of his coat collar.

' "Let me go!" he cried angrily. "You can go the other way, but I'm going this way."

'He was struggling as he spoke, and when I tried to pull him up again, the substrata began to shift, at first quite slowly, then faster, and soon we were enveloped in a cloud of dust and sand, whilst blocks of lava and pumice rolled down round us. Now he realized the danger for the first time and wanted to turn back, but it was too late. . . .

'In the end it was as if we were progressing in a mist. We could see nothing ahead of us, nothing to the side, but suddenly we ran into a hard object and the next moment we fell head over heels on to the mountain road, with pumice, gravel and sand continuing to hail down on us.

'I helped Ibsen to his feet and now I saw that we had run into the wall which is built to a height of about a foot or so each side of the road. Our clothes were covered with dust, we had a few grazes here and there, but otherwise all was well. Ibsen stood still for a moment, took a deep breath as he looked up, and said:

' "What a devil of a speed."

'Then he went on, in deep silence. We both felt that it had been a matter of life and death.

'When we reached the piazza, Ibsen brushed himself down very carefully, folded *The Fatherland* into a cornet, and saying "Now we'll blow that critic for a while", strode puffing across the piazza, to the great astonishment of the guests in front of the café.

'Just beyond the café there was a wretched little cigar shop, and there Ibsen bought a couple of the worst cigars that the peasants smoke, and when he had done this, he took out his notebook and carefully noted down what they had cost.

' "Do you write down that sort of thing?" I asked in surprise.

' "Yes," he said. "I have to keep very careful accounts of my expenditure, now that I'm married. When I was young, I didn't do it."

'Not until then did I realize that Ibsen's circumstances had been poor, and probably still were.'

These memories of Ibsen by Vilhelm Bergsøe have been fairly generally forgotten, both in Norway and in his home country, Denmark. Many works on Ibsen refer to them, giving a few details of literary interest. But I have given them this amount of space here because they give such a vivid and lively picture of Ibsen as, during a significant epoch of his life, he appeared to a young writer who was close to him personally and with whom he felt in harmony without at any time having to reveal himself to him. In the literature on Henrik Ibsen, these pieces of writing have a special position, and they should not be forgotten or relegated to footnotes. A minor query to end with: I wonder whether Ibsen refrained from noting down in his notebook the fogliettes of wine they had just drunk?

Ibsen's manuscript was ready in the middle of October and he was able to send it off in safe hands. I should think that it was on that day, after delivering his colossus, that he suddenly had time to write to his step-mother-in-law, Magdalene Thoresen, who had meanwhile moved back to Kristiania, beginning the letter with apologies for the long delay. He is pleased that Suzannah's sister has married and is to live in Copenhagen: '. . . for I do not think she is especially suited to conditions in Norway, and if there is any disparagement in this, then it applies to the conditions and not to her.—I never understand how you can bear it up there! Life up there, such as it is now for me, is something indescribably restricting; taking the spirit out of your being, and the strength from your will; that is what is so damnable with such petty conditions, and they make your soul petty.'

It is the *conditions* at home that he hates, not Norway herself. Beneath this hatred runs an undercurrent of homesickness, which during these years finds lyrical expression. But he looked on the 'conditions' with a mixture of hatred and contempt not only because of all the cowardice, stupidity, narrow-mindedness and hypocrisy, but also because he himself had so often been obliged to play the weakling's degrading role in these 'conditions'. He also knew that his own soul had been in danger of becoming too petty.

It appears from Ibsen's letter that at this time he had some hope that in Denmark he would find a spiritual milieu in which it would be possible to breathe and live, but *Peer Gynt*'s fate more or less crushed these romantic dreams of the future.

The next instalment of *Peer Gynt* was received by Hegel at the end of October, and this time the publisher did not let months go by. The poem was as impractically long as *Brand* and had many more Norwegian words and ideas, but now the manuscript went to print, and on November 14, 1867, it was published.

Now Ibsen awaited the reaction in Scandinavia in a state of considerable tension, and it was primarily what the Danish critics would have to say that he could not wait to hear. But the first reaction came in a letter from Bjørnstjerne Bjørnson, who had not had much to say in favour of *Brand*, but who as early as November 18, 1867, four days after *Peer Gynt* came out, wrote an enthusiastic letter.

'My dear Ibsen!—I am so grateful for *Peer Gynt*, that I cannot remember any book in all my years as a writer which has impelled me to give so warm a handclasp; I have warmly received.... I love the loyalty to our great purpose, from the Danish cause to the greatest ideals. I love your indignation, I love the courage it has endowed you with. I love your strength, I love your mischief; ah, was it not like the smell of the sea on the coast after the suffocating air of the sick-room; my mind filled with laughter, daring, recklessly truthful, as the trifles became trifles, and the great things gave splendour and fire to my yearning. I could take to cursing in good Norwegian, for I have for too long spoken French in the salons.'

And in *Norsk Folkeblad*, Bjørnson soon wrote an enthusiastic review. Ibsen could then rest assured that the debate was in full swing in Norway, and there he knew it would become an issue. With even greater excitement he waited for young Brandes, but most of all for Clemens Petersen. The review came out in *The Fatherland* on November 30th, but it did not reach Ibsen until over a week later. It is the measure of how sensitive he still was beneath his self-confidence, that he took this review as an annihilating blow, an assassination. This it was not, but it was very derogatory. Clemens Petersen had not discerned very much of the poem's meaning and intention. Ibsen was seized by an utterly unmanageable rage, and it was over the innocent Bjørnson that he poured it, in the most furious letter he had ever written. He knew what close friends Bjørnson and Petersen were, and that Bjørnson was in Copenhagen at the time, so he suspected Bjørnson of playing a double game:

'Rome, December 9, 1867

'Dear Bjørnson,

'What kind of infamy is it that at every turn comes between us? It is as if the Devil himself personally came and shadowed us. I have received your letter. When one writes as you write, then there is no deceit in one's mouth. Things are given which do not allow themselves to be imitated. I have also written a reply from a grateful heart, for it is not praise one is grateful for, but to have been understood, that makes gratitude unspeakable. And now I have no use for my reply and have torn it to shreds. An hour ago, I read Mr Clemens Petersen's review in *The Fatherland*. If I am *now* to answer your letter, I must begin in another way: Please may I acknowledge the receipt of the honoured communication of this and that date with the attached review in the named newspaper. If *I* were in Copenhagen and had someone there who was as near to me as Clemens Petersen is to you, then I would have knocked him unconscious before I would have allowed him to commit such a tendentious crime against truth and justice. . . .

'Clemens Petersen has a great responsibility, for Our Lord has set him a great task. Do not think that I am a blind cowardly fool! You may think that I in my quiet hours rummage and probe and dissect quite politely in my own bowels—and in the places where it hurts most. My book *is* poetry, and if it is not, then it will be. The concept of poetry in our country, in Norway, will bend itself to fit the book. There is nothing stable in the world of concepts. Scandinavians in our century are not Greeks. He says that the strange passenger is the concept of anxiety! If I were standing at the place of execution and could save my life with that explanation, it would never have occurred to me; I have never thought of that; I slipped the scene in as a caprice. . . .

'I am however glad of the injury which has been inflicted upon me; there is God's help and decree in it, for I feel my strength grow with my indignation. If there is going to be war, then let it be so! If I am not a writer, then I have nothing to lose, I shall try as a photographer. But our contemporaries up there, one by one, person by person, I shall take on myself, as I have done with the language reformers, I shall not spare the lives of mothers and children, nor the thought or sentiment behind the word in the soul of anyone who earns the honour to be included.—

'My dear Bjørnson, you are a warm and blessed soul, who have given me more that is great and magnificent than I can ever repay, but there is something in your nature which can easily cause your good fortune, and just *that*, to become a curse to you. I am right to tell you this, for I know that under the crust of filth and nonsense I have been serious in my calling. Do you know that all my life I have drawn away from my own parents, from my whole family, because I could not remain in a state of semi-understanding. What I have written here is probably somewhat incoherent, but *summa summarum* is: I do not want to be an Antiquarian or a Geographer, I do not *want* to develop my aptitude for Monradian Philosophy; briefly, I simply do not want to follow good advice. But one thing I do want, even if external or internal forces drive me to tearing the roof down on to my head—I always want— so help me God, to be and remain

Your faithful and honestly devoted

Henrik Ibsen'

Unfortunately Ibsen did not send the letter straight away. For despite Ibsen's unbridled rage, Bjørnson could not take what Ibsen had written as directed at anyone else but Clemens Petersen. But next day Ibsen wrote a very long addition which *must* have wounded Bjørnson deeply. Ibsen's rage is still intense, but colder, and more poisonous:

'I am not in correspondence with home—but all the same I can tell you something from there. Do you know what is being said there in Norway as long as Carl Ploug's paper is read? They say: It can be seen from Clemens Petersen's criticism that Bjørnson is in Copenhagen.

'If you have reported on *Peer Gynt* in *Norsk Folkblad*, then they say: Diplomatic touches, but not fine enough.'

Later in the postscript comes an assurance that it is not Ibsen who thinks such things, but others. 'That I don't mistrust you in this matter, you will see from the fact that I am telling you all this. I neither stand nor ever will stand on my supporters' side against you. In relation to your friends—that's another matter.'

That this letter is in every way deeply unjust to Bjørnson does not make it any the less interesting as a psychological document. Clemens Petersen's article had been a philosophical-aesthetic, literary analysis which showed that *Peer Gynt* did not measure up by *his* yardstick, and the only remarkable thing is that Ibsen had not been able to perceive this. Perhaps he did have some premonition of Petersen's verdict when he was walking across the piazza in Ischia with Bergsøe, a criticism by Petersen rolled up into a cornet, like a trumpet in his mouth. On the other hand it is quite correct, as Ibsen conceitedly asserts, that if this was not poetry, then anyhow the concept of poetry would with the years bend itself to conform with his book. It is also amusing to note Ibsen's angry refutation of the idea that 'the strange passenger' is the concept of anxiety and his insistence that this scene is pure caprice. For Petersen's interpretation has since been accepted and acclaimed and, within the choir of inner voices which populate the last act of *Peer Gynt*, 'the concept of anxiety' is hailed as an idea drawn from Ibsen's deepest psychological instinct—the kind of caprice which might be called genuine inspiration.

Bjørnson took Ibsen's letter, anyhow to begin with, as an attack of insanity, a kind of spontaneous Italian mental disturbance. Later Ibsen's aggression must have made a deeper impression on him, for the reply he wrote to it is the last letter but one that he wrote to Ibsen for many years.

Bjørnson's reply is very long indeed, filling over eleven pages of a book. Bjørnson makes persistent and elaborate attempts to calm the rabid Ibsen down, describing conditions in Norway and Denmark, saying in what respects he must agree with Clemens Petersen, and why, despite *Peer Gynt*'s obvious lack of wholeness and unity, he is still attracted and moved by the book. Naturally he cannot resist one or two sarcasms, otherwise he would scarcely have been human.

Ibsen for his part had been sitting there in Rome, bitterly regretting what he had written. When Bjørnson's long reply came—not until Christmas morning—he did not at first pay any attention to the sarcasm, but only realized with inexpressible relief that Bjørnson was apparently still his friend

'That load of rubbish I sent in my last epistle has in the meantime caused me to have not one single pleasant and satisfactory hour. The worst thing a human being can do against himself is to do an injustice to others. Thank you, with your great spirit, for taking the matter as you did! I foresaw nothing but dissension and bitterness for a long time to come, but now, afterwards, I see it as something so natural to you that you took the matter in just this way and in no other. I read your letter over and over again, every day, and read myself free of the painful thought that I should have wounded you.'

So they both took it in the wrong way, each wounding the other and on second thoughts feeling hurt, and at that communications broke down between them.

A small detail in Bjørnson's reply, and in Ibsen's reply to that letter, is worthy of notice. In his reply, Bjørnson mentions a rumour that both of them are to be honoured by decorations: 'Shall we not agree to refuse? To me it is all so loathsome; is it not the same to you?'

But Ibsen did not quite agree:

'On the matter you mention, "the order", I must, according to my deepest convictions, remain in complete disagreement with you. We belong to a monarchy and not a republic. . . . From the State we receive money; royal power presents us with an honour, for it respects public feeling, whose existence it acknowledges. Why refuse the one form of expression when we have not refused the other for the same thing? Let us look deeply into ourselves! Is it our intention in future to become ascetics? Do we intend to decline every well-meant festive occasion, every speech of praise, etc?'

But life went on, and Ibsen's attacks of rage, his 'paroxysms', abated, he was able to establish that the sales of *Brand* were not just a flash in the pan, but that on a solid basis he now had the whole of Scandinavia talking; also that in Norway he was regarded as a champion of the conservative forces against national language reform and nationalism. That Peer Gynt also had wider scope both for the world and the future, Ibsen discovered only with the passage of years.

But the thoughts that had erupted like a volcano in his furious letter to Bjørnson had set his mind in motion. In his reply, Bjørnson had told Ibsen among other things, that he ought to write a satirical comedy, and Ibsen himself had threatened to become a 'photographer', in other words to attack the enemy and the 'conditions' so that everyone could recognize himself.

It was while he was busy with such thoughts in the spring of 1868, that he began to feel himself more and more rootless in Rome, and was forced to move on. He could not go home and he did not want to; and he no longer desired to go to Denmark either. So it came about that at the beginning of May he left Rome, travelled through Florence to Berchtesgaden in the Tyrol and, after a few weeks in Munich in the autumn, settled in Dresden at the end of October, 1868.

10

Over to Farce

IT took Ibsen time, both after *Brand* and after *Peer Gynt*, to absorb the influence his work had had on the outside world, before he could seriously concentrate on something new. As late as three and a half months after the book had been published it is still the controversy about *Peer Gynt* that is occupying his mind. He writes to Hegel:

'How is *Peer Gynt* going? So far as I can see from newspaper reports, it has been very well received in Sweden, but do the sales confirm this?

'It seems that the book has roused a great deal of fuss in Norway, but that does not worry me in the least; but both there and in Denmark they have found much more satire than I had intended. Why cannot one read the book as a poem? For that is what I have written it as. The satirical sections are fairly isolated. . . . My work will perhaps be a play for the theatre, and it is to be hoped that it will not be long before I get to work on it seriously.'

And it is no doubt possible that for a time he felt empty, written out after two such immense volcanic eruptions, each in its own way a break through in dramatic poetry. As with the scorpion on his desk in Rome, after such an explosion he must have felt 'normal' again.

It is clear that he had nothing else in mind in the form he had used for his last two works. Now that he had made his claim for ideals and had set up its counterpart, he had no more principles to formulate for the time being. Now the time had come to turn his sights from the abstract to the concrete. It was also natural for him to use the knowledge which he had acquired from more than ten years practical work in the theatre and a number of attempts, some of them successful, to master this dramatic form.

As I have said before, I have always, perhaps wrongly, believed that Ibsen had at first meant the fourth act of *Peer Gynt*, the one covering Peer's manhood years, to be set in Kristiania, but had afterwards decided that this would enlarge the scope of the play too much. Following the same line of thought, I have also always believed that Stensgaard in *The League of Youth* originated in an attempt to put Peer's manhood years in a Norwegian setting. But after that, the desire to write a satirical farce, or a comedy of Norwegian life, got the upper hand, and not until he had got going on *that*, did he permit himself to draw at will upon this secret spiritual source, both for Stensgaard and the others. He became in fact what he had threatened—a photographer—a designation which when he was a young theatre critic, had been his worst term of abuse.

Turning from the sources of *The League of Youth* to its dramatic quality, it has always surprised me that so many Ibsen scholars mention this play in the same breath and almost on the same level as his great dramatic poems. In our time, anyhow, *The League of Youth* seems to be a somewhat clumsy and overloaded farce, full of tricks and complications, with incessant side-issues and contemporary gibes, containing almost sheer caricatures rather than human beings.

It would naturally have created a storm when it came out, for there were plenty of people who felt themselves caricatured, no doubt many more than in fact were. And inevitably the play was taken up by the Right and regarded as an attack on the Left. But for the person who reads *The League of Youth* today, it is a matter of complete indifference whether Prime Minister Richter made a fool of himself with his persistent and temporarily unsuccessful attempts to marry money, or whether the peasant leader, Ueland, is the model for Lundestad, the play's wily fox.

It is of much greater interest that Ibsen has obviously borrowed features from his own father for his glib bankrupt, Daniel Hejre; and the fact that the milieu is the Skien of his childhood is also interesting, but only inasmuch as it confirms what we already

know, that Ibsen's ties with his own father were always negative
and insubstantial and that his hatred for the conditions at home
was deep-rooted.

But the justification of the play is that Ibsen is trying his pren-
tice hand at a genre which he has not attempted before. He uses
new materials, often with masterly skill. For the first time he
writes about individual human beings of his day, and in the
tongue of his own time. Instead of imitating a variety of styles, as
in all his previous work, he lets all these caricatures, these 'animal
faces', express themselves each in his own individual manner.
What they express is often tediously repetitive, but the portraits
are usually very lifelike. It is also worth mentioning that several
of the situations recur in different settings as leading themes in
Ibsen's later plays, for example, Landowner Bratsberg's crisis
when he learns that one of his nearest and dearest has forged a bill
of exchange.

The play is not great, the main character is totally revealed from
the first moment, and possesses none of *Peer Gynt's* redeeming
dimensions or nuances. But technically it is well turned and has
some good acting rôles.

Ibsen obviously did not get going on this new play until after
a considerable incubation period. As late as at the end of September, 1868, he writes to Hegel that he is now to live in Dresden,
and says:

'In Dresden I shall write my new play—more of that later. I hope
that will be complete by Christmas, and as this is too late for
publishing and performance for this year, it will have to be left.
I shall send you a copy and then perhaps we could come to some
agreement on what else there is to do. I am very pleased with my
new *peaceable* work.'

It was not until October that he began to get a move on. On
October 31, he writes from Dresden to Hegel:

'My new work is going ahead rapidly. It will be in prose and
wholly for the stage. The title of the play is *The League of Youth
or Our Lord & Co:*, Comedy in 5 acts. It is about the frictions and
currents of present-day life, and will, notwithstanding that it takes

F

place in Norway, apply equally to Denmark. I find myself in a happy and reconciled state of mind and am writing accordingly. . . .'

It did not really become a conciliatory farce. The next bulletin goes on December 22 to Hegel, who has in the meantime protested about the blasphemous title:

'My comedy has now got as far as the 4th act. I think it will amount to about 180–200 pages, which is suitable. Your suggestion with reference to the title will be followed; it is quite right, and I myself was half-way towards the same thought from the beginning. The expression would anyhow not have annoyed anyone, *when the play has been read*. There is not a single word on religious matters in it, but no one could know that beforehand, and so, one could easily cause offence with the subtitle. So, away with it!'

The industrious Ibsen slaved away at his new art form, writing draft after draft. Not until the beginning of May did he send the end of the manuscript to Copenhagen. It was sent to the printers at once, but Ibsen wanted Gyldendal to delay the book temporarily, as he intended to send the play to all three main Scandinavian theatres, counting on it being accepted. And so it was in the early summer, which says something for the position Ibsen had attained all over Scandinavia with his great dramatic poems.

There were other matters, however, that were taking up much more of Ibsen's time and interest that summer than this 'peaceable' comedy, into which he had put so much craftsmanship that he could proudly boast that he had let the dialogue speak for itself without a single monologue directed at the audience— without even a single 'aside'.

The first distraction was P. F. Siebold, a German man of letters familiar with Scandinavia, who had been so taken with *Brand* that he wanted to translate it into German and generally launch Ibsen in Germany. To begin with Ibsen had been doubtful whether *Brand* were translatable, and one cannot wonder at this. He knew his own worth as a lyric poet and knew how many nuances would be lost if the translator were not a poet of quality. Nevertheless the idea soon captivated him. To win through in Germany would be the equivalent of gaining a European reputation, which at that time meant world recognition.

During the spring and early summer of 1869, Ibsen began to be more and more enthusiastic about this plan and suggested that Siebold should consider *The Pretenders* too. He is very willing to co-operate over effective publicity. There must be laudatory articles about him in the serious papers. The real centre for publishing activities is Leipzig, and he is willing to travel there and work for his cause. In order to become known in Germany, he also renews his connection with his old friend from Rome, Lorentz Dietrichson, who is now making his career in Stockholm as a curator, private tutor to the royal family and also as a professor. Ibsen asks Dietrichson to write about him in the German papers.

We have seen something of Ibsen's burning and justifiable ambition. We have also heard a little of his well-founded misgivings about the petty 'conditions' at home, his suspicion—even of Bjørnson, and increasingly of Bjørnson—that friendship decided official opinion. So perhaps it was necessary for him to use the same methods?

That summer, also, he was invited to be one of the Norwegian delegates to a conference in Stockholm on the orthography of the Scandinavian languages, to formulate a common code of rules for all of them, so that they could be as closely linked as possible.

One would have thought that Ibsen was an obvious choice for the delegation. He was read more widely in neighbouring countries in his own language than any other Norwegian author, even Bjørnson. He had worked on Norwegianizing his language and knew more about the problems than most philologists. And his own orthography and use of language had hitherto been very varied. In the same letter he spells the same word in several different ways, he uses traditional Danish spelling, and he tries to spell according to spoken Norwegian; in fact he is very inconsistent.

However, in the end it was only as a substitute that he went off to Stockholm at the end of July, 1869. He had many other interests besides orthography to attend to there, for he knew he had gained a large public in Sweden and that *there* he had not yet been slated by any personal enemies. He knew that he might be offered a decoration. He knew that Dietrichson was closely connected with the royal household, and he had just persuaded Dietrichson to introduce him in German translation into serious German publications. In his letters to Dietrichson, he stresses that his opponents in his own country should not be mentioned; although it would otherwise have been natural for his friend from his early years in Rome to emphasize by this means the dramatic nature of Ibsen's later rise to fame. But no, the biography must just say that his country has honoured him with a life-pension and in other ways. In addition, it is important for him to have his new play performed in Stockholm, if possible at the same time as in Copenhagen and Kristiania.

To finance the trip, he had applied for and received a large grant of three hundred riksdalers to make a study-trip to Sweden. On July 20 he travelled north. His stay in Stockholm became a triumphal procession. The orthographic conference itself lasted only a week, from July 25 to 30, but produced considerable results, anyhow so far as Ibsen was concerned. After this, his spelling is considerably more consistent than before.

After the conference, however, Ibsen remained in Stockholm for almost two months. He explained this in a letter to his brother-in-law, J. H. Thoresen: 'I am living here in an incessant stream of festivities, so that hitherto I have not passed a single day without invitations to dinner and so on.' And this homage went on through August and September; he enjoyed it and needed it.

Lorentz Dietrichson, with his good connections both in Stockholm's best society and in the city's literary circles, was delighted to set the stage for this triumphal procession. He says a great deal about it in his memoirs.

'It was a stirring summer that year in Stockholm. The Crown Princess of Denmark was celebrating her marriage, which had brought a number of royal heads together in Sweden's capital city. Henri Martin visited Stockholm. Orthographic experts, including several of the most important linguists in Scandinavia, visited Stockholm, and Henrik Ibsen visited Stockholm. At Ibsen's request, I rented a couple of rooms for him in Herkules Bakke, between Brunkebergs Square and Regeringsgatan, and when he arrived, he installed himself there. The author of *Brand* was expected to have an old, stern and serious face, and an elegant young man appeared, in a velvet frock-coat, cultivated, lively and charming. One could not liken *Brand* to *Brand*'s author, and several people expressed their surprise openly to him, some simply disappointment, but soon he had taken them all by storm, especially the ladies. One of the first houses into which he was introduced was that of the Limnell family, well known for their generous hospitality to all illustrious travellers, as well as the less illustrious. The husband held a senior post in the railways and his wife, the widow of the well-known editor of *Aftonbladet* (Evening News), Rektor Svedbom, was much admired for her intelligence, her warm heart and her personal charm. She was the soul of a wide literary circle and I myself, ever since my arrival in Sweden ten years earlier, had enjoyed excessive hospitality in this house, so naturally I took Ibsen there as soon as possible. The family lived in their pretty villa, *Lyran*, by Lake Mälare during the summer and there Ibsen spent more than one lovely summer evening, and soon won everyone's hearts in this circle. That was also why, the following year, he addressed to Mrs Limnell his famous "Balloon Letter to a Swedish Lady".'

Dietrichson tells how Ibsen's great poem came to Stockholm the following year and how he, Dietrichson, was the first to read the poem aloud to a reverently admiring inner circle of literary personalities. The Norwegian-born authoress, Laura Kieler, has maintained that it was *she* who was the first to read it, in Limnell's house, but Dietrichson is no doubt right. Dietrichson goes on:

'But back to Ibsen's stay in Stockholm. At that time he moved among a number of Stockholm's most intellectual families.

When the wedding festivities and the orthographic conference were over, and royalty from both literary and State empires had gone their way, the great writer-prince remained behind. He obviously enjoyed Stockholm, and in addition an idea began to go round in certain circles that would soon become reality. Ibsen was to be invited to take part in the opening of the Suez Canal. The idea no doubt came from King Carl XV (who had probably read *Peer Gynt* and noticed that the fourth act was partly set in Egypt). Mr Demirgian, the unfortunate oriental who at that time played a great part in the court of King Carl XV, had the task of making the necessary arrangements.'

Dietrichson was also to have gone, but illness prevented him. Ibsen and he nevertheless left Stockhom at about the same time:

'But before that, the Director and players of the Royal Dramatic Theatre in Stockholm had planned for our enjoyment a farewell party in the Hotel du Nord. .... One evening when Ibsen was at the Dramatic Theatre, King Carl XV had him summoned to his box, and soon after that to the Palace, where he invested him with the Order of Vasa—that was Ibsen's first decoration.'

Not until September 29 did Ibsen leave Stockholm, where he had basked in his fame and popularity and must have displayed considerable social charm, in stark contrast to the impression he gave in later life of being a closed, withdrawn sphinx.

Before he left, he had received a message to say that the Royal Theatre in Copenhagen had also accepted *The League of Youth*, on good terms. It was to be performed in Kristiania in October and at the Dramatic Theatre in Stockholm in November. With the contracts in his pocket, he no longer had any reason for holding up the publication of the book, and he asked Hegel to put it on the market. He writes to his brother-in-law about the forthcoming trip: 'I have received a special invitation from the Viceroy of Egypt to be his guest for one or two months in his country and to be present at the inauguration of the Suez Canal. Everything will be paid for, including the journey from Paris and back again.' He goes on to give instructions on the administration of his finances while he is away, and says that he wishes to ask permission to use the remaining half of the grant he had had for the journey to Sweden for the Egyptian trip instead, and that this should not present any difficulties, for 'I am on especially good terms with the King and he is pleased I am going down there'.

So then he went south, first home to Dresden for a few days and thence to Paris, Marseille and Egypt.

II

The Long Maturing Spell

THE distinguished gathering of guests invited to the opening of the Suez Canal had already reached Egypt when the starting signal was given for *The League of Youth*. The greatest uproar was naturally in Kristiania, because of the many references to Norwegian politics and certain virtually named Norwegians. There is no doubt that Ibsen borrowed features from Bjørnson's public manner for Lawyer Stensgaard, but many people also saw portraits of Richter, Johan Sverdrup and other prominent personalities.

The première took place in Kristiania on October 18th and perhaps it is best to allow Suzannah to relate what happened, through the letter which gave Ibsen his first news of the play's reception:

'Dresden, October 2, 1869

'Dear Ibsen,

'I have received your letters and from them seen that all is as well with you as it could be. Sigurd says too that it is the thought of this that consoles him, and I say as he does, seize and enjoy everything offered to you. It is not every day one is guest of a King.

'But while you are enjoying to the full the glories of the south, you can imagine the storms in Kristiania over *The League of Youth*. On the first night, the first three acts received tempestuous applause, but in the fourth act, when Bastian speaks of what the nation is, whistles began to come from the third row from a couple of students engaged in the struggle for the new Norwegian language. How do you like that?

168

'According to *Morgenbladet*, the play went excellently; Krohn's and Isaksen's performances works of art; all the actors received excellent reviews in *Morgenbladet*. The evening ended in deafening applause.

'But now for the second evening: your benefit performance was settled in advance, for it was sold out before it began. As Lundestad ended his first speech the whistling began, and though it was time and time again drowned by applause, still they did not give up. The curtain had to be lowered. The producer had to go out and ask for quiet so that the play might continue; but the noise mounted to such an extent that the gaslight had to be extinguished at the end of the play. . . .'

At the third performance there were fights in the theatre, but the play was performed fifteen times that season and eight times in the next. In Stockholm the play opened on December 11, and despite the opposition of the theatre-censor, Carsten Hauch, the Royal Theatre in Copenhagen put on *The League of Youth* on February 16th the following year. Great success all the way.

But it was *The League of Youth* that made the break between Ibsen and Bjørnson definite and prolonged. As late as September, Bjørnson had written to Ibsen in Stockholm saying that he was delighted with the new comedy, for he had always thought that Ibsen had special talents in that direction. But on October 20, two days after the première, he writes to Rudolf Schmidt, a young Danish critic: 'Not a syllable from me about *The League of Youth*, and take my advice, not one from *you* either.'

On November 30, Bjørnson speaks out in another letter to Schmidt: 'Ibsen's play calls the young Norway a scheming, egoistical society, which abuses the name of freedom to conceal its ambitions and covetousness. He then invents several people, through whom he executes the young Norwegian nation. This is how it is understood here by his friends and everyone else follows suit. *This* is what I call murder, and everyone after me.' And later: 'Everyone sees that he has involved me, *but everyone pretends not to see it*—for Ibsen's sake, naturally. It was left to a Dane to present this view, that to the public I was Stensgaard. . . .'

This time Ibsen was not hurt by the storm his play provoked at home. Now he had entered a new period of his life. His stay in Stockholm had satisfied him that he was recognized as one of the great cultural leaders in Scandinavia, so they were welcome to make a little fuss in that small corner of the world, on which he was no longer dependent. Now he had started on the longest journey of his life, and it appeared that for a long time to come he would be fully occupied with assimilating new impressions from his travels and from world politics, from the Franco-Prussian war and from the annexation by Italy of the Vatican State. . . .

From a fragment that has been preserved, it appears that he probably meant to write a longer account of his travels, but that he put it aside after a description of a single day of the long boat trip southwards, up the Nile, to the first waterfalls, where the Aswan dam is today. The description of the countryside and the life of the people is extremely lively and shows what an exceptional journalist Ibsen could have been. He is, among other things, absorbed in studying the Arab, the Oriental:

'The Oriental associates only with his superior or his subordinate, never with his equal; his mind is as if spellbound by the same stillness and muteness as that which binds the landscape. A lethargic dream-life seems secretly to envelop him. I think, therefore, that caffeine, tobacco and opium do not put him into an abnormal state, but only stimulate what is natural to him.

'As things are, one can easily see what a fearful problem this government has to solve, having to bring in a whole new civilization. The main task is not in fact bringing modern improvements to something already in existence, but recreating in the future the whole spiritual habitus of the individual, breaking down the prejudice of a thousand years—yes, to a certain extent doing violence to nationality itself. Only a fearlessly autocratic government could achieve such measures. Representation of the people on a European model would naturally result in soft rubbish about "human rights", and would, like the River Nile, flood the task with oratorical water, but would hardly deposit its fertilizing mud on anything but the phrase itself.'

This brings us to the heart of the inner conflict which has lain dormant in Ibsen's previous work, but which now becomes and remains a driving force. Not merely in appearance is there something paradoxical and deeply divided in his relationship to the world around him. It is evident from everyone's impression of him that from his childhood in Grimstad he had been a kind of compulsive logician, with a deep need to push arguments to extremes or even to turn them upside-down to see whether he could not then arrive at different conclusions from those of tepid conventional thinking. In Grimstad he was opposed to all accepted ideas. In his years of toil in Bergen and Kristiania he made all kinds of attempts, often unsuccessful, to adapt himself to currents he thought were the least unattractive of the alternatives available, whilst in a narrower circle of friends he was argumentative, even quarrelsome. The same was true in Rome. He was not joking when he carried on passionate discussions on why a starving writer should prefer to eat the door-key rather than become a shop-assistant; the problem of whether twice two is four on other planets was not an excuse for an argument; he takes it up again in a letter to Georg Brandes five years after his argument in a café in Rome.

So at first he had been an agitator and then he had tried to adapt himself. After that, he had read the gospel to his people in two great dramatic poems as no writer has done before or since; after which he was acclaimed by conservative forces for attacking the claptrap talked by the advocates of progress. He, who wanted his people to 'think big', was now more hated than anyone else by those of his countrymen who had at least attempted to think about progress, to think big.

The same paradox is apparent in his political thinking. Having studied the Arab peoples he declares that for them autocratic government is necessary. At the same time, he is a fanatical enemy of the State. He goes further than the theoretical anarchists: the State must go. It is at this time that he writes the poem 'To my Friend the Revolutionary Speaker':

'They say I have become "conservative",/I am what I am all my life/I don't believe in making moves/upset the game and you have me fast./ ... You grieve for torrents over the world./With pleasure I place a torpedo under the ark.'

And later, he complains in a letter to Georg Brandes that the Paris communes have compromised the idea of revolution for long years ahead.

It is in a letter to Brandes just over a year later that his political philosophy is clearly articulated, against the background of his revulsion for both sides in the Franco-Prussian war:

'And so far as the question of freedom is concerned, then I think it is limited to an argument about words. I will never agree to making freedom synonymous with political freedom. What you call freedom, I call freedoms, and what I call the struggle for freedom is nothing else but the gradual awakening to the idea of freedom. The person who possesses freedom in a different way from something that is sought, possesses it dead and without spirit, for the concept of freedom contains the idea that it gradually expands during acquisition and if therefore during the struggle someone stands up and says: now I've got it—then that shows he has just lost it. But it is precisely this dead possession, with a certain static concept of freedom, that is a characteristic of State societies, and that is what I have said is not good. Yes, no doubt there can be good in possessing the freedom to vote, freedom from taxation, etc., but for whom is this good? For the citizen, not for the individual. But there is absolutely no need for the individual to be a citizen. On the contrary. The State is the curse of the individual. Away with the State! I shall be in on that revolution.'

Two more reflections: 'Exchanging of forms of government is no more than wavering over degrees, a little more, or a little less—all evil.' 'The State has its roots in time; it will be better in time. Greater things than that will fall: all religion will fall. Neither moral concepts nor artistic forms are immortal. . . .'

Whether his philosophy made him an anarchist or an arch-individualist, it was a source of fresh inspiration when he began seriously to dissect human beings in his contemporary dramas.

He spent the winter of 1869–70 at home in Dresden, tidying up one or two loose ends. There had been 'three bears from the old North' at the magnificent inauguration of de Lesseps's engineering triumph, the Suez Canal; besides Ibsen and the Norwegian Egyptologist, Lieblin, there was a young Danish literary figure, Peter Hansen. He and Ibsen became close friends and his company must have been both entertaining and relaxing in the midst of a gathering which otherwise consisted entirely of high-ranking titled personages from all over the world. It is to Hansen, in the autumn of 1870, that Ibsen writes the letter which has been extensively quoted in this book and which is inevitably quoted in all books on Ibsen, as it is outstanding as an open-hearted autobiographical document. The letter hints that Hansen had thought of writing a comprehensive biography for a collection of Ibsen's poetry, but so far as is known, all Hansen did was to include Ibsen in an anthology of Scandinavian writers which he published in 1870.

But Ibsen had many small irons in the fire. *The Pretenders* was to come out in a new edition and the spelling was to be in accordance with the new rules Ibsen himself had helped to formulate. This in itself was a time-consuming job. In addition he wished to have the lyrical parts of it set to music, a task which was undertaken by the Danish composer, Peter Heise. For now the play, backed by Ibsen's reputation, was to have its chance in the theatre. The Royal Theatre in Copenhagen this time accepted it, without even consulting their resident censor, Carsten Hauch, who was then eighty years old.

There was now the task of making a collection of Ibsen's widely scattered lyrical poetry. Ibsen had probably not taken the trouble to keep newspaper-cuttings or copies of them during his time in Kristiania, and anyway his papers there had been dispersed after the auction. During the orthographic conference in Stockholm, Jakob Løkke, schoolmaster and old friend of Ibsen's, no doubt on his own initiative, had undertaken to track down such of Ibsen's poems as were available in various publications, and this involved Ibsen in a great deal of work, choosing and discarding, filing and revising. . . .

When publication date at last drew near, he was kept busy with types, format, the arrangement of the verses on the pages and much else. His choice of poems is a curious mixture of exaggerated self-criticism and practically none at all. He was very severe on the lyrics of his youth. It is evident that there was a good deal of festive 'ding-dong' verse written to order as hack-work in his Kristiania years, which he did not now wish to acknowledge and basically never had acknowledged. But he also rejected several fine pieces. The few poems he had written in exile were naturally included; they were written for no other reason than that his heart needed airing. He added at the last moment two very long poems, which take up a disproportionate amount of space in relation to the rest. One is the controversial 'Balloon Letter to a Swedish Lady', written a year after the events he is disputing, incoherent, entertaining in parts, and with many sidelights on the times, often quoted by Ibsen-scholars, but quite unworthy of inclusion in a collection which contains so many of the finest concentrated reflective lyrics ever written in Norway.

There was one more poem which is scarcely even comparable to the rest; 'Rhyming Letter—to Mrs Heiberg', which owes its inclusion to the circumstances in which it was written.

In the summer of 1870, the year after he had conquered Stockholm, Ibsen took a trip from his home in Dresden to Copenhagen. His intention is obvious. Hegel and his firm were the main pillars of his growing reputation. After the early confusion over *Brand* and its subsequent success as a best seller, Hegel realized that here was an investment. And Ibsen, who during the years after 1864 despised both Norway and Sweden, put his trust, for good reasons, in Denmark and considered going to live there. Then came *Peer Gynt* and the sharp Danish criticism which shook his faith in Denmark. After that came his recognition in Sweden, and in the meantime his enemy and Bjørnson's friend, Clemens Petersen, had gone into exile.

Now the time was ripe for conquering Denmark, as he had Sweden the previous year. Copenhagen was for him the cultural centre of Scandinavia, and he wished to make personal contact with cultural circles there, besides, of course, nursing his connection with Gyldendal and in other ways consolidating his position. There are many small signs—we shall return to one of them—that his eventual aim was always the conquest of Norway. His basic mood at that time is expressed in the little poem he put at the end of his collection. Three of the stanzas are quoted here to put his visit to Denmark into the right perspective:

Burnt Ships

He turned the stem
Of his ship from the north
seeking legendary traces
of more brilliant gods.

He burnt his ship;
blue-black smoke
like a strip of bridge
northwards flying.

Towards the snow-country's cabins
from the sunny shore's brushwood
a knight rides
every single night.

Although things did not go quite so well as he had hoped, he did much to strengthen and define his status in Denmark. Behind the friendly façade, opinions among the Danish cultural circles had always been tinged with scepticism. Ibsen naturally met all the leading cultural personalities, and the one who made the strongest impression on him was the greatest actress of the Danish theatre of the century, Johanne Louise Heiberg, whom he had admired since his first trip to Copenhagen almost twenty years earlier. That admiration led him to write her the lengthy rhyming letter, and later to include it in his collected poems, a distinction which it by no means deserved.

Ibsen met no royal personages on this visit, and it was he himself who had to get something done about obtaining the

Order of Danebrog. It was Mrs Heiberg who pleaded for him with a minister, who chatted to another minister, so that at last some time after he had left Denmark, the prize was won.

His delight over the order was great and genuine. Home again in Dresden, he also started up a veritable crusade to obtain the Turkish order which the Khedive had half promised all his Suez guests, in exchange for the sackful of honours the guests had brought with them from their respective home countries to hang on prominent Turks. He received it in the end, a magnificent cross, which also delighted him.

He gives some explanation of this perhaps childish desire, in a letter to the Armenian adventurer, Demirgian, who stood high in the favour of King Carl XV, and who had arranged Ibsen's trip to Suez, but who had to leave Sweden shortly after the death of King Carl XV. Ibsen writes that he has been promised the Turkish order.

'This honour was extremely flattering to me, *as it will be of the greatest use to me in my literary position in Norway.* It will also be some compensation to me for the neglect I have suffered at home, in that the Order of St Olaf has been presented to several artists, painters and musicians, whilst I have been passed by—and this regardless of the fact that I stand faithfully on the side of the government and support it with my pen and all my abilities.'

In our eyes the last lines of this quotation are deeply compromising for Ibsen—we know he had no sympathy for tepid liberalism, which he considered never got to the roots of evil; and it sounds absurd that he, who was willing to torpedo Noah's ark and thought the State should be abolished, should be protesting his faithful support for it simply in order to achieve something as narrowly vain as an official honour, an order.

But if all of us suffered Ibsen's misfortune of having every single written word, private and public, examined and exposed in later years, on the whole few would come out of it better than he. His writing to a Marshal of the Royal Household is an explicable, even though a not entirely likeable hunger for honours, and his arguments seem to him to fit the case. It is said that he used to sweep his hat off for grand landaus with royal or aristocratic coats of arms on their doors, as they passed him in the street, even if there were no one in them. Many witnesses also agree that for some years he walked the streets wearing his orders in full array, not just the small buttons or ribbons that represented them.

But underneath all he writes on this matter there is the same refrain: 'This will be noticed in Norway; this will annoy someone, but will make everyone value my writing even more.' It is the knight who every night rides northwards to 'the cabins of the snow-country'. Inevitably, his single-mindedness was rewarded in the end: he received the Order of St Olaf, Norway's greatest honour.

We are now approaching the enormous odd man out in Ibsen's dramas, the great ten-act play, *The Emperor and the Galilean*, which he had in mind for nine whole years before he found a form for it, and which later he always considered to be his life's main work.

Many learned scholars are agreed on this. Within the ten acts whirl ideas and opinions, protests and remonstrances, a portrait gallery of long rows of colourful personalities twisting and turning past Julian's outward and inner gaze; and he himself is a victim of incessant interwoven moods, courage and fear, faith, doubt and scepticism, hatred and love, in an everlasting self-consuming brooding.

There is sufficient food for conjecture and research, but for the general reader these eternal philosophizings gradually become too kaleidoscopic and deteriorate into tedium towards the end. There is no place in a biographical portrait for detailed analysis of a colossal work of this kind: one can only indicate its heights and depths. But in order to point out any feature of *The Emperor and the Galilean*, it is wise to look at the work from several different angles.

We have seen Ibsen's success from devoting two years to consolidating his position as one of the great cultural leaders of

Scandinavia. When his collected poems came out in 1871, Gyldendal printed a first edition of four thousand, which was at that time a very great number for a collection of poems. And in every other way he was now secure.

From time to time during these years he had written to his publisher that he had a new play on the stocks, shortly to be launched, but obviously this was not quite correct. We know that he had already begun to plan what was to be *Pillars of Society*, but without really going ahead with it.

It was another theme that harried him; a subject which had impressed itself upon him in Rome back in 1864, and which he had then discussed with Lorentz Dietrichson and written to Bjørnson about, and then taken out again, over and over again, without really being able to draw the keel for it—the drama of Emperor Julian, who fell from Christianity and went over to paganism.

Rome itself and its surroundings, with all its memorials of ancient times, naturally set Ibsen's imagination working; here he saw before him the setting of his very first dramatic poem, *Catiline*. And of all the remarkable figures of antiquity, Julian the Apostate appealed more strongly to him than any other. Ibsen, too, had set himself against Christianity and its accepted norms, and was a seeker after new and different spiritual ground, driven by doubt and scepticism and an intense craving to find something new to believe in.

Certainly, in Ibsen's day there was no dearth of new ideas, views of life and philosophical trends. On the contrary, the accepted norms were being departed from in all directions. Marx carried Hegel's philosophy on to materialism. Schopenhauer was attacking on other fronts, and at the same time the natural history of the world was beginning to take shape.

Did Ibsen read a great deal of the innumerable philosophical theses, books and controversial papers which were circulating at the time? Obviously not all that much. I think Gerhard Gran puts his finger on something very characteristic when he quotes Emperor Julian's angry remark in the second act, to Basilius of Caesarea. First Julian asks in despair: 'Where shall I seek and find?' and Basilius replies: 'In the holy men's scriptures.' And then Ibsen exclaims on his own and Julian's behalf: 'The same answer of despair. Books—always books! When I went to Libanius, then it was books, books! I come to you—books, books, books! Stones for bread! I cannot use books—it is life I am hungry for, life, face to face with the spirit. Did a book make Paul see? Wasn't it a flood of light which struck him, a vision, a voice?'

There are many indications that Ibsen had a certain fear of theorizing books. Georg Brandes reproaches him for it. To understand such fears, one must go back to his childhood. He established himself then an *independent thinker* with a kind of 'superiority-feeling' that he managed things better than stupid adults did, anyhow better than his father. And this continued. Every time he came to theoretical books, he felt himself misled, and when he tried to use his new-found knowledge in his writing he always discovered that this knowledge was like clinker, making his writing less lively than it would otherwise have been.

For my part, I am convinced that the reason for Ibsen's lifelong reluctance to educate himself in philosophical ideas was that, as a profound original thinker himself, though he liked hearing about others' conclusions, he was afraid of allowing himself to be led astray by seductive arguments.

Ibsen's reply to Brandes's reproach is wholly characteristic. In a letter of May 18, 1871, he says:

'I have often thought about what you once wrote, that I have not acquired the present standpoint of knowledge. How could I lay my hands on it? But is not every generation born with the suppositions of the day? Have you never noticed in a collection of portraits from the previous century a strange family likeness between the different people of the same period? It is the same spiritually. What we profane people do not possess in the way of knowledge, I think we have to a certain extent as an idea or instinct. And a writer's task is also essentially to see, not to reflect; for myself, I see a danger here.'

He certainly did not shy away from factual knowledge of Julian and his day; on the contrary, it would provide him with

material for characters, scenery and minor rôles. In much the same
way as the Roman landscape had done, it would serve to populate his imagination. Many sources can be indicated; many indeed
he himself has named in notes which have been preserved. And
he frequently writes letters asking for more information on Julian.
There is, on the other hand, nothing to show as to sources for
Julian's psychology. Ibsen's aim was not to give an historical
picture of Julian, but to recreate him with a message for Ibsen's
own time, a time which in many ways he saw as similar to Julian's
but with the signposts reversed; a time retreating at full speed
from centuries of fossilized religion, but now moving *away* from
Christianity.

We may well understand why Ibsen's conclusions were nine
years in the making. Julian was a seeker, a man on his way down
into the substratum beneath his own time's thinking. So was
Ibsen. In the play, Julian fanatically dissects what he believes in
and causes it to disintegrate, gradually seeing new truths behind;
which in turn he attacks and demolishes.

The play began in Ibsen's mind as an ordinary five-act tragedy,
but even in his days in Rome the vastness of the scope became
apparent, so that he talked extravagantly about writing a play
of nine acts; and when he set himself to work in Dresden in 1871,
for a while he thought that it would be a trilogy. That must
have been so early in its existence that he still thought that through
hypotheses and antitheses, Julian would ultimately reach a
synthesis, arriving at clarified truths. But it did not work thus.
The final truths, like the glittering portal in *Peer Gynt*, retreated
ever farther away. Instead of a play about Julian's third kingdom,
it became the drama of Julian's struggle; what interests the reader
today is neither Julian's conclusions nor the reasoning which
brings him to them, but his burning desire for recognition. This
is why the dramatic effect is lost towards the end, for the possibilities of a climax of perception grow steadily less.

To give a short outline of *The Emperor and the Galilean* is as
fruitless as trying to detail the action of a large battle painting. The
action is intensified, falls apart, and is intensified again. One
feature of the play, however, deserves special mention here, for it

has been little noticed: while all Ibsen's other dramatic works deal with personal conflicts and therefore contain people of both sexes in a true dramatic balance, in the cast-list of *The Emperor and the Galilean*, which contains at least fifty to sixty performers, there are only three women, of whom two have walk-on parts and the third only one big scene.

But this scene is central to what is otherwise a colossal continuous drama on Julian alone. It is very pungent and foreshadows Ibsen's later contemporary dramas. After many complications Julian has gained his beautiful Helena, the sister of Emperor Constantinus and the woman who has been his dream. But because he is a dreamer, a brooder, an artist, when at last he has acquired her, he is more taken up with his own thoughts and with the phenomenon of ecstasy in general than with physical esctasy inspired by her. In the meantime Emperor Constantinus has her poisoned and in her fantasy-orgies before she dies she cries out that she has never loved Julian, but only his virile rival, Gallus, and that her apparent devotion to religion has been utterly physical, so that she is pregnant by her own priest.

The scene is melodramatic, but it is melodrama with gripping psychological perspectives. Here Ibsen penetrated with one clean cut the layers of an overwrought female mind. The frail, weak Julian hears that Helena has never loved him, at most she has loved only the brutal power of which she hoped he was master; but for the person Julian, with his inky fingers and book dust in his hair, she has felt nothing but loathing. On the other hand, she has loved his executed rival, the virile Gallus; and she has loved the most powerful of them all, Christ, so ecstatically that she believes that it is Christ himself who has made her pregnant through one of the priests.

Ibsen's struggle with his dramatic material took time. From the correspondence with Hegel, it appears that he had always hoped it would go more quickly, and as early as April 9, 1872, he writes: 'About *Julian*, I will soon have completed part two. The third and last will be child's play.'

It was not child's play. On October 14, Ibsen writes to

Edmund Gosse, who was now acting as his first propagandist in Great Britain: 'I am working daily on *Julian Apostate* and hope to be able to have it complete by the end of this year.'

But then new difficulties arose. In February, 1873, Ibsen writes to his old friend Ludvig Daae, asking for information on a number of things connected with the spelling of Greek names and endings. At about the same time, Ibsen gives his publisher the news that now his work is really complete:

'Dear Mr Hegel, Herewith I have pleasure in informing you that my great work is complete, and more happily concluded than any of my earlier ones. The title of the book is *The Emperor and the Galilean, a world-drama in two parts*. It contains Part One: *The Secession of Caesar*, play in five acts (170 pages). Part Two: *Emperor Julian*, play in five acts (252 pages). Don't let the words *world-drama* frighten you! They are created in the same way as *folk-drama, domestic-drama, national-drama*, etc., and are in their right place, for my play deals with both heaven and earth.' (Later he revises the title slightly and calls it instead *A world-historical play*.)

In this letter he promises to send forty-eight pages a week of clean copy, but not until October 17, 1873, was the book on sale, and it is then—as he writes to his brother-in-law Thoresen in Kristiania—'a very thick volume of 512 pages'. It was printed in a first edition of four thousand copies, and a further two thousand copies had to be printed shortly after the new year of 1874. In contrast to nearly all Ibsen's earlier works, it met almost no opposition. It was read with greedy interest, interpreted and discussed far and wide, but with respect, almost veneration. If it did not actually arouse enthusiasm, it caused an immense stir, far beyond the boundaries of Scandinavia.

Naturally *The Emperor and the Galilean* is never performed on the stage in its entirety. Even with the briefest of intervals, it would take something like twelve to thirteen hours. There have been attempts to perform it in various cut versions, but without scenic success. On the other hand, it should be mentioned that the

Norwegian Radio Theatre, fifty years after Ibsen's death, broadcast it as a serial in ten instalments, one act at a time, almost without cuts in the first five acts, but with considerable cuts in the last, which from a dramatic viewpoint are very much weaker. The broadcast included a résumé of each act, and was such a success that it was later repeated twice.

12

Increasing Praise

THREE years went by between *The League of Youth* and *The Emperor and the Galilean*, and four more years were to pass before Ibsen's next dramatic work was completed. During the years in which he fought tirelessly for recognition for his Julian, he had many other activities which took up a great deal of his time and restricted his creative work.

Along with Hans Christian Andersen and Bjørnson, he had now become Gyldendal's biggest seller, and thus had the opportunity not only of publishing his collected poems in larger editions, but also of rewriting and republishing a number of his earlier plays, *Lady Inger of Østråt*, *The Warriors at Helgeland*, *The Pretenders*, *Love's Comedy* and *Catiline*, all of which had aroused disgracefully little attention outside the locale when they were first published. Now they were assured a large sale all over Scandinavia and theatres everywhere were willing to reassess their views on several of them.

But the success of *Brand* had aroused attention outside Scandinavia too, which naturally did not surprise Ibsen, but which made it necessary for him to foster his new connections, make agreements and carry on an extensive correspondence (which he had to do himself, for there was no one else to do it for him). It was during these years that Ibsen began to acquire a European reputation.

But let us make a brief digression and take a look at the writer as he sits working in Dresden in the early 1870s. His daughter-in-law, Bergliot, whose source is always Suzannah, relates: 'Henrik Ibsen's working-day now becomes more and more disciplined, with a definite timetable, and Mrs Ibsen keeps everything that may distract him away. Both from outside and inside.'

It is no secret that Ibsen wished to be a painter, but few people know how much it cost Mrs Ibsen to dissuade him:

'She really had to struggle with him. Even on days when Henrik Ibsen was not in a good mood, Mrs Ibsen forced his pen into his hand. After a while he saw that this was the right thing to do. "When you're not in the mood to write," he often said later to Sigurd, "then you must nevertheless do as I do, just sit down at your desk and then inspiration comes of its own accord." Thus she drove him gradually into greater concentration. Even in the early days of their marriage, she tried to keep distracting friends and acquaintances away.

'There was no one who could inspire him as she did. If he was depressed she knew how to raise his spirits. One must oneself have heard her reveal her fantastic faith in him to understand how she has given him strength through the years. When destructive criticism depressed him, she was not despondent. Her eyes blazed and she said: "You with your genius, what do you care about what that donkey writes." And it always ended with him going back to his work feeling liberated.'

Bergliot Ibsen also sheds light on another side of their family life. She writes of Sigurd:

'He was disciplined early, but he was thrashed only once. His mother brought him up to be obedient from his earliest years. And she had her own methods. When, for instance, she was going into town, and they had no maid, she had to leave him on his own, so she placed a piece of cotton on the floor and told him that he might not go beyond it. Sigurd himself could remember this, and related that the piece of cotton had hypnotized him so much that he remained sitting on the floor, staring at it until she returned.

'But he was not always so easy. He could also be extremely naughty, and then it was as if he had a devil in him. Then he might knock over plant pots so that they flew out of the window and Mrs Ibsen said later: "My hair stood on end."'

Otherwise it appears from this account that they lived a retired and economical life, so that at school Sigurd was ashamed of his homemade clothes. About the evenings she says:

'Every evening after homework was over and done with, Henrik Ibsen played cards with Sigurd, and each time, he let Sigurd win. But then catastrophe occurred. One evening Henrik Ibsen won. The boy was so put out that he threw down the cards. But after that Henrik Ibsen would never play cards with him again, and they began to play chess—which they continued to do until Sigurd was grown up.'

And a last glimpse:

'When Ibsen completed a new work, he read it out aloud to Sigurd and his mother. This tradition he continued to the end. I can remember that when I married Sigurd, Henrik Ibsen said to me, after he had completed a new play: "You mustn't take offence, Bergliot, if I don't ask you to listen. But I'm used to reading to Sigurd and his mother only." And I understood this very well. Those three had a communal life.'

In the summer of 1874 his relations with Norway became complicated and delicate and had several phases, the first being the great poem I mentioned earlier, written for the tenth centenary celebrations of Norway's unification, at the erection of the Harald Monument at Hafrsfjord in 1872. Ibsen was also asked to write the celebration poem, and was very suspicious to begin with, asking in letters to Norwegian friends, whether the person who had commissioned it had any mandate to do so, whether anyone else had been asked to do it, so that he would be low down on the list of speakers, etc. . . . He wrote the poem, but made conditions regarding who should read it (no actors, thank you) and how it would otherwise be publicized.

Finally he believed that all was in order; but this was not so. This is what he said about Norway in a letter of September, 1872, to his business manager and brother-in-law, Thoresen:

'I do not think I can reckon with much sympathy from up there, when I see such typical Norwegian inconsiderateness as was dealt out to me by the so-called Harald Committee last summer. They request me to write a poem for reciting in Haugesund. I write the poem. They ignore it at the celebrations and sell it like other hack songs, hitherto without even considering offering me one single word of explanation for this mysterious matter.'

The letter then continues with a stream of embittered abuse against this, that and the other in Norway, and threats that as 'national satirist', he will make them suffer for it. And now it is not just the liberal opposition he attacks, but 'an absolutely indefensible cowardice, indulgence and compromise in nearly all of those who should be the defenders of the foundations of our society'.

His rage subsided, temporarily, when in the summer of 1873, he had delivered *The Emperor and the Galilean*. But even before its publication, he basked in the honour of being chosen as the representative for Denmark and Norway at the great art exhibition in Vienna in July, 1873. He was proud of the fact that he had collected quite a number of medals for Danish and Norwegian paintings, and as an almost professional painter, he had undoubtedly been able to add some weight to his vote. While he was there, he also learned that King Oscar II, in connection with his coronation, had presented him with the honour he most desired, the Order of St Olaf.

Otherwise he was scarcely reconciled to his home country, and during these years he suffered constant irritations over refusals of applications for an increase in his artist's pension and refusals of applications for grants—the authorities no doubt considered that he earned enough as it was.

Shortly after *The Emperor and the Galilean* was put out, he had the brilliant idea of having *Peer Gynt* put on the stage. A new edition of the book was to be published, and so he wrote to Edvard Grieg and asked him whether he would not consider composing the music. With Grieg's music, this play has been performed all over the world for almost a century, it has become Norway's uncrowned national-romantic festive play, in spite of

what was thought when Ibsen conceived the idea in Rome in 1867.
It is worth quoting some of Ibsen's instructions:

'The first act is to be kept intact, with only a few cuts in the dialogue. Peer Gynt's monologue on pages 23, 24 and 25 I would like treated either melodramatically or partly as a recitative. The wedding scene on page 28 needs, with the help of a ballet, to be made much more of than as it stands in the book. A special dance tune must be composed, to continue quietly until the end of the act.

'In the second act, the scene with the three milkmaids on pages 57–60 should be treated musically according to the composer's discretion, but there must be devilry in it! The monologue on pages 60–62 I had thought of as accompanied by chords, that is, as melodrama. The same applies to the scene between Peer and the woman in green, pages 63–66. Similarly there must be some kind of accompaniment to the scenes in Old Man Dovre's hall, in which though, the dialogue should be cut considerably. Also the scene with the boyg, which is given in its entirety, must be accompanied by music, bird-song must be heard, and bell-ringing and hymn-singing in the distance.

'In the third act I need chords, but sparingly, for the scene between Peer, the woman and the little troll. Similarly, I had thought of a slow accompaniment from page 109 until the bottom of page 112. (That is Åse's death.)

'Practically all the fourth act is to be omitted from the performance. . . .'

Let that suffice, although the instructions for the fourth and fifth acts are equally minute. Ibsen tempts Grieg with a suggestion that he wants to send the play in to Christiania Theatre, and that they should together request the sum of four hundred riksdalers, of which Grieg shall have half. He also reckons that the play will be performed in Copenhagen and Stockholm too.

Grieg, who was acutely in need of the money, but who basically could not stand *Peer Gynt*, reluctantly agreed to provide the music. Ibsen was so encouraged by Grieg's reply that he almost immediately wrote to the Swede, Ludvig Josephson, who was then the energetic head of Christiania Theatre, to ask whether his theatre wished to be the first to put on a performance of the play. The letter to Josephson was sent from Dresden on February 6, 1874, and Ibsen must have had some vague idea that, although Grieg had asked for a postponement so that he could write the music during his summer holiday, it would be possible to sell it in the twinkling of an eye, so that the play could open the season in Kristiania. Ibsen had in fact thought of visiting his home country the following summer for the first time for ten years, and then it would have suited him admirably to have a world première of *Peer Gynt*, with Grieg's music and all the trappings, in order to celebrate the occasion.

But it did not happen like this. The summer came and went and still Grieg remained uninspired. Here are a few short extracts from Grieg's letters to Bjørnstjerne Bjørnson, which show both the romantic Grieg's attitude to the work itself, and his struggle to compose the music.

On September 17 he writes to Bjørnson about, amongst other things, the music for Olav Trygvason:

'As a matter of fact, if I had received your text, I would have refused Ibsen and avoided *Peer Gynt* with its many pitfalls. I hope to have completed this work by the autumn (it is only a question of fragments here and there). . . .'

In October Grieg is in Copenhagen and writes:

'I recently saw H. C. Andersen, who could now be rightly called Gaga Andersen—he's in his second childhood! But talks about you with his old admiration, whereas Ibsen is loathsome to him, and *Peer Gynt* the worst thing he has ever read. I cannot but admire how it sparkles with wit and gall from beginning to end, but it will never have my sympathy. For me it is, however, the best thing Ibsen has written. Am I right in this? You don't imagine that this is a voluntary choice on my part, do you? I was asked by Ibsen last year, and naturally boggled at writing music for this most unmusical of all subjects. But I thought of the two hundred [riksdalers] on the journey, and made the sacrifice. The whole thing hangs like a nightmare over me. . . .'

In January, 1875, he has progressed no further and writes:

'It has gone as you predicted with *Peer Gynt*. It still hangs like a nightmare over me, and it will be hard to get it away before the spring. It was the need for money, or rather the offer of money, that persuaded me and that was wrong, perhaps, but travel and so much delight stood before me.'

At the end of February, 1875, he still had not completed it, and writes from Leipzig:

'My stay in Leipzig and *Peer Gynt* are in the same state; I cannot decide how long I shall be before completing this work here, so I shall now work like a horse.'

And on March 17, he writes from Leipzig about Ibsen:

'He wrote to me a short time ago that *Peer Gynt* is not to be performed this season—to my great delight, as I am now working quite calmly here, before going south.'

Not until the end of July, 1875, does Grieg tell Ibsen that now the music is ready. The world première is in February, 1876.

This music became a powerful influence not only on Edvard Grieg's later world fame, but also on *Peer Gynt's* reputation. The explanation of the fact that for three generations it 'romanticized' the play, blunting its sharp teeth, is to be found in the fragments of letters which are quoted here. Grieg's temperament was as distant from Ibsen's as possible, and his melodies were bound to bring conciliatory features to this 'most unmusical of all subjects'.

But back to the spring of 1874. Much of Ibsen's time was devoted to absorbing the extraordinary sales and prestige of *The Emperor and the Galilean*—this happened nearly every time he published a major work. The routine task of correcting proofs for new editions of earlier works also took up time, even if it is undoubtedly true that the fourteen-year-old Sigurd was allowed to deal with the spelling. But at last, on July 8, 1874, the following information comes from Dresden: 'To Miss Henrietta Hofgaard, Kristiania. In reply to your pleasant information in your letter of

3rd inst., may I inform you that it is our intention to arrive in Kristiania on the steamer *Århus* on Sunday July 19th, at 6 p.m. Yours faithfully, Henrik Ibsen.'

The steamer was still the only practical method of reaching Kristiania from the south. Naturally Ibsen travelled via Copenhagen, to talk business with his publisher. As early as this he had already begun thriftily to save money, and constantly requests Hegel to place it in safe investments. To his brother-in-law Thoresen in Kristiania—with whom, incidentally, he is still on formal terms—he writes that he hopes soon to be able to live off his dividends and his writer's pension, but this is to be kept strictly confidential. He was careful to avoid actual speculation—his father's example frightened him—but he is much occupied with acquiring the best possible yields. At the same time, he is still confronted from time to time with old debts from his Bergen days. During his stay in Kristiania that summer, he is sensibly advised to buy property, which will pay him handsomely, and he tells Hegel that several of his friends have become wealthy in this way. But he has his reservations, and finally chooses to put what money he has in Norway into the recently founded company that is to run trams in Kristiania—progressive, sensible and secure.

Ibsen, Sigurd and Suzannah arrived in Norway on July 19 and settled in with Miss Hofgaard in Pilestredet 7. It is clear that he is still anxious and sensitive, from a letter to his old friend, Birkeland of the 'Dutchmen', in which he refuses an invitation to a trip to Maridalen, saying:

'It is my intention during my stay here to avoid anything that may look like a public occasion, and I think in this respect that I am freer if I do not accept the committee's invitation. I shall speak to you of my thoughts on this matter and I imagine that you, as a thoughtful man, will approve.'

He could not avoid knowing that he was both respected and feared, but that did not set his mind at rest; and he wanted at all costs to avoid being used by either of the opposing camps. So he mixed quietly with his old friends, made a brief trip to an archaeological congress in Stockholm to revive old connections, but otherwise kept himself to himself.

However, he had stayed in Kristiania as long as until the end of September for very good reasons. It would have been very unlike a man of Ibsen's ambitious and purposeful temperament to have attempted to state his position publicly and clearly. He feared acclaim from the liberal camp, in which at that time he suspected sinister intrigues against him. At the same time he was heartily opposed to the ruling party conservatism which had taken him to its heart after *The League of Youth*. So any acclaim must come from a neutral quarter.

Originally, he had undoubtedly considered a large gala performance of *Peer Gynt*. As this was now out of the question, his conversations with Josephson, director of the theatre, were aimed at using the theatre in another way to mark his visit. Two of his plays were especially suited to this, and both were included in Christiania Theatre's current repertoire. One was *Love's Comedy*, which had originally provoked conservative citizens into saying that he deserved thrashing rather than a grant, but which now in view of his success had been published in book form again. During the 1873–74 season it had been a formidable success in the theatre, and had been performed no fewer than fourteen times. This play could be used to indicate his radicalism.

The other play was *The League of Youth*, which since its controversial première in October, 1869, had remained in the theatre's repertoire and had been performed altogether twenty-seven times. That would suitably emphasize Ibsen's loathing for the leftist section of the community. Naturally, Josephson was more than willing to use Ibsen's presence in his home country to celebrate with both plays the theatre's most profitable author.

Although I have no proof that it was through his own efforts that Ibsen, despite his shy withdrawal, was lionized in Kristiania during the first half of September, this was most likely the case. All that was needed now was a neutral institution which would be able to turn the Ibsen revival into a genuine occasion.

The theatre's plan was to perform *Love's Comedy* on September 3 and 8, and then *The League of Youth* on September 10, *Love's*

Comedy on September 11 and *The League of Youth* on September 13. The neutral institution was the Norwegian Student Union, Ibsen's first public forum, in whose journal his first work, *Catiline*, had been first reviewed, and to which Ibsen had been an energetic contributor and editor during his first year in Kristiania.

Everything worked out well. Ibsen had promised to be present at the theatre on September 10, and he was given an ovation. The students went in procession with their Union and Choral Society's banners to Pilestredet and acclaimed him wildly. Unfortunately the speech that he made has not been preserved, but the references to it in the papers are so precise that it seems probable that they were taken from the manuscript. Certainly, the speech was not improvised. In it, Ibsen is at first quite frank about the doubts and anxiety he has felt at returning to Norway, because of past bad feeling. Now that he has been received with such honour, he wishes to make an explanation and a confession.

He says first that it is not about himself that he has written, but that he has felt he had some responsibility in what had happend in the country. And what is writing? He had come late to the realization that in writing it is essential not merely to *see*, but so to convey impressions that the recipient can view them through the author's eyes. ... Only that which has been fully experienced can be seen and received in this way, and experience is precisely the secret of modern writing. Everything that he has written during the last ten years, he experienced spiritually. But no writer experiences anything in isolation. What he experiences, his contemporary countrymen experience together with him. ...

Continuing to analyse his literary achievements, he says that fitfully and in his best hours, he has given expression to what stirred 'vividly and greatly as something beautiful within him!'; but that sometimes he has also written about the opposite, about what his introspection revealed as impurities and dregs within himself.

He believes it is right to say this to students in particular, for they have the same task as the writer; to clarify to themselves, and through this to others, the earthly and eternal questions which concern the time and society to which they belong. In this

G

respect, he himself has continued to be a student: a writer is by nature long-sighted and he has never seen his native land in all its vitality so fully, so clearly and so closely, as from a distance.

He confesses in conclusion that the greatest cause of despair for the Emperor Julian at the end of his life is the recognition that he will be remembered with respectful appreciation by clear and good minds, but his opponents are rich in the love of warm, living human beings. The unexpected warmth and generosity of his reception by the students this evening was the richest reward of his visit.

Even if his speech had been carefully prepared before he knew whether the students' reaction would be warm or chilling, it is a testimony to what he wanted to do with his writing and of what he had feared and hoped of his visit to Norway. And he meant it, anyhow at the time, when a few days later he wrote to Hegel: 'I have been received with extraordinary goodwill by everyone. All previous ill-will has now gone.'

This proved to be true up to a point, but several decades were to go by before Ibsen was able seriously to consider settling in his own country. Provisionally, he retreated to Dresden and worked hard for the next few years at the dissemination of his work and acquiring for himself a reputation in other countries—a little in England, a mention or so in France—but first and foremost in Germany where he lived, which he knew for him would be the gateway to the rest of the world.

He had many obstacles to overcome. Pirate translations of his work began to appear in German. At first he probably encouraged this, for it was more important to be recognized in Germany than to receive a little money for the translations. As his reputation grew, he was also exposed to attacks from German quarters, because his writing from the time of the Danish-German war was taken to be anti-German, and he had to defend himself. But gradually, as his own youthful fiascos began to be hailed as successes in Scandinavia, he realized that there were many tempting opportunities that made it necessary for him to go systematically to work to secure his rights.

This took up a great deal of his time and resources for several years. He had to find translations that would not detract from his work and which he could control himself; he had to make contacts and offer his plays to strategically important theatres. When he moved in the spring of 1875 from Dresden to Munich, it was not, as he himself said, just because Dresden was an expensive city to live in, but chiefly because in Munich there was a rich cultural milieu which would be to his advantage.

In Dresden he had enjoyed the opportunity provided by his loneliness to grapple with 'Julian', and read aloud or play cards with Sigurd and Suzannah beneath the lamp in the evening. Now he needed contacts, and he acquired them.

Oddly enough, it was again Bjørnstjerne Bjørnson who was to prepare the way for him, this time quite involuntarily. Bjørnson's peasant stories had long since been translated into German and had made his name known there. But it was in 1875 with *A Failure* that he made his real break-through in Germany. This brilliant play, popularly and simply written with an immediate stage appeal, took Germany by storm, partly because business conditions in the country made the play extremely topical. So when Ibsen offered his plays, at first translations of *The Vikings* and *The Pretenders*, the directors of theatres all over Germany were more than willing to believe that what came from Norway might be good.

The first performance of Ibsen outside Scandinavia was given at the Court Theatre in Munich in April, 1876, and was a great success, with many calls for the author. Later the same year, the play was put on with outstanding casts, both in Vienna and Dresden.

Meanwhile the Duke of Meiningen's famous theatre had given a guest performance of *The Pretenders* in Berlin in June, and later that year it was performed in Schwerin. Ibsen was also invited to visit the Duke of Meiningen in his castle, where he was welcomed with enthusiasm and was decorated by the Duke with a Saxon order. A little later *The Emperor and the Galilean* was published in English. In Poland, the first book on Ibsen's work was published and in the course of a few years Ibsen's name became world famous and much was expected of him. These expectations he richly fulfilled with the series of contemporary plays which now followed, from *Pillars of Society* to the epilogue *When We Dead Awaken*. The plays which now come from Ibsen's pen were epoch-making in the history of the theatre—so much so that the last decades of his century and the first decades of our own have rightly been called Ibsen's era. He developed and perfected realism with a mastery no one could match, and at the same time raised it from drama to tragedy.

Brand and *Peer Gynt* would in any event have secured Ibsen a lasting place in the cultural life of *Scandinavia*, but it was his contemporary dramas which made him a world writer. He had tried his hand as a realistic social writer with *The League of Youth*, but more as an exercise in polemics with characters and dramatic effects than by way of searching psychological depths.

But with *Pillars of Society*, Ibsen took a long stride forward in the direction of the kind of writing that was to become his own. He had still not achieved the supreme combination of realism and simplification which came to mark his masterpieces. The play has many disfiguring scars from his battle with the material—in particular, he had not yet managed to limit it and there is far too much of it for a simple play. As a psychological and realistic play, it is nevertheless a milestone in the writing of the day.

Ibsen conceived the basic idea as early as when he wrote *The League of Youth* and before he had to thrust all his other writing to one side in order to create Julian. There is a wealth of material— sketches, notes and drafts—which show how the play gradually took shape. He wished to confront the world of his day with the simultaneously comic and tragic conflict between words and deeds, between morality and practice, and he had originally thought of it as a comedy. It did in fact become something of a comedy in the end.

Much has been written about the play's setting being the real town of Grimstad, which it undoubtedly was. It is obvious from his notes and drafts that, in this new method of writing, Ibsen has made use of naturalistic settings. Against this background move concrete characters, whose moral make-up he wishes to dissect—not as a photographer this time, but as a painter of plausible people of his own time. The significance of the name, Grimstad (hideous town) cannot for one moment have been lost on him and must have stimulated his imagination.

But the plot which was to unfold there changed as his thoughts matured. It is easy to trace the introduction of the subsidiary story of the old, unseaworthy ship which is unscrupulously sent to sea to meet certain shipwreck. While he was in Kristiania in 1874, there was a great deal of publicity about Samuel Plimsoll, the British Member of Parliament, and his fight to bring in stricter measures regarding seaworthiness. And it is clear that the place of women in this enclosed society is drawn from Camilla Collett's writing and Aasta Hansteen's public appearances. Ibsen at this time had been seriously awakened to women's place in society and the psychology of women in general.

All this is merely the material from which he builds. He places the rotting American ship in Consul Bernick's shipyard and Aasta Hansteen in the family; but then the material grows while he struggles with it. The main character, the Consul, slowly takes shape—a man with good intentions, who commits senseless acts, which become gradually greater moral betrayals and finally sheer unscrupulousness hidden behind an increasingly moral mask. As the play progresses, mercilessly, his past catches up with him.

This John Gabriel Borkman in swaddling clothes is thus surrounded by all the women he has betrayed. His youthful love whom he betrayed to marry money, his wife whom he betrayed by pretending to love her, his sister whom he cheated of her inheritance, his daughter who was born out of wedlock after his affair with the actress—through his exposure they all appear and can call him to account. The portrait gallery is also enlarged and made colourful by minor characters and minor conflicts.

But what raises this play far above *The League of Youth* is that so many of these people are seen from within—not illuminated with platitudes or external character-drawing; each has his or her own personality and destiny. Even if the form is not wholly successful, the picture he wishes to see not precise enough and the psychological analysis lacking in depth, the play's underlying dramatic appeal is so great that it still has life in it.

For two whole years after laying the keel, Ibsen worked on it, and he thought he was over the worst. Not until August, 1877, does he write to Hegel: 'Tomorrow I shall send you the end of the manuscript, of which only the last one and a half pages are missing, but I shall not have time to copy that bit if this letter is to go by the evening's post, which is of importance to me. . . .'

This time Ibsen took great care to provide for both performance and publication. In Scandinavia, his name had not lost its magnet in theatres since Ludvig Josephson's version of *Peer Gynt* with Grieg's music had been such a success at Kristiania Theatre in February, 1876—there alone it was performed almost forty times in that same year. But now that the theatre in Bergen was open again and there was a theatre in Gothenburg, tour-directors all over Scandinavia were after this new play of Ibsen's. The book, which Hegel was allowed to publish after Ibsen had his other contracts arranged, was brought out in an edition of six thousand, and seven weeks later four thousand more copies were coming off the presses.

Ibsen had himself taken steps to have the play translated into German and sent to as many theatres as possible—the laws at this time were such that if a pirate translator should appear first and offer his translation to theatres, the theatre dealt with the translator only, not the author. Nevertheless, after a few months, two pirate translations appeared alongside the one that Ibsen had arranged.

It is a measure of his break-through that four months after the play had been published in Denmark, in Berlin alone there were notices of five different theatre performances at the same time.

One theatre alone was left out in the cold this time—Kristiania Theatre, which Ibsen had excommunicated when after considerable losses and a fire in 1877, it had used this as an excuse to rid itself of both the opera performances and the important but expensive Ludvig Josephson, and had appointed the writer Johan Vibe as manager, against strong opposition from the board. Ibsen writes about this to his old friend Hartvig Lassen, the theatre's literary consultant:

'I did not say to Mr Vibe that the theatre board has tied Josephson's hands, but I said that the *institution* of direction has been a hindrance to and a burden on him. And I went on to say that it would have been more in the interest of the theatre if the direction had got rid of itself instead of getting rid of the manager and opera. [Ibsen himself, of course, had experience of theatre boards.] And look at the man you have made Josephson's successor. He was here in Munich this summer, and he talked like a five-year-old child about the appointment he had received.' '*Pillars of Society* was first performed at Kristiania Theatre about eighteen months later.'

Even before *Pillars of Society* came out, when the manuscript had only just gone to the publishers, a small event occurred which gave Ibsen immense and lasting pleasure: Uppsala University awarded him an honorary doctorate at their fourth centenary celebrations in the autumn of 1877. Naturally he went there to receive the honour, and for the rest of his life he liked to be addressed as Doctor.

I have dwelt much—some readers may feel too much—on Ibsen's weakness for honours, my object having been to show how even a very confident genius can also have an ultra-sensitive mind, with a compulsive need to acquire a bulwark to protect him against insults from the outside world. But his honorary doctorate was quite different, far more than just a salve for his old wounds. It was the academic world's recognition that his work was equal to the best that had been achieved by scholars of the time.

We have heard that Georg Brandes, his friend and fellow crusader, had reproached Ibsen for not making himself sufficiently aware of the philosophical knowledge of the day, and that Ibsen had replied that a writer's task was to *see*—to think and experience. He appears to have come just as far in his own way as the scholarly researchers had in theirs. That one of Scandinavia's leading centres of learning had welcomed him into their midst as an honorary member gave him clear confirmation of this, a fact which undoubtedly must have greatly encouraged him and stimulated him in his efforts to go on.

Before we go on to consider his first true dramatic masterpieces, which were now in preparation, there are two small features of his personal life which give a corrective to the picture of Ibsen the man as his daughter-in-law saw him.

One is connected with the trip to Norway which he let Suzannah and Sigurd take whilst he went to Stockholm. He himself did not want to go to Norway; his dissociation from the petty bickering in his home country had become even more insuperable with the years and in addition he had again tried in vain to get an increase in his writer's pension. But after nearly twenty years' absence it was time for Suzannah to visit her home again. Sigurd was nearly eighteen and apart from their stay in Kristiania in 1874 he had never seen his own country.

It is, however, not the trip to Norway itself that is interesting, but the correspondence between the three of them. It is full of a warm and intimate love, which shows that Suzannah had been something more to Ibsen than the stern guardian we have been allowed to see.

They obviously arrived in Norway just after their last reading aloud of *Pillars of Society*, and her first impression of Bergen is: 'Everyone there was as if straight out of *Pillars of Society*, so lifelike, yes, even Rørlund; as Sigurd said, he could not fathom how you could have known everything, such as how the people of the town streamed down to the quay; it was like that there.' After speaking of her pleasure at seeing the countryside again, she goes on to say: 'I think of you every day. . . . It seems to be so long since I left, and yet it is only five days.'

Ibsen's letters are equally loving and cheerful, and his worries about his growing son are as comically paternal as those of most fathers: 'I hope that you are having a good time up there, but watch out for all kinds of carelessness and keep an eye on Sigurd and your money and do not let those people from Sogn and Hardanger rob you.' And to Sigurd, amongst other things, the following warning: 'Do not risk bathing up there, where the water is cold and can easily bring on death-like cramps.' Ibsen knew this from his own experience, for he himself once in his youth had nearly drowned in Bergen, when in midwinter he had fallen into the water in a somewhat animated state and had been rescued at the last moment. But Sigurd was there in the summer. In a later letter: 'In nearly all the Norwegian papers I read about accidents, brought about by the careless handling of loaded rifles. You would be extraordinarily unkind to me if you do not keep a long way away from people who handle such weapons.' Then there is the marvellous sentence: 'If an accident occurs, please see that I am telegraphed at once.'

After returning to Munich, he is unhappy and misses them: 'Now however I am pleased to be back and at peace again, although I am by no means particularly happy; it is unpleasant to have to eat out every day, I do not like the food, the evenings are long, cold and dismal, I sit alone at home all the time. . . .'

The second corrective concerns the picture one is so often given of Ibsen's alleged stinginess and lack of hospitality. We have heard that in Rome he had social inclinations and interests. In Dresden the family were still living in very restricted circumstances. They were saving systematically, for Ibsen was terrified of leaving his wife and Sigurd in the kind of circumstances he himself had had to struggle with. But in Munich he had at first developed quite an extensive social life and was very hospitable, particularly to Norwegians. Then it came to his ears that one of his many Norwegian guests—almost certainly someone battening on his food and drink and growing fame—did not think that what he was offered was good enough! Ibsen was enraged. He himself considered the food and drink Suzannah prepared, expecially a *mead* she brewed, the best in the world, and here were his guests turning up their noses at it. Thereupon, says his daughter-in-law, he closed his door, in future choosing his few friends with more care.

There is one puzzling point about his guests. A young literary figure from Norway, John Paulsen, went to Munich in 1876 and frequented the Ibsens' home, both then and later. It is one thing for Ibsen to have believed in his extremely slight talent and persisted in applying for grants for him, but it is quite another, and one which is really incomprehensible, that a brilliantly intelligent man like Ibsen should have kept up the innocently

open-mouthed admiration to which this John Paulsen himself
testifies in his memoirs of Henrik Ibsen. Ibsen did in fact tire of
him later on.

Ibsen's programme for his future work had changed somewhat
over the years—it had matured and clarified, as he himself has
indicated in his letters and his speech to the students in 1874. His
purpose now was to experience for himself the problems which
confronted people in his day, and to present to them the predica-
ment defined by Lona Hessel (Aasta Hansteen) in the summing up
of *Pillars of Society*: 'No, it is the spirit of truth and freedom that
are the pillars of society.'

Almost inevitably the problem of women's place in society
then became the main theme in Ibsen's writing. He uses it again
and again, always in new variations—not as propaganda, but as
part of his character-drawing. For the question is whether the
emancipation of women might not have been the most fundamental
social change that took place in this century, a bloodless and often
invisible revolution. After centuries of autocratic male society,
liberal ideas about human rights and freedom slowly began to
clear the way for a demand that women too should have the
right to be human beings—simply fellow-human beings.

We know already that Ibsen, both in theory and in practice,
had valued and often romanticized women from his youth onwards. But as long as his writing was essentially concerned with
ideas, most of the plays took place within the head of one thinking
person or another, and that person a man, whether he was called
Brand, Peer or Julian. *That* was the battlefield for man's struggle
with trolls, spiritual forces and philosophies. Now it is different.
All round that humbug pillar of society, Bernick, hums a swarm
of living women characters and it is they who give the play life.
After this, Ibsen's male characters are never again allowed any
peace from this main problem; and this in a great measure
explained how he became one of the most original creative dramatists of his time. In *that* bloodless revolution he was, more than
anyone else, the victorious revolutionary thinker.

As an obvious first choice, Ibsen took up the married woman's subordinate position in the home and society. No doubt this idea was encouraged by the visit to Munich in the spring of 1877 by the much-respected authoress and feminist, Camilla Collett, sister to the great Wergeland. In her writings Mrs Collett had fought tirelessly for the cause of women, but apparently in vain. She was then nearly seventy years old and seems to have become bitter and frustrated. The story goes that once when she was to live for a while in Copenhagen, the *grande dame* of Danish cultural circles, Johanne Louise Heiberg, let her a villa. Camilla Collett did not appear to be particularly satisfied. When Mrs Heiberg asked her what the matter was, Mrs Collett replied sourly: 'I had thought of something with pillars.'

During her visit to Munich she spent much time in the Ibsen home, and naturally talked about women's rights. The argumentative Ibsen teased her by making many conventional comments on women's place in society, which he could hardly have meant, and he was amused by her annoyance. But every evening Ibsen had to accompany his elderly friend back to her hotel, and then they talked together. In a letter written twelve years later Ibsen says, 'It is many years since you, through your spiritual life's work, in one form or another began to become a factor in my writings.'

It was not until eighteen months later, however, a whole year after *Pillars of Society* had come out, that he began to write his new play. In the autumn of 1878, after a stay in Gossensass in the Tyrol, he had again settled in his favourite Rome, where, as he wrote to Hegel on August 2nd: 'I hope to have time to complete my new work.'

The first notes for this play are dated from Rome, September 19, 1878, and are headed: 'Notes for modern tragedy.' They begin:

'There are two kinds of spiritual laws, two kinds of conscience, one in man and a wholly different one in women. They do not understand each other, but woman is judged in practical life according to man's laws, as if she were not a woman, but a man.

'The wife in the play does not know the ins and outs of right and wrong, natural feeling on the one side, and belief in authority on the other, confusing her.

'A woman cannot be herself in today's society, which is an exclusively male society, with laws written by men and with prosecutor and judge who judge women's conduct from a male point of view.

'She has committed forgery, and this is her pride, for she has done so from love of her husband, to save his life. But this man with his everyday honesty, stands firmly planted on the law's foundations, and regards the matter with a male eye.

'The mental struggle. Depressed and confused by her faith in authority, she loses her faith in her moral right and ability to bring up her children. Bitterness. . . .

'. . . everything must be borne alone. The catastrophe approaches mercilessly, inevitably. Despair, struggle and defeat.'

I have quoted this very clear synopsis of *A Doll's House* almost in its entirety because it shows the way in which Ibsen begins to work from now on. It looks as if the play is ready, so to speak, and the added cast-list is virtually identical to the final one, except that the names are altered slightly later on. There must have been many months of systematic thought before these notes were written—manipulation and fining down of the external intrigue and the inner mental struggle, pruning away of minor characters and subsidiary plots. The simplification that he had not quite managed for Consul Bernick, has now been carried out consistently. It is of course possible that there were notes and papers which were destroyed before the résumé of September 19, but this is not likely for in that case the résumé would have been longer and more detailed as an aid to memory.

It is exciting to follow his methodical planning even further, even if many rough drafts have clearly been destroyed. A fuller synopsis, which is close to the arrangement of scenes in the complete work, is undated. Then comes the first complete draft, in which the beginning of the first act is dated May 2, 1879. So it has taken six months' work to get as far as that; but by contrast it has taken him only three weeks to draft the first act, as the end is dated May 24. The second act was begun on June 4 and finished on June 14. The third act was begun on July 4 and finished on July 14. The fourth act was begun on July 18 and finished on August 3. On September 20, Ibsen was able to say that now he had finished it, but for strategic reasons the book was not sent to the bookshops until December 4—this time in a first edition of eight thousand copies, and even that did not suffice. The next three thousand went into print that same month and a third edition came out in February the following year. Even before the book was out, Ibsen had arranged for a German translation, and the play was duly offered to all the theatres in Scandinavia and the German-speaking world in which he was interested.

It was while he was wrestling with his doll's house, after he had written the résumé, but before the first draft, that Ibsen struck a practical blow for the feminists, obviously with the idea of gaining experience. At the annual general meeting of the Scandinavian Society in Rome, on January 28, 1879, he put forward two proposals. One was that women should be eligible as librarians, and that was passed. The other, extremely revolutionary for those days, was that women should be eligible as members of the society. The proposals were put forward in January and were considered at meetings on February 13 and February 27. They created a tremendous stir.

Ibsen's argument for including women as members fills over seven large pages of a book. After pointing out that some energetic women had succeeded in forcing their way into membership nineteen years earlier, he asks: 'Is there anyone in this society who dares to maintain that our ladies are all beneath us in education or in intelligence or in knowledge or in artistic talents? I presume that not very many would venture to maintain any such thing. . . .' Ibsen's proposal failed by a single vote to obtain the necessary two-thirds majority: nineteen members voted for it and eleven against. He left the meeting in a fury and refused to speak to those who had voted against it.

He took his revenge a little later, when to the committee's astonishment he accepted an invitation to the society's annual party, revelling in the opportunity of wearing all his decorations, for it was a gala night. Gunnar Heiberg, then twenty-one years old, has given an amusing account of the evening, of which here is a fragment:

'He sat on his own. We all thought that he had forgiven his fellow human beings and some thought that he had even had regrets. . . .

'Suddenly he walked out on to the dance floor and said: "Ladies and Gentlemen!"—The moment was dramatically expectant. What was going to happen? Would he confess his sins? He could not possibly want just to make a valedictory speech then, not he! Not Ibsen! Then, covered with all his decorations, he made a truly thunderous speech: No one escapes great ideas. Not even here! In this society! In this puddle! He did not use the word puddle, but the contempt in his voice announced it loudly.'

His proposal had been received as if it were a criminal attempt on the life of society. And it had especially annoyed him that the *women* had intrigued and agitated against it.

'He shook his head with its grey mane. He folded his arms across his chest. His eyes flashed. His voice shook, his lips trembled and he thrust out his lower lip. He looked like a lion, or much more, he looked like the later enemy of the people, Dr Stockmann. And he repeated over and over again: What kind of women are these, what kind of ladies, what kind of females, ignorant, fundamentally uneducated in the most fundamental way, immoral, on the lowest of levels, the most wretched—the ——

'Crash! A lady, Countess B., fell to the floor. Like the rest of us, she was expecting a dreadful word. But she forestalled the course of events and fainted.'

Ibsen completed his punitive sermon, went out to the cloak-room, took his overcoat and went home.

We do not know whether Ibsen had enough sense of the ridiculous to smile a little at his scathing denunciation of the same ladies whose admission to the society he had been almost pathetically anxious to justify. But that evening must have been unforgettable for others besides this young Ibsen-enthusiast, and for Ibsen himself, a source of real delight and new strength for his work on his play.

Before going on to give a fuller account of the fortunes of *A Doll's House*, a digression is necessary. It has often been said that the Norwegian-Danish authoress, Laura Kieler, is the model for Nora, and that the situation was suggested by her marriage. Mrs Kieler believed this herself, and had some grounds for her belief. To put it mildly, she was a somewhat persistent admirer of the great writer. Profiting from the success of *Brand*, at twenty years of age she wrote a continuation in novel form, called *Brand's Daughter*. Later on, she met Ibsen in Copenhagen, visited him in Dresden and also sent him immature manuscripts which he firmly refused to recommend for publication.

He became paternally, slightly humorously, interested in this tense young lady and her marriage, and both the lark and the doll's house are words he used with regard to her long before the play was thought of. It is also true that she incurred debts without her husband's knowledge and, though she did not commit forgery, the consequences were such that for a while she had to go into a home for nervous troubles.

Perhaps too her husband appears here and there in the character of Helmer, who is after all just a typical husband before the last scene, when he becomes something of a human being. But there the similarities end. The woman Nora is not copied from anyone; she was conceived and given birth by Ibsen and she has no characteristics in common with what we know of Laura Kieler. *A Doll's House* is an elaboration of two minor elements in *The League of Youth*—old Bratsberg's mental crisis when he hears of his son's forgery, and the character of Bratsberg's daughter-in-law, Selma, who dislikes being nothing but a pampered family pet. Not that it matters where Ibsen got his material. What matters is the process, plainly showing in the synopsis and the various drafts, whereby these characters became living people, inextricably bound to each other in a taut and simple main conflict.

The furore *A Doll's House* caused all over the world during the next few years can only partly be explained by the keenness of Ibsen's perception and the strength of his creative genius. Whether this was feminism, whether what she did was legally indefensible, whether she ought to have remained with Helmer despite everything; these were the things which caused a storm over the whole of Europe. But the reason why the play is still performed on stages all over the world, from Peking to New York, from the far north to Australia and Argentina, in societies where Nora's social position is no longer relevant, is that the mental conflicts the play propounds are universal and timeless and the taut dramatic simplification is achieved without any of the *human beings* being simplified away.

To return to the play's immediate fortunes. In book-form, it came out in Copenhagen and Germany in December, 1879, in Finland in 1880, in England in 1882, in Poland in 1882, in Russia in 1883, in Italy in 1884. The Royal Theatre in Copenhagen put it on as early as before Christmas, 1879; in January, 1880, it was on at the Royal Dramatic Theatre in Stockholm and Christiania Theatre; in March, 1880, it went to Munich—and then it spread all over Germany and Austria and thence all over the world.

To conclude, one famous episode. In Germany, the moral indignation provoked by the play was in many places much stronger than its purely dramatic impact. There were demonstrations and counter-demonstrations in theatres. When a famous actress, Hedvig Niermann-Rabe, was given Nora's role, she flatly refused to allow the play to end in tragedy—she would not let Nora leave her children. When Ibsen realized that she was determined to have her own way, he agreed to make a new ending:

'... for use in an emergency ... according to which Nora does not leave the house, but is forced by Helmer to the door of the children's bedroom, where they exchange two remarks and Nora collapses at the door and falls to the floor. ...

'This alteration I have myself to my translator called "a barbaric act of violence" against the play. It is entirely against my wishes when it is used, but I harbour the hope that it will not be used in quite a number of German theatres.'

It must be added that this same actress some years later performed *A Doll's House* in its proper form and with considerably greater success. So far as I know, eighty years passed before there was another attempt to use this false ending. A Swedish actress then refused to abandon the Helmer home and, with the help of her husband, who was the producer of the play, had her own way and went on tour for the State Theatre with her 'barbaric act of violence'.

13

The Great Scandal

IBSEN let about eighteen months elapse between sending in *A Doll's House* and deciding on his next subject. All the evidence is that in the meanwhile he roamed round brooding, irascible and quarrelsome to many people, receptive and open to a few. There was much to brood over, both in world affairs and within himself. In the constant attempts to trace sources of inspiration, influences, impressions which might have given food for thought and material for more plays, there has been one influence which has often been too little noticed and that is the influence of his own writings.

For quite a number of years after his rise to fame, many new editions of his earlier works were ceaselessly being published. In some of them he made alterations and to some he added introductions, but anyhow he constantly re-read them—if for nothing else, to see whether there were any misprints.

What is noticeable in his later plays is the number of conflicts and relationships Ibsen now salvages from earlier works and uses again. After his struggle with form and content in *A Doll's House*, he is aware that he knows his art thoroughly. Purely intuitive psychology is now his main interest. He knows the explosive dramatic effect, both in the written word and on the stage, of binding destinies together so that they cross each other at a tragic point of intersection. He is now combining in a manner uniquely his own the techniques of classical tragedy with the conflicts and predicaments of his own time.

By the autumn of 1879, the family have already moved back to Munich so that Sigurd can continue his studies there. Ibsen's attitude to Norway is clearly ambivalent, but with a distinct undercurrent of mistrust. In the summer of 1879, in a letter to Bjørnson, he flatly refuses to join in a campaign for a purely Norwegian flag, without the union insignia, on the basis that: '. . . it is quite unimportant whether our politicians win any more freedoms for society, as long as they do not win individual freedom. . . . There are not twenty-five free and independent personalities in the whole of Norway. It is not possible for them to exist [unless we] . . . take away signs of prejudice, narrow-mindedness, dependency and baseless authority, so that the individual can sail under his own flag. . . .'

He expresses the same revolutionary view in a letter of thanks he sends in December to his 'carissimo' Lorentz Dietrichson, from whom he has received a propagandist poem: '. . . it seems to me doubtful whether it is feasible for us to bring about better artistic conditions in our country, so long as the spiritual soil in all directions is not cleared, cleaned and drained of all swamps. So long as a people think it more important to build religious meeting-houses than theatres, so long as they are more prepared to support the Zulu Mission than the Museum of Art. . . .' (Ibsen is here referring to the time after the fire and repairs to the theatre in Bankplassen, when the idea of acquiring a large modern theatre for Kristiania was revived. He then prepared an estimate for a theatre with 1,800 seats; but the National Theatre was not completed for another twenty-two years, and even then it only had 1,000 seats.) At the same time he hints in his letters that he might consider moving to Kristiania, when his son, he hopes, is to complete his law studies. He did not want to live there for good, but just for Sigurd's period of study. This plan, however, soon came to an abrupt end.

In May 1880, he has an idea which he ventilates to Hegel:

'I have at the moment plans for something new, on which I should very much like your opinion, and so I am briefly outlining them for you.

'I do not think I am wrong when I seem to have noticed that the introduction of the new edition of *Catiline* has been read with considerable interest. What if I now wrote a whole little book of about ten to twelve sheets containing similar information on the external and internal circumstances under which every single one of all my literary works have come about? In connection with *Lady Inger* and *The Vikings*, in this way, I would thus wish to deal with my stay in Bergen, with *The Pretenders* and *Love's Comedy*, I would describe my subsequent period in Kristiania, and after that my Rome life with *Brand* and *Peer Gynt*, etc. etc.— I would naturally not attempt any interpretation of my books: it is best that the general public and the critics are allowed to play about as they like in that field—anyhow for the time being. But I want to tell of the circumstances and conditions under which I have written,—naturally all with the greatest discretion, and leaving open wide scope for all kinds of guesswork.'

It was probably at about this time that he began to make notes for such an autobiography, but Hegel must have advised against it; anyhow nothing came of it but a few brief notes on his childhood years in Skien, from which a little has been quoted in this book.

In the summer of 1880, he began his campaign to get Sigurd admitted to complete his studies at the faculty of law in Kristiania. He also sent Suzannah and Sigurd to Kristiania to make the arrangements and when difficulties arose he himself wrote a letter to the King (the government) about making the matter the subject of a royal ruling, so as to get round the regulation that to be able to take a Norwegian law examination one must first have taken a Norwegian so-called 'second-exam', which included Latin and Philosophy. Sigurd was no doubt more than qualified in both subjects, even if not exactly according to the curriculum in Kristiania, so for him such a 'second-exam' would mean a wasted year. He writes bitterly to his father about the unfriendly reception he has received from the Ministry. With his excellent results in the German examinations (and his famous father) he feels deeply insulted and says conceitedly: 'Such an exam even with top marks will be the equivalent of degradation.' He concludes that he would like to complete his studies in Italy.

Ibsen soon telegraphs his consent and writes from Berchtesgaden, where he is on holiday: 'What would you have gained
by acquiring a Norwegian law degree? It was never your intention to become a civil servant up there. The only positions there
which you could desire, you can obtain nevertheless; you can
become a professor or go into the diplomatic service. . . .'

To Hegel, Ibsen expresses himself quite sharply a month later,
on October 25: 'All foreign universities are open to him, and
we are now returning to Rome, where he will complete his law
studies and then become naturalized. I shall at some opportunity
raise a suitable literary monument to that black theological
gang which at present rule in the Ministry of Ecclesiastical
Affairs.'

After Ibsen's arrival in Rome at the beginning of November,
the first hint reaches Hegel that there is something definite afoot:
'I am wrestling now with new literary plans, which I hope in the
course of a few months will have matured sufficiently for me to
begin to get to grips with the real work.'

Months of bad temper went by—during that winter in Rome,
he is said to have been difficult company even for his friends—
and not until March 22, 1881, does the first indication come that
work has really begun. In a letter to Hegel, he says: 'I want to tell
you in confidence that I am writing a new book, which will be
ready by the summer. It will probably come to about twenty
printed sheets; this work interests me very much and I feel certain
that the book will also be received with interest by the public.
For the moment, however, I do not want to say more about the
content, but later I shall perhaps come back to it.'

It looks from this as if while he was working on it, he had no
idea that the witch's brew he was now concocting would
occasion the greatest sensation and scandal of the century in the
cultural life of Scandinavia, and with echoes all over the world.

For him, and also for us who can look on it from a safe distance, *Ghosts* is a logical and obvious continuation of the programme of work to which he had announced that he would
dedicate his life and to which, on the whole, he managed to
adhere. This adherence to a grand design prepared beforehand is

perhaps the reason why he was able to reach the pinnacle of his achievements when he was over fifty years old.

The doctrine of evolution and the problem of heredity were highly topical subjects at this time and leave their mark on much of the literature of the age, partly in the form of optimism, a belief in constant progress, and partly in the form of pessimism, naturalism's searchlight on the phenomena of degeneration. The problem of hereditary disease interested Ibsen very much: as a good psychologist and an incorrigible moralist, he thought that evil deeds, betrayal and deceit in human matters, hit back at the betrayer, at Peer, Stensgaard and Bernick. That children suffer for their parents' misdeeds, he not only knew from his own life, but saw all round him. What then was more natural than that he should turn to the unmentionable disease which was a consequence of a strict moral code for women and a wholly different moral code for men. Women were in duty bound to remain good and virtuous within the boundaries of marriage, while men could ravage freely, whether married or no, and buy themselves cheap eroticism anywhere.

The unmentionable disease was at that time much more widespread than we can imagine today, and caused secret misfortunes even in the best of families. Ibsen himself never mentions the disease—syphilis—by name, but turns the searchlight on to its fatal consequences as they shape the destiny of a woman—a Nora who has remained in a crippling home and too late experiences the tragic consequences.

When the play was published, it was taken as a tragedy about venereal disease, and Oswald was thought to be the central character. Without fundamentally intending it to be the main point, Ibsen had touched on one of society's worst cancers. He had exposed not only man's sacred right to a double code of morality, but also a whole taboo world, which everyone knew about and whispered about in corners, but no one dared mention aloud.

We now know the deepest meaning of *Ghosts* and so the play still survives dramatically, despite science's rejection of the picture of Oswald's disease. The real point of the play was to describe a different phase of the oppression of bourgeois woman. Both Nora and Helene Alving have allowed themselves to be married off, not for love, but because others decided things for them and because this was accepted practice. Both have tried to adapt themselves to marriage, as society demands of them. Neither of them has succeeded. Whilst Nora finally breaks away, Helene Alving remains in her home, and her increasing hatred of her husband's penchant for dissipation has turned her alienation from him into a positive rejection, so that he really has no alternative but to take his pleasure where he can find it.

The tragedy lies in her own feeling of co-responsibility. She has, though with increasing reluctance, followed suit, though she has finally seen through the wretched hypocrisy on which her life has been built. She has done three things to atone. She has taken her dead husband's illegitimate daughter, Regine, into her house: Regine's mother, the maidservant, was duly married off to the blackmailer and carpenter, Engstrand, but the threat of exposure hangs in the air all the time. Secondly, she has sent her son away to be brought up in less unhealthy surroundings. Thirdly, she has rid herself of her husband's fortune, the price for which she in her time had earlier sold herself to him. That the money is used to build a home for fallen women is at the same time a biting irony and an atonement.

Then all falls in ruins around her in a tragic avalanche. Oswald comes home, apparently liberated, proclaiming his *joie de vivre*, but inwardly undermined by his hereditary burden, mortally ill and depraved, and the first ghost which appears is just a little too much port and an attempt to seduce that more than willing social climber, the maidservant, who he has no idea is his half-sister.

The tragedy develops at a steadily increasing pace. The institution burns, the son's insanity breaks out and as the curtain falls Helene Alving is faced with her fearful choice: shall she or shall she not answer Oswald's prayer to help him out of this life? Ibsen himself was asked directly by William Archer whether she gives him the poison or not, and he replied: 'I would never dream of settling such a difficult question!' For Mrs Alving both possibilities are equally tragic.

Ghosts retains its full theatrical and psychological power up to this day, despite the fact that the picture of Oswald's disease is no longer valid, and despite the contrived nature of the fire—logical and symbolically correct though this incident undoubtedly is. The basis is not only the dramatic mastery with which the play is constructed, but first and foremost the perspectives it gives to a woman's mind, a woman who, through her tragic destiny, achieves maturity, purification, catharsis.

A letter to Hegel in June, 1881, indicates that the material he had first considered in the spring was different from what finally appeared in *Ghosts*, but that now he has put everything else on one side, and Helene Alving is beginning to take shape. He writes about money and wishes to:

'. . . take this opportunity to say that a change has taken place in my literary plans for the summer. The work I wrote about earlier has been temporarily put to one side, and early in this month I began to tackle some material for a play which has long occupied my thoughts and which has now penetrated so deeply into me, that I could no longer possibly let it lie. I hope to be able to send you the manuscript by the middle of October. I will tell you the title of the play later and today will only note that I am calling it "a domestic drama in three acts". I need not add perhaps, that this play has nothing whatsoever to do with *A Doll's House*.'

This time it took him no longer than three months to write the play. *Ghosts* was published in the middle of December, but even by then it had dawned on both Ibsen and Hegel that there would be a storm over it, for on November 23 Ibsen writes to Hegel that '*Ghosts* will perhaps cause alarm in certain circles, but that cannot be helped. If it did not, then it would not have been necessary to write it'. Hegel must have been soothed or anyhow have reckoned that the possibility of a sensation would not damage sales, for this time the first edition ran into ten thousand copies. The fury the book roused caused the greater part of the edition to be returned and thirteen years went by before it was sold out.

From December, 1881, and throughout the whole of 1882, a

hurricane continued to blow all through Scandinavia over Ibsen's play. And it was not only the conservatives who let out a howl. The liberals too, and most radicals, were so shaken by the explosion that they neither realized what a masterpiece it was, nor that there was balance in it. Most people thought that Ibsen through the mouth of Mrs Alving, wanted to legalize incest and advocate sexual licence and nihilism. Even such a wise and radical personality as Alexander L. Kielland wrote to Brandes:

'This accumulation of horrors interests me—frankly less for its own sake than for the insight it gives me into this refined, careful, decorated, somewhat snobbish person, who like Nora, has always had a secret desire to say damn it in the middle of all that refinement, and who has now summoned up the courage—God knows where from—suddenly to get some fresh air in a wild outburst.'

In Norway, only Bjørnson and Professor Peter Olrog Schjødt defended it. Ibsen writes of Bjørnson's defence in January, 1882: 'The only person in Norway who has stepped out freely, boldly and courageously in my favour is Bjørnson. That is like him. He has in truth a regal disposition, and I shall never forget him for it.' Ibsen was indeed right, but that was not what he had thought before.

Of course, later on more defenders began to make themselves heard—Amalie Skram and Camilla Collett—but they were drowned in the torrent of abuse. In Denmark, Georg Brandes tried to defiend it, but it was a letter from the Danish author, Sophus Schandorph, originally a theologian, but later a follower of Brandes, which particularly delighted Ibsen and drew from him a reply which he very much wanted Schandorph to make public:

'That such alarm should occur, I was prepared for. Even if some of our Scandinavian critics have no talent for anything else, they at least have an undeniable talent for fundamentally misunderstanding and misinterpreting those authors whose books they undertake to judge. . . . They are trying to hold me responsible for the sentences which some of the play's characters utter. And yet there is in the whole book not a single sentence, not a single utterance which is the voice of the author. I was very careful about that. . . . And they say that the book preaches nihilism. Not at all. It preaches nothing whatsoever. It only points out that nihilism lurks under the surface, at home as elsewhere. And so must it necessarily be. A Pastor Manders will always egg on a Mrs Alving or two. And just because she is a woman, she wishes, once she has begun, to go to the utmost extremes.'

The theatres also hermetically sealed their doors, both in Scandinavia and Germany, not daring to offer their public such fare. The play's first performance—strangely enough—took place in Chicago in 1882, and later on it was put on in Helsinki by August Lindberg, who had permission from Ibsen to take it on tour round Scandinavia and did so for several years with great and increasing success. In Kristiania, young people went in procession with torches to acclaim him, whilst there were whistles for Schrøder, the director of the theatre, who had rejected the play.

In the outside world, it caused a sensation wherever it broke through and to some extent introduced a new era in the art of the theatre. In many places it was banned; everywhere it was loudly abused. It did not reach London until ten years later, and it may be of interest to note the collection of abuse which William Archer amused himself by gathering up and which Francis Bull gives in his introduction to the play in the Centenary Edition. The play was described as 'naked loathsomeness' and Ibsen himself as 'an egoist and a burglar, a crazy, cranky being'; and '97 per cent of the people who go to see Ghosts are nasty-minded people, who find the discussion of nasty subjects to their taste in exact proportion to their nastiness'. 'Old Ibsen is as dead as a door-nail.'

14

An Intermediate Play
and New Maturing

THE first few months after the publication of *Ghosts* contained
Ibsen's first major defeat for many years. The antagonism at home
surprised and infuriated him and made him wish to defend himself against all the distortions and misinterpretations to which he
had been exposed. That it also worried him is no more than
hinted in his letters. For the last time in his life he writes very
aggressively, prodigal of explanations, and again deeply grateful
to the few who defend him, although he must have seen that even
its defenders misunderstood the play.

But the distance from the despised puddle in Scandinavia was
now great enough to enable him to calm down quite soon.
Opposition could shake him but not crush him. And it now suited
him to return to the subject with which he had been occupied
before Mrs Alving came along and shook him by the shoulder,
demanding life.

Looking back over Ibsen's achievements so far, we find that
in one way *An Enemy of the People* is a reversion to a form of
writing that he had already abandoned. Both his doll's house and
his ghosts come from a spiritual workshop which created living
human beings, seen in relation to their day, but conditioned by
their inescapable destinies. *An Enemy of the People*, on the other
hand, is an extrovert, popular play, an argument sustained by two
real people, supported only by 'types'. It is written by an experienced and important dramatist and is alive enough in its way: but
it has no more to it than that.

He might have tackled it less superficially if the great scandal over *Ghosts* had not lured him out of his habit of self-criticism. Now, however, his fury changed to cheerfulness and he saddled his hobby-horse—that the mob is never right, that democracy is half-hearted and liberals all cowards and humbugs.

It is a letter to his friend Olaf Skavlan, written only a few weeks after the publication of *Ghosts*, that gives the background to the change which had come about in him. In it he says:

'Recent times have been rich in experience, learning and observation for me. I was naturally prepared for my new play causing a howl in the camp of the stagnant men, and it does not disturb me any more than would a pack of chained dogs barking at me. But the alarm I have observed among the so-called liberals has given me a great deal to think about.'

Then he scoffs at the leftists busying themselves with abjuring all responsibility, and writes the sentence we have already quoted about Bjørnson's regal disposition. But the others:

'But what of all these terrified freedom-fighters? Is it only in the political field that the campaign for liberty shall be allowed in our country? Is it not first and foremost the spirit which needs to be freed? Such servitude that we cannot even enjoy the freedoms we already have. Norway is a free country inhabited by imprisoned people.'

On the stage, Dr Stockmann is often depicted with Bjørnson's facial features, and everyone is agreed that Ibsen had been thinking of both Bjørnson and Jonas Lie. That he also thought of himself, and perhaps with a smile remembered the evening in Rome when he made a countess faint, is confirmed not only by the hero's name, originating from the place in Skien where Ibsen was born, but also by the hero's almost too direct expression of opinions which were really Ibsen's own.

Among the godparents of the play was the father of Ibsen's German writer friend, Meissner, a doctor in Teplitz in Bohemia in the 1830s, who was stoned because he ruined the resort's season by pointing out that there was cholera in the town. Another was the apothecary Thaulow in Kristiania, who when Ibsen was there in 1874 was still carrying on a somewhat temperamental campaign against the organizers of a kitchen which had been set up to make cheap food available to the poor, but instead was run on purely profit-making lines.

It is easy to see that the play in its final form is a counterpart to *The League of Youth*. The printer Aslaksen, as well as several other characters mentioned in *An Enemy of the People*, is taken directly from *The League of Youth*. The play has a certain social purpose, which is evident from the second of the two unusually friendly letters which Ibsen writes to Bjørnson at this time.

In this letter, in which he declines to come to Norway for the twenty-fifth anniversary of *Trust and Trial*, he writes that he has been taking a great interest in Bjørnson's travels during the last few months:

'I have received confirmation of so much of what I suspected in relation to the standpoint of society at home. And I have had constantly to ask myself the question: is it good that politics so completely outstrip social tasks? And this is undoubtedly happening in Norway at the moment; social questions are not coming out at all at home, and although they are still occupying the whole of the rest of Europe to an overwhelming degree, the masses out here do not bother particularly much about politics.'

(It is in this same letter that Ibsen utters his well-known dictum that while Bjørnson's works stand in the first rank of literature, he himself would nevertheless have chosen as an inscription for a memorial to Bjørnson the words: 'His life was his best writing. And to realize oneself in one's vocation, I think, is the highest a human being can attain.')

An Enemy of the People is essentially a social document—the eternally topical story of capitalist enterprise polluting the town's drinking water with waste, and the vigorous, fearless doctor who is stoned when he wants the town to pay for expensive reforms.

As early as March, 1882, he wrote to Hegel:

'It will be a peaceable play this time, which can be read by the city fathers and the merchants and by their ladies. It will be easy for me to complete and I will see to it that it is ready fairly early on in the autumn.'

On June 21 he was able to say that he had finished the rough draft on the previous day.

'It is called *An Enemy of the People* and is in five acts. I am still somewhat uncertain whether I shall call the play a comedy or a straight play; it has much of the character of a comedy about it, but also a more serious fundamental basis.'

When he sends the rest of the clean copy of the manuscript, he writes:

'My occupation with this work has amused me and I feel it as a loss and a vacuum now that I have finished it. Doctor Stockmann and I get on so excellently with each other, we are in agreement on so many points, but the doctor is a more confused person than I, and in addition has several other peculiarities which mean that people will tolerate from his mouth things which they perhaps would not tolerate so well if they had been said by me.'

Hegel, who undoubtedly looked with horror on the thousands and thousands of copies of *Ghosts* returning to the firm's warehouse, was considerably reassured by his reading of *An Enemy of the People*. Many publishers would have cut such a controversial author down to a fairly modest first edition, but Hegel went up to ten thousand copies this time too, and they gradually sold, but much more slowly, and it took about ten years before a new edition was necessary.

Ibsen took mild pleasure in revenging himself on the theatres in Scandinavia. Not one of them—and he had for several years now been the greatest attraction at them all—had dared risk *Ghosts*. Whereas before he had been very careful to see that theatres were allowed to read the plays before they came out in the bookshops so that they should not be tempted to think that good sales would damage attendance, this time he did not send the play to one of them, but allowed the book to be published

and waited with amused confidence for theatre directors to come
and beg. This they all did, sooner or later. Ibsen knew that this
was a good stage play. Successes then followed thick and fast.
The play is still performed on stages all over the world, and for
two reasons: the social conflict is and always will be as topical
today as when it was written; and despite all his oratorical,
rhetorical, Nietzschean, anarchic, temperamental excesses, Doctor
Stockmann offers many great actors a brilliant part, which they
force their theatre directors to allow them to play. Nevertheless,
among the scenic masterpieces Ibsen hatched out after he was
fifty, *An Enemy of the People* takes a modest place.

While Ibsen was completing the clean copy of *An Enemy of the
People*, other things were claiming a good deal of his attention.
In the summer of 1882 he experienced the triumph of his son
Sigurd receiving his law degree in Rome and a month later in the
same city receiving a doctor's degree with distinction. Sigurd was
at this time much taken up with his wish to become a naturalized
Italian citizen and to seek a career in the Italian diplomatic service.
He had not forgotten that in his own view he had been discourt-
eously received in Kristiania. He was altogether a very self-confident young man, much encouraged by his father, who always
admired him and idolized him.

However, through good connections a position was found for
the young lawyer in the Swedish-Norwegian Foreign Service,
first in Kristiania in 1884, then a spell in Stockholm, and then
later in Washington and Vienna, until 1890, when his career
ceased abruptly. But we shall return to this later.

During the following two years it was not simply for Sigurd's
sake that Ibsen took such an interest in political conditions at
home. During the years 1883 and 1884 the long battle between
the Swedish-Norwegian monarchy and the Norwegian national
assembly became much more violent. It caught the attention of
the whole population from the moment when Parliament, at the
end of April, 1883, after a week's debate decided to bring a case
to the Court of Impeachment against the government installed
by the king in 1880, in order to put it out of office. The case

continued until the late winter of 1884 and ended with the king having to submit, a triumph for parliamentarianism.

Ibsen followed all this eagerly. In June, 1883, he gave vent to the following heartfelt sigh in a letter to Brandes:

'I am wrestling at the moment with the draft of a new dramatic work in four acts. Diverse lunacies tend to assemble inside one in the course of time, and one very much needs an outlet for them. But as the play will not deal with the Court of Impeachment or absolute veto, nor even the pure flag, it is unlikely to gain much attention from Norwegian quarters. Let us hope that there are, however, ears to be found elsewhere.'

It is in this same letter that he defends Doctor Stockmann's attack on democracy, by saying that in ten years' time perhaps the majority will have gone over to Stockmann's side, but by then Stockmann will have progressed ten years!

'In my own personal case, at least, I perceive such consistent progress. Where I stood when I wrote my various books, there is now a considerable compact quantity of people, but I myself am no longer there, I am elsewhere, further on, I hope.'

These are indeed prophetic words.

At about this time, he also wrote a few more lines which are worth noting. Lucie Wolf, the actress, whom he had known since her début in Bergen in 1853, had written asking him to write a prologue for her thirtieth jubilee. Ibsen's reply is friendly, but reluctant; first because prologues and epilogues should be banished from the stage, for only dramatic art belongs there and declamation is not dramatic art; secondly because verse has done the art of acting much damage. Verse form in dramatic writing will be destroyed. Art forms die just as the absurd animal forms of the past died out when their time was over.

'I myself have during the past seven or eight years written hardly a single verse, but have exclusively pursued the far more difficult art of writing in simple truthful realistic prose. It is through this language that you have become the excellent artist that you now are.'

It was with this far more difficult art that he was now concerned. But in January, 1884, he still had not put pen to paper.
He wrote on January 22 that he had 'had one of those periods
during which I sit at my desk only with the greatest of reluctance.
But today I have been out and bought new paper, new ink and a
new pen, on account of a new play with which my thoughts are
occupied at present.'

He got started at the end of April. He wrote to Hegel:

'And now a little about myself. All through the winter, political
complications in Norway prevented me from tackling my new
dramatic work with undivided attention. But now at last I have
emerged from all that confusion and am writing with full force.'

Some quite full notes, drafts and corrections to *The Wild Duck*
have been preserved. The first notes were presumably written
more than a year before he bought ink and paper to write the
play, and are interesting because the play he then had in mind was
much more of a social document than the one which finally
emerged. The social presentation falls in line with the views Ibsen
expressed in letters, for instance those to Brandes and Bjørnson
at this time. He also began to sketch the characters, and several
times incorporated real people in the sketches, not to use them as
models, but to borrow details for which he could find a use. The
first sketch of Hjalmar Ekdal can be placed and dated exactly
because of its origins in a real literary figure and photographer in
Kristiania, Eduard Larsen, whom Ibsen had known in his youth
and who had taken the first known photograph of the author.
This was at the time when photography broke through in
Norway and as a profession had a certain attraction, particularly
for young men with some artistic inclinations. Ibsen knew several
of them. Among others, D. F. Nyblin, one of the actors during
his time as director of the theatre in Møllergaten, abandoned the
theatrical profession and established himself as a photographer,
becoming the capital's most fashionable portrait photographer.

It appears from these notes that Alexander L. Kielland also
provided food for Ibsen's imagination, but this was for the very

first sketch of Gregers Werle, who turned out very different in the end. Very many other people passed under the review of Ibsen's inner eye and contributed in a greater or lesser degree to the human beings in *The Wild Duck*. But at all events it is certain that the play changed character during its formation, becoming something quite different from what he originally planned and from anything his public expected from him.

What chiefly distinguishes *The Wild Duck* from his other contemporary plays is its *compassion*. The stern apostle of ideas and chastiser of society has gone, and it is almost as if this new, changed Ibsen is disputing his own earlier ideas. He now considers the problems of everyday life as a wise and indulgent judge of human character.

Again the construction is so that it is as if secret cog-wheels were engaging, driving the characters towards their destinies, so that their past overtakes them with all its force. And this time it is not one or two main characters who are three-dimensional, but two whole families—the Ekdals and the Werles.

I will give a brief outline of some of the play's characters, not to attempt an analysis of this, the richest of all Ibsen's contemporary dramas, but to indicate the balance within every single destiny. First Hjalmar Ekdal, the personification of 'living a lie', with limited abilities and large pretensions, with lazy adaptability and his father's dark past to excuse everything. He is in every way a sham and an egoist, and Ibsen allows him to expose himself so completely that if, as so often happens on the stage, he is caricatured by the actor who represents him, he becomes nothing. But if he is so represented that his childish, naïve charm is allowed to emerge, he becomes, despite everything, so human that his fate is moving. That Ibsen, even before the world première in Bergen, was careful to see that Hjalmar was not allowed to be caricatured, is clear from a letter to the twenty-seven-year old producer and director of the theatre, Gunnar Heiberg, in which he writes: 'The most difficult point is the performance of Hjalmar Ekdal's part. What the actor in question must give here, and first and foremost, what he must refrain from, will be obvious to you after reading through it.'

Look next at Gina Ekdal, her destiny irremediably common-place. Seduced by old Werle, married off to Hjalmar, whom she protects and looks after, she tries to reconcile herself to life and make the best she can of it. She has become a wholly different person from the character Ibsen outlines in his first notes, where he writes that the photographer's marriage with 'the immature wife is in a way a "true marriage"', in that during their married life he has deteriorated, or anyhow has not matured. Now he cannot do without her. The same thing has happened to her.' But this does not happen to Gina. In the final version she has grown into a modest, but warm-hearted and genuine person, whose struggle with life has something heroic about it. Then the past appears and crushes everything.

Or look at Old Ekdal. Apparently a purely 'theatrical' figure— the naïve lieutenant fooled by the sharp merchant into crimes which he has not understood, but which he alone has to pay for. And he too, with his remaining instinct for self-preservation is defended by Ibsen to the last. He is at the same time the most down-to-earth and the most imaginative of this shipwrecked family. It is he who is the inventor of the dark loft, the dream-land for all losers. At the same time he is totally free of conscious pathos and sentimentality, and this is precisely what makes him pathetic.

Then there is Gregers Werle. For decades he was understood as the idealist of the play, forced to flee from home when he saw through his father, a genuine seeker after truth, even if he invol-untarily causes unhappiness when he tries to atone for his father's sins by helping his fellow human beings. Then half a generation after Ibsen, and not without inspiration from his dramas, science thought up a number of general laws of psychological behaviour. The results were popularized into catch-words and then Gregers Werle was appointed commander of the 'Oedipus complex', with the consequence that for some years he was presented as a pure psychopath. He is this too, but not very much more so than a number of normal moralists. In years to come, he will probably find his rightful place in this remarkable play, in which the characters change as the times look differently upon them, but persistently stay alive, because audiences all over the world become involved in their destinies, identifying themselves with some of them and reacting against others.

Even the play's little heroine, Hedvig, and its great villain, the merchant, father and daughter, both menaced by the dark of blindness, have been considered in different lights over the years. Hedvig was for a long time the star part for great actresses who wished to interpret her sacrificial death, but who nearly always made her more melodramatic than tragic. It is her simple devotion to the man who she thinks is her father, but who repudiates her, which gives her the child's courage to sacrifice her life. It is her touching simplicity which to this day has brought her un-scathed through actresses' fearful interpretations of her death. And I wonder if her counterpart, the merchant Werle, will not also one day receive his true interpretation? He has in fact almost water-tight arguments, so to speak, for all his baseness. He is much more than the villain Ibsen was to use as the play's evil spirit. Interpreted by a really great actor, he too can become one of the play's main characters.

There are only two other features of *The Wild Duck* which should be noted before passing on to the later dramas. Now that Ibsen has mastered the technique of tragedy, by unifying time, place and action so that his characters *have* to behave as they do, now and then he makes use of dramatic caricatures on the peri-phery of the play; people who are not human and were not thought of as such, but rather as 'contrast-characters', who with their distance and sudden conspicuous behaviour are stones which splash into the pool and set the waves in motion. *The Wild Duck* has its Relling and Molvik, and the later plays their equivalent intruders in the action.

In *The Wild Duck*, for the first time, Ibsen makes dramatic use of symbols. *The Doll's House* is sheer realism, but in *Ghosts* the first indication comes—in the very title. In *The Wild Duck*, the symbols become clearer and this time not only in the title but in the very symbolism of the dark loft.

The Wild Duck was written between April 20 and June 13, 1884, in Rome, and a clean copy made in Gossensass. It was sent to Hegel on September 2 with a letter, a few lines of which must be quoted here:

'... the people in this play, despite their multifarious defects, have nevertheless become dear to me during my long daily association with them, but I have hopes that they will also find well-disposed friends in the great reading public and not least among actors and actresses, for without exception they offer rewarding parts. But the study and rendering of these people will not be easy. . . . This new play has in some ways a place on its own in my dramatic production; the method diverges in several respects from my earlier work. However, I do not wish to say more on this. The critics will, I hope, find these points, and will anyhow find various things to dispute and interpret. In this way I think that *The Wild Duck* might lure some of our younger dramatists into new ways, and that I consider desirable.'

Ibsen was right, to the extent that more or less all European dramatic writing in the next generation was directly or indirectly influenced by *The Wild Duck*. But when it came out, it roused more astonishment and confusion than enthusiasm. Both supporters and opponents were disappointed. Henrik Jaeger said: 'The public does not know what to think and will not be much the wiser from the criticism that appears, for one paper says one thing and the next something else.' Or, as *Aftenposten* puts it: 'One can ponder and ponder where Ibsen wishes to go, and not find out.' Messages and prophecies were expected of Ibsen, but he did not oblige.

The disappointment Ibsen admirers felt over *The Wild Duck* is expressed most clearly nine years later by the great Swedish writer, Hjalmar Söderberg in the periodical *Ord och Bild*, when he considers that the time of 'crisis' in Ibsen's life occurred with *The Wild Duck*:

'It shows all the signs of having been written under the influence of the great miscalculation in the author's life. *I read this drama*, writes Edmund Gosse, *on the deck of a steamer. It was on the Atlantic, the winter the book was published, and I shall always connect the thought of these sad pages with the sight of the bleak picture of the sea in turmoil.* It is undeniable that Ibsen's pessimism in *The Wild Duck* is his most bitter, most grey and most oppressive—a dark room in which on all sides the walls are for ever receding—and what Ibsen has written since seems to me in its essentials to bear the impression of being a brilliant man's attempt to kill time.'

More recent times have judged *The Wild Duck* differently. Sigurd Bødker described it in 1904 with the words: '*The Wild Duck* is the master's masterpiece.' In 1918, Nils Kjaer wrote: 'I wonder whether any Norwegian literary work has been more admired and loved!' And Ibsen's lifelong champion in England, William Archer, who to begin with did not appreciate the play, in 1923 called it 'Ibsen's greatest play'.

15

Visit to Norway and
Renewed Exile

The Wild Duck was published in the autumn of 1884 in an edition of eight thousand. Despite the surprise and disappointment in rightist as well as leftist circles, it was at least read, discussed and performed. A second edition came out before Christmas the same year and the play was produced in all the permanent theatres of Scandinavia in the course of a few months—it was very successful in Bergen, and in Kristiania it was billed twenty-two times during that season.

Usually when Ibsen had completed one of his great dramatic works he felt empty, for everything that he had systematically moulded together in his imagination had then abandoned him and was now in print and on the stage. His experiment was complete, the results delivered, the laboratory was deserted, and he had only the usual troubles of speeding his new creation on its way. But this time he was much taken up with practical matters. In February, 1885, his son, Sigurd, moved from Kristiania to the Swedish-Norwegian Foreign Department in Stockholm, to begin with obviously as a kind of probationer, for Ibsen took pains to see that his business manager in Kristiania, the bookseller Lund, had sufficient money for Sigurd to live a carefree life in Stockholm until later that winter, when he would be able to earn his own living.

Ibsen now began to feel restless in Rome, presumably partly because Sigurd was no longer there or in need of him. He considered going to live in Germany again, and cherished a little dream, inspired by Bjørnson, of perhaps going to live somewhere

near Kristiania, but far enough away from the town to be left in
peace by intruders from the left or right. Politically he had swung
violently over from right to left at this time, although he had
preached to both sides in turn so emphatically that both feared
him and he regarded both with mistrust. As he himself had
admitted to Rikke Holst Tesselt, he was never a courageous man
in his youth when it came to a confrontation. Now he hesitated
no longer to enter into personal controversies or ruptures, even
with his best and oldest friends.

This was precisely what happened during his visit to Norway in
the summer of 1885. Except for his stay in Kristiania in 1874, this
was the first time he had visited Norway for twenty-one years.
As late as at the end of April, 1885, he had no thought of travelling to Norway.

He writes to Hegel:

'Where we shall choose to stay this summer I still do not know
definitely, but possibly it will be either the Tyrol or Lake Con-
stance, where I hope to be able to work in peace and have my new
play ready by the autumn at the usual time. It is doubtful that we
shall return to Rome after that. For several reasons it would be
expedient for me to go and live in Germany again for a year,
where I would be in a better position to conduct some literary
business matters than from down here. In addition I should in
that way then bring my home somewhat nearer, and just lately
have seriously begun to think, if possible, of buying a small
villa, or more accurately a country house in the proximity of
Kristiania, near the fjord, where I could perhaps live somewhat
isolated and exclusively occupied with my work. The sight of the
sea is what I miss out here and this grows from year to year.'

What made Ibsen suddenly change his plans for the summer is
not known. He had probably discovered that his new play was
not yet anywhere near ready for writing, and also the trip
Suzannah and Sigurd made up to the North Cape the previous
year had evidently made him wish to see at least the west of
Norway again. But the fact that Sigurd was able to take leave

from his job in Stockholm had probably counted most, for then this inseparable trio were able to be together in Norway, in Molde, which Bjørnson had described with such lyrical enthusiasm that it had overcome even Ibsen's scepticism. Perhaps it would be possible to find a place there for the future?

So he and Suzannah unexpectedly travelled northwards at the beginning of June, 1885, naturally via Copenhagen, where his publisher duly fêted his world-famous author. Ibsen arrived in Kristiania in June, and June 10 did in fact become something of a turning-point in his life.

On that day the National Assembly, by-passing the government, was debating a private motion from Bjørnstjerne Bjørnson concerning a writer's pension for Alexander L. Kielland. Ibsen sat in the diplomatic box and listened to the debate. For several reasons he did not feel whole-hearted sympathy with Kielland. He considered him something of a sybarite and an idler, and thought he had come by his literary success too easily and quickly. In this he was wrong; and Bjørnson showed a truer instinct in his enthusiasm for Kielland. Apart from Ibsen's own prose, there is no prose-writing of that day which has been less affected by time and linguistic development than Kielland's.

But that Kielland deserved his writer's pension Ibsen completely agreed, and the parliamentary debate was a shock to him. The Supreme Court case had revolved round the government's access to the National Assembly—that is, their duty to be responsible to parliament. But on this occasion the Liberal government was not represented in the debate, and this cowardice and hypocrisy administered the death-blow to Ibsen's belief in the Norwegian Liberal Party. The motion was defeated by fifty-six votes to fifty-three. And in general he discovered in Kristiania that the political climate, which he had looked on with indulgent irony from a great distance, was not just a brief cold spell, but an ice-age. He had not previously understood that the Liberals' persistent but often narrow-minded and compromise-ridden struggle against the monarch and bureaucracy and for democracy had left such scars that there was hatred and bitterness on both sides. Old friends were no longer acknowledging one another.

Most of Ibsen's old acquaintances, the 'Dutchmen', were now on the extreme right wing, and he felt more rootless and homeless in Norway than ever. He rapidly abandoned any thought of settling down there. But at the same time he seems to have been looking for some tide of opinion with which he could be happy to swim.

The only place where he thought there was hope was among the workers. As we know, Ibsen in his youth had had great sympathy for the workers' first political movement in Norway, the Thranites. After this had been crushed the remaining workers' unions had gone over to becoming a form of society for popular education, but at this point in the middle of the eighties, their aims were mainly political and they were being infused with the steadily growing socialist doctrines in Europe.

Ibsen can have known little about the strength of the socialist element in the worker's union in Trondheim, but it was with obvious delight that he received an invitation to go to Trondheim and be fêted with a procession of banners. He went to Trondheim and there gave the first and last political speech of his life. According to the paper *Dagbladet* he said to Bjørnson at the station platform at Kristiania: 'Greet all that are young in heart in Norway and ask them to be loyal, and say that I want to be with them as the pivot of the left, as the left pivot. What appears to be madness in the young, will finally become the germination. You can be sure of that.'

In his speech, after alluding to the progress that has been made in the country since his last visit eleven years earlier, he continues:

'But my visit home has also caused me disappointment. I have realized that essential individual rights are still not secured as much as I had thought or should hope for and expect under the new régime. The majority of our rulers do not grant the individual either freedom of belief or freedom of expression outside arbitarily fixed limits.

'So there is still much to do here, before we can be said to have reached real freedom. But our present democracy is not likely to succeed in solving these problems. There must be a noble element in our parliamentary life, in our government, in our representation and our press.

'Naturally, I am not thinking of nobility of birth, or nobility of money, or nobility of knowledge, or even that of ability and talent. But I am thinking of nobility of character, of the spirit and of the will.

'That alone is what can free us.

'This nobility, with which I hope our people will be endowed, will come to us from all quarters. It will come to us from two groups, which have not hitherto been damaged irreparably by party pressures. It will come to us from our women and our workers.

'The reforms of conditions in society, which are now being undertaken in other parts of Europe, are essentially concerned with the future position of women and workers.

'It is this I am hoping and waiting for and will work for as much as I am able.'

After this, he could with peace of mind go on to Molde and spend his holiday with his wife and son. He writes to Hegel: 'After a few hectic days in Kristiania, I was glad to go north to Trondheim, and now we are here in Molde, one of the most beautiful spots in the world, as far as panoramic views are concerned. . . . But nevertheless I should not want to live here for any length of time, and so nothing will come of my thought of buying property here.'

The fact was that even in idyllic Molde, the party battle between right and left was raging so furiously that he could not remain unaware of it. The Liberals in the town held a reception for him, but the Rightists stayed away. The Rightists held a reception for the Prince of Wales and Gladstone, who were visiting the town, but did not invite Ibsen. Even the best friend of his youth, Lorentz Dietrichson, who was also holidaying in Molde, was now very reserved. As Ibsen wrote later: 'During daily intercourse a pettiness of mind and spirit became more and more obvious, a weakening of character, a feeble deferring to other people's judgements and thoughts, which could be nothing but repellent to me.'

Open rupture, however, did not occur until the end of September, after Ibsen had stayed with old acquaintances in Bergen, and then toured round the coast to Kristiania. Dietrichson was at this time chairman of the Student Union, and at a meeting on September 26th, Frits Thaulow, the painter, put forward a proposal for a torchlight procession for Ibsen, before his departure for Copenhagen three days later. Somewhat offended, the committee and chairman accepted the proposal and Dietrichson, together with another committee member, sought out Ibsen and asked him when it would suit him to receive the torchlight procession. He did not mention that it was not on the committee's initiative that this had come about. Ibsen, nevertheless, declined, saying that he did not wish for a student celebration on his departure. From this episode grew a very bitter controversy between Ibsen and Dietrichson, lengthy feuds in the press, protest meetings and demonstrations and the formation of a liberal student union, whose first action was to invite Ibsen to be a honorary member.

Ibsen's letter to the Student Union from Munich is too lengthy to quote, as it runs to over seven pages. It will suffice to quote the first telegraphic exchange of comments between these two old friends, who in correspondence had previously addressed each other as 'carissimo'. Dietrichson's telegram runs:

'You replied to my invitation to a torchlight procession that your grounds for refusal were a dislike of all public appearances and your previous refusal to the worker's union. Have you since given someone authority to repudiate your own reply and thus my rendering of it to the students, and stated another reason?'

He is referring to remarks made by Ibsen to Ove Rode, Margrethe Vullum's son by her first marriage, brought up in Norway but later Danish Minister of the Interior and editor of the paper *Politics*—remarks which Rode had repeated at a Union meeting. Ibsen's answering telegram is unequivocal:

'Your account of my refusal was incomplete. I said, amongst other things, I do not wish for student jubilations at my departure. I really meant: I do not feel akin to a student union under your leadership. Tell the students this. Henrik Ibsen.'

This is strong stuff, and it sounds like something much more than a sudden outburst of rage. Although later he was reconciled to some extent with Dietrichson, it is as if he was using this episode to slam the door behind him. All thoughts of settling in Norway are abandoned and all personal friendships in his native country broken off. Not until six years later did he return home to live, undoubtedly chiefly for the sake of his son, Sigurd.

In October, 1885, he acquired an elegant apartment in Munich and writes: 'We live spaciously and handsomely here now in Munich's best and most magnificent street, paying only half of what our apartment cost us in Rome.' He lived in this apartment for six years, a creature of habit and an introverted brooder, cold and reserved.

When it comes to both his methods of work and his notes, he is always equally optimistic in his letters to Hegel, expecting the plays to be started and completed more quickly than they were. Then he proceeds from the first methodical roughing out of drafts when he thinks everything is clear in his head to the alterations and polishing of the last clean copy and, as always, the dispatch of the manuscript at the last moment in order to reach the shops before Christmas; a whole year later than he had hoped.

This maturing process is the same each time and gradually Ibsen became less particular about covering his tracks and tearing up his rough drafts—perhaps because he himself no longer objected to posterity examining his seams—so that this preliminary work is a veritable gold-mine for scholars. The deplorable thing, however, is that the research has hitherto been carried out only by *literary* scholars, whereas in this preliminary work there is also a mine of information for research about the theatre, for teachers of dramaturgy and the techniques of drama; the author has left his workshop all in order and open to anyone who wishes to follow the plays from early notes to drafts and on to the small time-consuming and painstaking alterations of nuances and finally to the complete version seen on the stage.

A few lines about *Rosmersholm* written by Professor Francis

Bull in 1932 at the time provided me with the key to this play.

'The Alving family at Rosenvold and the Rosmer family at Rosmersholm are doomed to destruction, riddled with degeneration,—the last living member is useless and doomed, but the dead live, Chamberlain Alving and Mrs Beate. "Ghosts" and "white horses" frequent the old mansion, the past appears again and again, people cannot free themselves from their heritage, and afterwards new light falls on everything that Mrs Alving and Rosmer would prefer to be rid of, but in vain tried to forget.'

So far, apt enough; but then Bull rises from pithy definition to inspired interpretation:

'In *Ghosts* there is the clashing of battle signals and shrill discords; the basic atmosphere of *Rosmersholm* is more elegiacally musical, but the two plays are like movements of the same symphony— they belong intimately together.'

This is exactly what the two plays are, movements of the same symphony. *Rosmersholm* has been called both Ibsen's most pessimistic and his most optimistic play. It may be interpreted either way. Whatever the interpretation, it is clear—and not only from his notebooks—that the Swedish writer, Count Snoilsky and Ibsen's impressions of the mansion at Molde, Moldegård, provided fuel for his imagination and that ghosts from his own earlier writings haunt the place.

Ibsen had been taken with Snoilsky's work from the beginning. In his diary of the trip up through Gudbrands Valley in 1862, he twice thinks he has recognized Snoilsky in a fellow-traveller, but they did not actually meet till 1864 in Rome. At that time Ibsen was annoyed with the Swedish-Norwegian Foreign Minister, who was vacillating over the Dano-German war. Snoilsky was a close relative of the Minister, so Snoilsky and Ibsen quarrelled. Five years later, Ibsen had changed his opinion of the Minister but so had Snoilsky, so they were in disagreement again.

Ibsen's friendship with Snoilsky was not very close but Snoilsky's personal destiny interested him very much. Snoilsky was thirteen years younger than Ibsen, but reached eminence when he was quite young. Then his promise was extinguished. He married into his own class, went into the diplomatic service and seemed lost to literature—a serious loss. But at about forty years of age, he burnt his bridges, obtained a divorce, resigned from the foreign service and married again. Then his lyrical writing suddenly began to flourish anew, swinging between inspired optimism and elegiac pessimism. Rebel and romantic, he found himself floating between the sky and the sea, like Ibsen's bird— too heavy for the air, too light for the waves.

Ibsen had sketched out the outline for *Rosmersholm* before he went to Norway in 1885. We do not know whether he had by then considered Snoilsky as a central character in this play, which was to be the counterpart of *Ghosts*. But anyhow, Snoilsky went to Molde and spent several days with the Ibsens there. He was accompanied by his new wife. His rejected first wife had died of tuberculosis after the divorce, but opinion had it that Snoilsky was to blame for her death. Ibsen's admiration for the new Countess Snoilsky was great and in a letter to Snoilsky he talks of 'your lovely, magnanimous wife'.

But here, as in all Ibsen's later plays, one might use a hackneyed turn of phrase and say that any similarity to real people is entirely coincidental. And in any case it does not matter. For *Rosmersholm* is a play about three creations of Ibsen's own, two (Rosmer and Rebekka) still living, the third (Beate) already dead.

Rosmer is a theologian, but gradually frees himself, not least through Rebekka's help, from what his Christianity, his pre-judices and male society have made him think. But when he dares to go outside the world of the spirit into reality, his nature is too feeble, his will too weak, his spirit still too soft to be inured against the storm he meets. Not least, he feels partially responsible for Beate's suicide, for she had had grounds for jealousy, for feeling herself rejected and thus betrayed.

But it is Rebekka who is the main character in the play, and she is in her way a new creation in Ibsen's writing. Both Nora and Helene Alving had solid roots in a realistic bourgeois milieu and thus consequently scruples and conventions to overcome.

Rebekka on the other hand, apart from the little portrait of Aasta Hansteen in *Pillars of Society*, is the first woman in Ibsen's contemporary writing who has brought herself up, as society has not been able to do it. In relation to the society into which she erupts, she is a revolutionary and a revolutionizer, independent in thought and will. Note that when everything breaks over her head and the battle is lost she is the first woman in Ibsen's writing who dares to talk openly about sex! And it is *that* confidence that is so shocking that it drives them both into the mill-race.

It is perfectly clear that Ibsen could not allow her to come from a normal bourgeois Norwegian environment. Rebekka represents a rebellion which in such circles would have been unthinkable. It would have been broken and subdued at its first appearance. Such instincts were reserved, by all the gods, for the husband. So Ibsen had to find an origin, a background that was sufficiently close for her to speak the same language and have read the books of the time, but sufficiently distant for her to be quite different. And Suzannah's and Sigurd's fantastic descriptions of North Norway during their trip to the North Cape in the summer of 1884 provided fuel for his imagination. Norwegians did not usually live under such natural conditions unless they were lost visionaries.

So, letting himself believe—whether rightly or wrongly is not important—that northern Norwegians had more of nature, the sea and rebellion in them than others, he fetched Rebekka and several other women characters from North Norway, to break into the brackish water of the stuffy fjords of the south.

Rebekka West is Ibsen's first deliberately realistic rebel, bent on more than just minor reforms. Social conditions compel her to work indirectly, through the good, wise and weak Rosmer. They fail so emphatically that a suicide pact is the only logical and psychological conclusion. *He* shows himself useless as a 'freed' person and *she* is entangled by his cast-off scruples. It is too crude to use the modern cliché that he is impotent. To Rebekka he is just that, ethically as well as physically. As a hyper-aesthetic and a brooder, he has undoubtedly also been the same with Beate. In a few years time, we shall no doubt see him interpreted on the stage as the personification of sexual anxiety, with all the associated behaviour patterns. He is in fact such an involved character that he comes to life under many interpretations.

The minor characters of Kroll and Brendel are very good parts, but their only purpose is to provide contrast to the main characters in their own very different ways. The hollow aesthetics of Brendel and their collapse are presented in a masterly fashion; Kroll is at the other extreme. Both have taught the theologian Rosmer something he had built on and then seen through. Brendel is the harmless parade figure, Kroll the man who causes the suicide; and Madam Helset represents the chorus of classical tragedy.

The outline of *Rosmersholm* was no doubt already sketched in Ibsen's mind in the late summer of 1885. As usual, he wrote optimistically to Hegel about the probable date of completion and as usual he miscalculated. The winter passed, and then the spring. He did not get started until the summer of 1856, and he finished about October 1. He writes about the manuscript:

'This play is to be regarded as the fruits of studies and observations which I had cause to make during my stay in Norway last summer. The play will, as far as I can see, not give any cause for attack from any quarter. On the other hand, I hope it will cause lively discussion. In fact I expect that in Sweden.'

In a letter to Brandes a month later he gives some insight into his method of work.

'The truth behind my persistent silence is that I am becoming more and more addicted to pursuing one single matter at a time, circling round one single series of performances, and while that is on, I push everything else to one side. Ever since my return here, I have been tormented by a new play, which was determined to emerge, and not until the beginning of last month did I get it off my chest. That is, that was when I got the manuscript out of the house.'

It is interesting to note that when the play did come out and a 'discussion group' of pupils at Aars and Voss school wrote to

Ibsen to ask him to clear up some obscure points, he was so touched that he replied to the schoolboy Bjørn Kristensen in February, 1887, as follows:

'The right to work runs fairly definitely through *Rosmersholm*. . . .

'But apart from this, the play deals with the struggle in which every serious person has to become involved with himself, to bring his way of life into harmony with his understanding of the meaning of things.

'Different spiritual functions do not in fact develop alongside each other, nor proportionately in one and the same individual. The instinct of understanding rushes forward from one convolution to the next. Moral consciousness, "conscience", on the other hand, is very conservative. It has deep roots in traditions and the past in general. From this comes individual conflict.

'But first and foremost the play is naturally a work about human beings and human destinies.'

16

Women, Women, Women

Rosmersholm was also received with some confusion and surprise when it was published, but Ibsen's European reputation had now grown so great that even the few attempts to show that his new play was meaningless and incomprehensible were made in more respectful tones than before.

The author himself, as usual, was busy arranging performances and translations. Again, Gunnar Heiberg won the race, in that the world première was in Bergen and was a great success, only the part of Kroll being criticized. Ibsen was still very mistrustful of the Christiania Theatre. He knew enough about the style of acting at this theatre to fear the worst when it came to his contemporary dramas, which exactly suited the Bergen theatre's youthful, adaptable and swift style, but did not come naturally to the old-fashioned, declamatory style which Bjørn Bjørnson had still not managed to eliminate from the theatre in Bankplassen in Kristiania.

So in December, 1886, and throughout January, 1887, Ibsen carries on a fairly long correspondence with Schrøder, the director of the theatre, explaining several of the characters in the play, to justify his demand for experimental casting.

At this time he was otherwise engaged, receiving an honour in Germany. From 1887 onwards, he was the tone-setting dramatist on German stages, and one of his most popular plays was now the controversial *Ghosts*. At first a festival week was held for him in Meiningen during the week before Christmas 1886, and the famous Duke, Germany's great theatre reformer of the day, awarded him an even higher order than before, an event he reports to Hegel with delight: 'You must not think that I mention

243

this from vanity. But I do not deny that it pleases me when I think back on the stupid denunciation to which the play [*Ghosts*] was subject for so long in our country.' He writes this letter on January 5, 1887, two days before he is to be honoured in Berlin with a reception and a private matinee of *Ghosts*, public performance of which was banned by the city's police. He would prefer not to go, but cannot 'refuse to appear, especially now that *Ghosts* has become a burning literary and dramatic question in Germany. I am prepared to meet considerable opposition in Berlin in the conservative press. But this too is a contributory reason for being present.'

It is not known whether during this winter and spring he was thinking about his next play, but as late as the beginning of June, he writes: 'We have now decided to spend the summer in Denmark, or more specifically in Jylland, where we are going at the beginning of July and where at first we shall stay somewhere on the coast. We shall not be coming to Copenhagen this time. I must have peace and solitude, so that I can get down to some serious work. This has not been possible this winter, as I have been busy with so many other things.' And a few days later: 'Both my wife and I will be extremely pleased to see the sea again.'

So in July, they went first to Frederikshavn, but then settled down in Saeby. Georg Brandes very much wanted them to come to Skagen, but this seemed to Ibsen too fashionable and full of distractions.

They stayed in Denmark until September, by which time the desire to honour Ibsen had been expressed in some quarters in Sweden. The first occasion was in the 'Gnistan' society in Gothenburg, when it is worth noting that in thanking them for their good wishes he added that 'he was able to appreciate this goodwill all the more, as his polemic interests were now in retreat and he felt that his writing was now on the way to assuming new forms. . .'.

At a reception for him in Stockholm on September 24 he produced some opinions which aroused a great deal of attention and were given various interpretations by the press afterwards:

'It is being said that I too, and in a prominent place, have contributed to creating a new era in the world. . . .

'On the other hand, I believe the times we are now in could with equal justice be described as a termination, an end, and that from them something new is being born.

'I believe that science's teaching on evolution is also valid in reference to spiritual life-factors.

'I believe that shortly there will be a time when political concepts and social concepts will cease to exist in their present forms, and out of them both will grow a unity, which at present carries within it the conditions for the happiness of mankind.

'I believe that poetry, philosophy and religion will blend together into a new category and a new life-force, which we who are alive today are on the whole incapable of imagining clearly.

'It has been said about me on various occasions that I am a pessimist.

'And I am that too, in so far that I do not believe in the immortality of human ideals.

'But I am also an optimist, in so far as I fully and assuredly believe in the germinating power of ideals and their powers of development.

'More specifically, I believe that the ideals of our time, in that they are fundamental, tend towards what in my drama *The Emperor and the Galilean* I suggested by using the term "the third kingdom".

'Allow me, therefore, to drink to what is to come—to the future.'

It was to be expected that these words of the old prophet would be the subject of discussion and argument. Had he said that he was a socialist? Well, perhaps so? So long as socialism was utopian, he possessed a life-long and unswerving sympathy for it.

Only a few months later, he answers a telegram which Dr Oscar Nissen sent him on his sixtieth birthday on behalf of the Kristiania Workers' Union:

'I beg you to tell the union's members that of all the classes in our country, it is the working class which is nearest my heart, and I beg you to add that in the future, which I believe in and hope for, there will be reserved for the worker conditions for life and social conditions which I welcome with lively joy.'

Ibsen went on to Copenhagen, where he was accorded much honour. Here he gave an interview to a journalist from *Social-Demokraten* who, like everyone in Scandinavia, had been pondering what he had really meant in Stockholm:

'And then it all came out in a question to him on his attitude towards the social question.

'At first his reply was not clear—anyhow it was neither the time nor the place to go deeply into this complex subject—and the writer simply said that he thought socialism had an immensely great future ahead of it, but that he was not sure about our party's forms and claims here in Denmark; and he referred to the differences between German and French socialists.

' "But on the whole," I said, "*Bjørnstjerne Bjørnson* has clearly and unequivocally proclaimed himself a fellow-believer. *He* is a socialist. What is *your* position, Dr Ibsen?"

' "*Well, I might be one too,*" was the writer's clear reply, and I realized where "the third kingdom" lay.'

It looks as if during these weeks, the wary Ibsen was opening up. Perhaps this was the result of the visit to him in Jylland that summer of a literary figure called Henrik Jaeger. Jaeger had long wished to write a biography of Ibsen, but Ibsen had declined to co-operate, partly because Jaeger had written with little understanding about several of his plays. But eventually he had agreed to such a book being published on the occasion of his sixtieth birthday in 1888, but only on condition that Jaeger made personal contact with him, so that Ibsen could prevent misunderstandings and misinterpretations. Jaeger went to Saeby and Ibsen was so expansive and forthcoming that Jaeger's biography became by far the best that had hitherto been written about Ibsen.

But back to the reception in Copenhagen at Hegel's, where the Danish writer, Hostrup, made a speech. A newspaper reported:

'Dr Henrik Ibsen replied in a remarkable speech. He described what he owed to Denmark for his summer stay here. He had known the mountains for a long time, but this summer he had discovered the *sea*. The smooth calm Danish sea, which one could walk right down to, without moutains closing the way to it; it had given his soul solace and peace. He had taken memories with him from the sea, which would be of importance both to his life and his writing.'

This does indeed sound remarkable, coming from the author of *Terje Vigen*. He probably meant no more than that now his mind was wrestling with the old romanticism of the sea, which had gripped him so many times before, perhaps most of all when he created his swooping seagull from North Norway, Rebekka West.

But many months were to go by before he put pen to paper. Outwardly, he seems to have done nothing but write a few letters, among other things in connection with the illness and death in December, 1887, of the irreplaceable Frederik Hegel; and after his sixtieth birthday on March 20, 1888, it took him many weeks to write letters of thanks to all those who had written to congratulate him.

The first draft of *The Lady from the Sea*, which had not yet then received a title, but had for a while been thought of as *The Mermaid*—is different from his usual drafts. It is a whole short story, and is dated as late as June 5, 1888, less than four months before the play was finished and sent in, and only four days before he set about his 'working manuscript'. It is an interesting document, because more than that of any other play it clearly shows how the action begins to take shape, while even as late as a week before the writing of the play, the background of events is still obscure.

Ibsen begins by describing the place. It is Molde, but reduced to a port of call for tourist boats and a resort with a sanatorium. The people fall into three groups. First, there are the residents, beginning with the solicitor—who later becomes the doctor, married for a second time and with two daughters by his first

marriage. (He had originally included these two young girls in
Rosmersholm as daughters of Rosmer, but he did not find a use for
them there.) Ibsen had originally planned to include several other
characters among the residents but he removed them all later on,
except for the superfluous hairdresser and the painter, Ballestad.

The second group are the summer holidaymakers and the
inmates of the sanatorium, and the third 'arriving and departing
tourists, who episodically become involved in the plot'. In the
finished play only three people from these two groups appear,
the young sculptor, the invited summer visitor, who became
Arnholm, and the stranger—who became anything but an
episode in the action.

He goes on to describe the atmosphere, and here too are obvious
reminiscences of his earlier environment. It is a small town which
wakes up only in summer. 'No vigour, no struggle for libera-
tion . . . limitations everywhere. From this, depression, like a
muffled lament over all human existence and behaviour.'

Then the romanticism of the sea begins:

'Has the development of man gone wrong? Why have we come
to belong to the dry earth? Why not the air? Why not the sea?
. . . The fascination of the sea. The longing for the sea. Man
related to the sea. Bound by the sea. Dependent on the sea. . . .
The sea possesses a power over moods, which has the effect of
willpower. The sea can hypnotize.'

Now we come to the heart of the matter:

'She has come from the open sea, where her father's parsonage
lay. Grown up out there—by the free open sea. Secretly betrothed
to the irresponsible young coxswain—dismissed midshipman—
resting throughout the winter because of damage to his ship in a
foreign port. . . .

'The secret in her marriage, what she hardly dares admit,
hardly dares think of: The imagination's fascination with the
past. With what is gone.

'Basically—in her involuntary imagination—it is with him that
she lives her married life.

'But—on the other hand—do her husband and children live wholly with her? Have not the three of them, as it were, a whole world of recollections between them.'

Then comes a preliminary outline of the first betrothed which is wholly different from the final characterization: in the draft he is overworked and morose and addicted to sea-bathing. Finally there is the young sculptor's 'vision' of the seaman's wife who is asleep, and the drowned seaman who comes back again.

As we see from the foregoing, Ibsen struggled long and hard to establish the characters and their inescapable destinies, and to place them in a credible environment. But how they came to behave when he got them living their own lives, was of less concern to him. As he himself said several times, it was not *he* who decided what his characters did; his task was simply to allow them to develop and show their true egos.

When he sat down at his desk on June 6, he was sure which combination of characters the play was to be about: the typical small town man, first thought of as a solicitor, later as a doctor, a widower with two daughters by his first marriage, married again to a woman 'from the sea' who was hypnotized by the sea— and by a dramatic youthful experience which meant that she did not live as one of the family into which she had married.

Thus he got on with writing the story of the Mermaid, as long as was necessary to make the scene clear to his inner vision. He included the minor characters to fill the environment, knowing perfectly well that he would cut most of them out again. It was many years since he had made use of large numbers of minor characters: in all his later contemporary dramas, they are indeed there, often in great numbers, but always invisible.

When he had prepared the framework in this way, he stopped without giving the story an ending, and went straight on to notes on the plan for the first acts.

As he stayed in Munich and wrote that summer, it was Rebekka West's spiritual half-sister, Ellida, who became the focal point of his imagination. The play took shape as a psychological study of hysteria-phenomena so vivid, so profound and clear that the advance of scientific knowledge has never been able to affect it.

The play is a mixture of realism and symbolic drama. In this case, as in *Rosmersholm*, Ibsen has made use of the symbols of the sea to explain certain phenomena in the female temperament which at the time had no scientific names. That there are hysterical features in Rebekka that force her to rebel to the point of desperation is clear enough. But with Ellida the hysteria has turned inwards, has become hypnosis, as Ibsen himself says—or neurosis, as we call it today.

It is this neurosis which makes her indolent in face of the environment she only half lives in, and at the same time constantly moody. Her neurosis comes to an acute crisis when the stranger appears and makes demands on her: like Ibsen and Rikke Holst, they had thrown their rings into the sea as a symbol of their eternal faithfulness. Then Ellida also becomes a rebel against her husband and society.

What then is the solution of this crisis, this rebellion? Ibsen lets her husband grow in the course of a few hours from a rather small, inert and drunken small-town doctor into a masterly psychologist. Wangel discerns that she is right when in her outburst she calls the marriage between them a business transaction in which he has bought her. And he lets her go.

The play's ending comes so abruptly, her release from her neurosis is so explosive, that it is difficult to make this *seem* psychologically convincing on the stage. The ending looks like an ordinary sermon on women's rights appended to a piece of otherwise profound psychology. Yet the ending is logical enough and psychologically right.

It did mean, however, that when the play was published, it was taken as propaganda for the struggle for the emancipation of women and for woman's right to decide freely for herself. Some of the greatest actresses in Europe—not least Eleanora Duse—seized with delight on the chance to interpret the play as such, and Ellida became one of their most memorable rôles.

The Lady from the Sea was published on November 28, 1888, in an edition of ten thousand copies. To say that it aroused agitation is putting it mildly. Despite Ibsen's forebodings, the book was received with considerable understanding in Norway, where, amongst others, the seventy-five-year-old Camilla Collett and Ibsen's own step-mother-in-law immediately announced themselves as the models for Ellida. In the press the book received very favourable notices, and at Christiania Theatre it became one of Ibsen's greatest successes. But in Sweden, Finland and in Denmark its reception was extremely mixed. Brandes refused to believe in the psychology of the play, and the Royal Theatre's censor, Erik Bøgh, advised against taking it on: he found it profoundly immoral, because it advised married couples to release each other when some male or female animal was 'fascinating' to the imagination or the senses. Fallesen, director of the theatre, accepted it all the same, but it was not a success in Copenhagen at first. Otherwise, the play was soon being performed all over most of Europe.

As usual Ibsen had a busy time seeing to his business affairs during the ensuing period, and there is nothing to show that he was seriously considering a new subject. But the summer and autumn of 1889 brought a dramatic development in his private life, an episode which in fact first became known after his death, when Georg Brandes, to everyone's consternation, made public a hitherto unknown series of letters in Ibsen's hand. These letters have been a cause of controversy ever since.

The purely outward course of events is clear and simple. Henrik and Suzannah Ibsen decided to go to the holiday resort of Gossensass, to spend the late summer and autumn there, as they had done several summers before, and this small seaside resort now wished to honour its world-famous guest by naming a square 'Ibsen Square'.

The formal ceremony took place on July 21 and the square lay so high up in this little Alpine town that the sixty-one-year-old author had some difficulty with the steep slopes, but he received the honours with great dignity. The following day, in the park by the hotel, Ibsen made the acquaintance of a young lady who was sitting reading alone on a bench. He had noticed her during the ceremony. The lady, or rather the young girl, was eighteen years old and belonged to Viennese society. She was of a romantic nature, had dreamy eyes and was called Emilie Bardach.

Ibsen had always been interested in young girls and this is not surprising. Every world-famous man—and Ibsen was that now—is an object of worship, not least from young girls, and his reputation as the champion of *women's* causes only served to enhance the worship. Besides it interested him to study young women, as he told Suzannah when she reproached him for allowing them to flirt with him; for he wanted to know whether their position in society really was as he had described it in his plays.

In addition it is reasonable to assume that he not only had a weakness for adulation in general, but also that he quite simply liked being adored by young women. No doubt sixty-one in those days was an even more advanced age than it is today, but Ibsen is not the only man in whom this weakness had survived and increased in old age. During the previous year, in North Jylland, his mild flirtations with several young girls had been sufficiently obvious to provoke controversy (still alive today) about which of two girls has left traces in the drama of the world: Ibsen is said to have told one of them that he wished to use her in his work and both have laid claim to being the model for his two portraits of Hilde.

But the story of Emilie Bardach was more serious than that. Emilie Bardach was romantic. She was in Gossensass with her mother, and whilst her mother and Suzannah talked about their problems, Henrik and Emilie went into out-of-the-way corners. Emilie fell in love once and for all: thenceforward she dedicated herself to becoming an Ibsen legend. She kept his letters as the treasures of her life and as soon as he was in his grave—she was then only thirty-five—she handed them over to Georg Brandes for publication. And in this way she also assured herself immortality—at least among Ibsen scholars, who will never cease to dispute over her rôle in Ibsen's life and work.

The drama of the situation was increased by the fact that the romance was observed at quite close quarters not only by Suzannah but also by another woman who also adored Ibsen, the twenty-four-year-old painter, Helene Raff, who was more intellectual and therefore more realistic in her love. She too kept a diary, and she was jealous of Emilie.

No one knows what in fact happened. Obviously nothing 'extreme' occurred, perhaps for several reasons on both his side and hers. But 'fires in old houses' are dangerous. Afterwards Ibsen wrote a number of letters, twelve in all, of which at least the first bears undeniable traces of love. With a priceless mixture of ordinary Ibsenish formal reserve and romantic love, he dreams—at his desk—of simply breaking with his gout-ridden Suzannah and going off into the world with this new young woman, who loves him so boundlessly.

It appears from his letter that one of the main subjects of conversation was the concepts of *Tollheit* and *Dummheit*, madness and stupidity. They both dissociated themselves from stupidity, and were to some extent devotees of madness, for Ibsen was inclined to call his unborn plays madnesses with which he was wrestling, while she was all for their committing 'mad deeds'.

Their association lasted two months, and then Ibsen returned to his desk in Munich and wrote his yearning letters, which gradually ebbed away in the course of the ensuing months, ending with him explaining firmly she must no longer write to him.

Only a year later, he spoke somewhat disparagingly about her to his young friend, Julius Elias, when in February, 1891, they were attending the première of *Hedda Gabler* in Berlin. He is said to have told Elias that *she* attached no importance to marrying a good young man, that she would undoubtedly never marry. What tempted her was captivating other women's husbands, or anyhow luring a husband away from his wife. She had been a demonic little *Zerstörerin* and had often seemed to him like a small beast of prey, who had chosen *him* as her victim. He had studied her very thoroughly. . . .

It attracted immense attention in Europe when Georg Brandes published these letters in Germany after Ibsen's death. Among the angry people was quite naturally Mrs Ibsen; but Julius Elias,

Ibsen's long-standing supporter, who was then in the process of helping her sort his posthumous papers, was angry too. Elias and Mrs Ibsen reduced the whole affair to a mere bagatelle, but Georg Brandes no doubt considered it refreshing that there was a crack in the sphinx's mask.

It would be out of place here to discuss to what extent there are features of Emilie in the play which Ibsen was brooding over when he met her, and which he completed the following year. Hedda Gabler is an extremely involved personality, composed of characteristics from many different individuals, and although Hedda's desire to play dangerous games and capture men from others might have been suggested by Emilie Bardach, her panic-stricken fear of scandal at least was not.

For more than ten years Ibsen had now concentrated almost entirely in his writing on the psychology of women: only *The Wild Duck* falls slightly outside the series of plays in which the study of various women, seen in relation to their environment, has been his main theme, the men in these plays being more conventional. It is a magnificent array of women that he has brought into the world, from Nora and Mrs Alving to Rebekka West and Ellida, and they are all seen with such clarity and psychological acumen that they have continued to live even when external circumstances have to some extent changed. But they also have another thing in common: they are fundamentally people who meet life boldly, positive in temperament and will, fully capable of a normal emotional life under different circumstances.

It is a logical development that a woman character with *opposite* tendencies, negative towards life, became Ibsen's next object of study. He certainly had no need to turn to Emile Bardach to find characteristics for her. The basic characteristic of this type is age-old and that it is not yet dead can be seen if one constructs an 'Ibsen play barometer' for the years after the second world war. *Hedda Gabler* is one of the most frequently performed of all Ibsen's plays. Perhaps it is symptomatic of a profound sociological truth that it is especially in the English-speaking world that this woman has had constant and huge success.

He did not have to take his Hedda 'from the open sea' or from
remote northern Norway. Neither was it necessary for him to
make her a woman who for conventional reasons, according to
the customs of the day, had married a little above herself. On the
contrary. Here he had a use for the general's daughter; and as he
says in his letter to his progressive French friend, Moritz Prozor:
'The title of the play is Hedda Gabler. By this I have wished to
indicate that as a personality she is to be understood as her
father's daughter rather than her husband's wife.'

Hedda Gabler is more intelligent than the previous main
characters, at any rate more intellectual, and she offers far more
detailed explanations of her own nature than the others do,
although the diagnosis is often based on self-deceit. Her most
prominent characteristic is cowardice—and it is undoubtedly
true, as Koht points out, that when it came to features illuminating
the psychology of cowardice, Ibsen did not need to go farther
than himself in order to learn. Cowardice had been a necessary
protection he had used to cover up his painful sensitivity, but at
the same time he felt it a humiliation to have to use camouflage,
because he had seen through both his own and others' cowardice
more profoundly than anyone.

But Hedda's cowardice is combined with, or has brought out,
a series of other negative sides in her character, curiosity coupled
with malice, joy in secretly causing unhappiness to quiet people;
and she compensates with arrogance for the self-contempt which
she does not wish to acknowledge. Towards the male sex, she
shows a mixture of fear of too close contact and contempt
because they are so easy to deceive.

To make this type quite clear, the woman who chooses to
develop indirectly, by intrigues and underhand means, Ibsen has
given her a husband who, as his character unfolds, is revealed as
constantly more and more innocent, out of touch with life,
pathetically naïve and an easy prey.

Hedda's anxiety becomes panic when she discovers that the
little contact she has had with life has made her pregnant, with
the consequence that she soon *must* face reality, instead of playing
the celebrated general's daughter and listening inquisitively to

bohemian confidences from suitors who can tell her about a world where terrible things happen.

The intrigue is spun with a mastery never before found in Ibsen's writing. His ability to simplify the intricate is quite exceptional. Nearly all the action in fact takes place off stage, and in the last draft even the scene leading up to the suicide; the piano-playing and the shot are moved out of view of the audience.

Here we should mention the special interpretation of the play which Ingmar Bergman, one of today's most famous producers, staged at the Royal Dramatic Theatre in Stockholm two years ago. To show how Hedda lives in her own world with no wish to be concerned with reality, he made the set so that behind and round his dark crimson Tesman drawing-room, with its heavy, fateful atmosphere, there was a kind of background world in the same colour. Hedda was there during the whole play, so that she too witnessed the scenes which, according to Ibsen's instructions, she is not supposed to hear. She was there from the rise of the curtain and she heard everything. She went into the drawing-room for the scenes in which she was supposed to be present and then left again to listen.

Ingmar Bergman's experiment put Hedda in new perspective. But nevertheless, it was not very successful. There was too great a distance between her and the other characters. In this interpretation Hedda was condemned to suicide from the very first moment.

Innumerable models have been suggested for various rôles in the play. Ibsen himself, in a kind of mixture of jest and seriousness, is said to have indicated Julius Elias as the model for Jørgen Tesman.

There was no enjoyable stay in Gossensass in the Tyrol that summer of 1890. Ibsen remained in Munich and worked. The play he was now working on was in a new style and broke new psychological ground, and the young painter, Miss Raff, who had now taken over Emilie Bardach's role as the author's young friend, but on a wholly filial level, is able to tell of many conversations on the psychology of women, on suicide, on free will and unintentional crimes. This time too, there is a profusion of notes by Ibsen, of which a number are perhaps used in the play, but a number are scraps of more casual origin.

Not until the latter half of November, 1890, has he finished and sent in the manuscript. For once he feels no melancholy over being separated from characters he has grown fond of, but deep relief at being rid of Hedda. He writes to his French friend Moritz Prozor:

'It is a strange feeling of emptiness for me, so suddenly parted from a work which for several months now has exclusively occupied my time and thoughts. But I must say it was good that it came to an end. The incessant association with these fictitious people in fact began to make me not a little nervous. With a respectful greeting to Countess Prozor, I sign myself. . . .'

Hedda Gabler came out before Christmas, 1890. It was published simultaneously in English, German, French, Dutch and Russian and was received with almost total confusion all over the world. A message was expected from Ibsen, if no more than pessimistic understanding of women's difficult position in society. But this female monster, this revolting female creature, received neither sympathy nor compassion. Even the cleverest literary experts, who over the years changed their minds about the play, sought in vain to find a solution to the puzzle. The only person in Norway to defend it was that Ibsen admirer, Gunnar Heiberg, who maintained that she was neither unreal nor incomprehensible. But he did not elaborate: he simply went on to jibe at all those who had written unfavourably about it.

This time too, Ibsen's new play was performed at a very large number of theatres round the world, but it was not until some years had gone by that the play's career on the stage began in earnest.

17

Home to Norway

THEN came new contracts, translations, stage rights, and later
that spring a triumphant trip to Vienna and Budapest, where
Ibsen was again honoured as one of the greatest playwrights in the
world. He had to be present at a long series of performances of his
plays, some good, some bad.

When he actually decided to return to Norway is uncertain. He
implies in a letter to Nils Lund, his Norwegian agent, in May,
1891, that he is thinking of going north for the summer. As late
as June, he writes about a 'summer trip' to Norway, but obviously
what he then wanted was to get to know the northern Norway
he had dreamed of ever since Suzannah's and Sigurd's travellers'
tales had set his imagination in action.

He and Suzannah arrived in Kristiania and soon went on, she to
Valdres, he to the North Cape—it has been noted that he did not
attempt to climb the North Cape, but remained on board ship.
Then back to Kristiania in August. It must have been at this time
that he decided to stay in Norway, at least for the winter, as in a
letter of August 11 he tells Gyldendal's new director, Frederik
Hegel's son Jacob, that he has taken an apartment in Kristiania.
'Naturally we are not considering staying here all the year round,
but will be travelling about, as hitherto. Thus it is only our point
of departure that has changed. This winter we shall stay here
though, and I have planned a large new dramatic work, which,
under any circumstances, it is my intention to complete up here.'

The apartment was in the commanding, elegant building
complex of Victoria Terrace, and it is described later by Peter
Nansen as large and uncomfortable, but definitely elegant.

There have been many guesses as to the reasons why Ibsen

eventually decided to settle in Norway. The fact that both his and Suzannah's health had deteriorated considerably may have given Ibsen the idea that the climate in Munich was at any rate not good for him; and Suzannah is said to have told enquirers that Ibsen wanted to die at home. Considering the indomitable will-power and capacity for work he showed during the next ten years, this explanation is hardly valid.

But it is more probable that he knew that he would be able to help his son Sigurd much more effectively from Kristiania than from Munich. Sigurd at this time was going through a crisis in his life and Ibsen was, as we have heard before, always eager to help him.

After Sigurd had been an attaché first in Washington and then in Vienna, it gradually became more and more evident that the Swedish Foreign Ministry wished to do everything in its power to place obstacles in the way of his career. As we know, Sigurd Ibsen was self-confident and not given to showing diplomatic caution. He was no doubt unsuited to subordinate positions and anyhow it did not suit him at all to see how subordinate Norway's position was in the Swedish-Norwegian Foreign Service. It may be mentioned that he defiantly continued to write his reports in Norwegian, although this was quite contrary to custom.

As early as December, 1889, the crisis grew acute. Now, Henrik Ibsen wrote an indignant letter to the Prime Minister, Emil Stang, insisting that the Norwegian government should intervene. The Swedish Foreign Ministry had obviously based its rejection of Sigurd's application for promotion on his lack of Norwegian legal qualifications. Now the Norwegian government would have to arrange to have such a ridiculous regulation altered! Ibsen threatened that with his world reputation he would bring about a great public settling of accounts.

It did not help, however. In January, 1890, Sigurd Ibsen resigned, went to Norway and started a campaign, which aroused a great deal of attention, on Norway's subordinate position in this field. To some extent it can be said that Sigurd Ibsen was the man who instigated the fight for an independent Norwegian Foreign

Service, a battle which fifteen years later brought about the break between Sweden and Norway. He was now writing political articles for Norwegian newspapers and journals, and it is understandable that his father wished to follow his activities at closer quarters.

There was undoubtedly a crisis in Ibsen's marriage at this time. When he went to the North Cape and she to Valdres, it was because they had quarrelled. And as there is not a single letter preserved from Ibsen to Suzannah during his North Cape trip, one can assume that the reason was the same, for Suzannah was very careful to keep Henrik's letters and in the ordinary way he was an extremely industrious and informative correspondent when they were apart. But we have more than just conjecture to rely on. A letter he wrote to Suzannah in Italy about four years later, the main point of which we shall return to in proper chronological order, reveals the crisis of 1891. In May, 1895, Ibsen writes:

'And now I come to the second main point of your letter. You insist that I shall take another residence. And, naturally, when you demand this so decisively, I shall do so. But in your letter you reproach me for taking our present one without consulting you. (You were in Valdres at the time and not in the kind of mood in which I could think of asking your advice.) When you now come home and find our new residence rented and furnished then you must remember that I have done this according to your own express insistence, and that this time too, I have not been in a position to consult you.'

It is nevertheless remarkable that we have no letters from Ibsen to Suzannah for the whole period from September, 1891, to May, 1892. This could possibly be because the crisis between them had become so acute that in her temperamental way she had burnt them all because they contained hasty and angry words. But this is hardly likely. That she did not destroy the letter of May, 1895, to which we shall return later, indicates that she was not in the habit of protecting her own future reputation by keeping the good letters and tearing up the bad ones; and crisis or no crisis, when the two of them were apart Ibsen felt a constant need to confide in her daily. Everything in short, indicates that several letters from him to her during this winter have been lost.

There is plenty of evidence that married life between these two old people was anything but idyllic. Both were explosive, bad-tempered and irritable by nature, but Ibsen was a man of habit and his need for Suzannah when she was away from him is so potent that his letters make almost comical reading. Both at Victoria Terrace and in Arbiens Street, they each arranged a fortress, each in a separate part of the apartment. The legendary wicked stepmother, Magdalene Thoresen, who was now much more sprightly than Suzannah, described them thus: 'They are two solitary people—each one alone—absolutely alone.' But it is just as certain that they were nevertheless indispensable to one another.

Not until this has been established can one begin to tell of Ibsen's last, moving and pathetic romance, which began when Suzannah was wintering in Italy and which continued for nine years. A friendship, a father-and-daughter love, a working partnership, and the last long shaft of sunlight on to a lonely old writer's life. For many years the only crack in the Ibsen-mask which could not be concealed was his letters to Emilie Bardach. Private matters such as his illegitimate son born when he was eighteen years of age were not talked about. There was silence on Ibsen's knowledge of the gossip round his parents' inharmonious marriage. And though everyone talked about his friendship with Hildur Andersen it remained on the gossip level until this fine artist died, over ninety years old, in 1956. She had by then systematically destroyed all letters and possessions which might have given her a place in the history of world literature, but she had told Professor Francis Bull enough about the friendship which had meant so much to her and to Ibsen for Bull to write a worthy memorial to her after her death.

Bull relates that Ibsen met her for the first time when he was in Norway in 1874. She was then a musical little girl of ten. She was the granddaughter of one of the very few people to whom

Ibsen remained devotedly attached all his life. This was Mrs Sontum in Bergen, his motherly landlady during his first year there, who cooked for him all the time he was in Bergen. How much she helped him financially and with credit is a secret between the two of them. But it is certain that Helena Sontum (called 'Madam' in Bergen, as was any woman who ran boarding houses, besides being married to a merchant, which merely gave her the title of Mrs), was a mother to him.

In 1874, in Kristiania, he must therefore soon have visited Mrs Sontum's daughter, now married to a Bergener, O. M. Andersen, whom Ibsen had also known in Bergen and who had become a city engineer and fire chief in Kristiania. It shows the closeness of Ibsen's relations with the Sontum family that when he returned to Norway he chose Mrs Sontum's grandson as his personal physician, transferring to Dr Edvard Bull on Dr Sontum's death.

When Ibsen came back from the North Cape in August, 1891, he again visited the Andersen household. The musical daughter, Hildur, was then on a walking tour in the mountains. She was already a fully qualified pianist and twenty-seven years old. A few days later she returned from her walking tour and Ibsen and Hildur became good friends, indeed they soon became such close friends that they later celebrated their friendship-day on September 19. And Hildur Andersen's self-effacing modesty had not sufficed to prevent that day from being memorable in the drama of the world. That is the date of which Hilde reminds Master Builder Solness when, ten years after their first meeting, she insists that he shall give her the kingdom he has promised her.

The young pianist became Ibsen's constant companion. She helped him furnish his apartment, she discussed with him his plans for plays. In addition, he very much liked company when he attended the theatre or lectures and Hildur Andersen even managed to lure the profoundly unmusical Ibsen with her to concerts.

Their first three visits to theatres took place in September, to gala performances held in his honour. Christiania Theatre honoured him with *Hedda Gabler* and with the hundredth performance of *The League of Youth*—no other play had ever been performed so often in that theatre. The third was arranged by August Lindberg, the Swedish theatrical manager, who for years had toured round Scandinavia with Ibsen's plays, and who at one time was the first to stage *Ghosts* in Kristiania. Now he did so again, and with Ibsen himself in the audience.

On October 7 Hildur Andersen was sitting beside him in the front row when the young Knut Hamsun held his first lecture on modern Norwegian literature. Hamsun had made his debut with *Hunger* the year before, and was now travelling round the country giving three lectures on literature. They aroused attention, partly because they contained witty and sarcastic attacks on Ibsen's writings, for which he had no good word to say, though otherwise, as Nils Collett Vogt remarked, it was by now almost sacrosanct in Norway.

Hildur Andersen has told Francis Bull that Hamsun grew visibly nervous when he discovered that Ibsen had accepted his invitation and had come to the lecture. And Ibsen's intense gaze increased the lecturer's nervousness and goaded him into increasing the violence of his attacks. She adds that a few days later Ibsen said: 'Well, I suppose you remember it is this evening we are to go together to Mr Hamsun's second lecture.' 'You don't mean to say,' she replied, 'that you want to hear that impudent fellow again?' Ibsen: 'You must see that we shall have to go down and learn how to write!'

Hamsun was attacking 'problem' literature, which he wanted to replace with a new psychological literature, which could illuminate the roots of the soul down to its most secret sources. Half measures were no longer enough and the divisions must be very much finer. The task was, while retaining the daylight of conscious life, to reach into the obscure and mysterious elements which had not yet been wholly explained.

That Hamsun discussed in one stroke all four great men— Ibsen, Bjørnson, Kielland and Lie—was in itself understandable, for they were all known to their contemporaries as writers of problem literature. His attack on Ibsen was the fiercest because he was the greatest; besides which, he really did loathe Ibsen, though paradoxically he admired Bjørnson.

Nevertheless it is remarkable that Hamsun at this moment in time was so short-sighted in his loathing of Ibsen that he did not realize that Ibsen had long ago embarked on the very course for which Hamsun had made himself spokesman. A number of main characters which Ibsen had created during the past decade betray by nuances in their personalities and behaviour the workings of the subconscious mind.

Ibsen and Hildur Andersen discussed the plans for his new play that winter, until February, 1892, when she went to Vienna to continue her music studies. But then they exchanged letters, and telegrams too, on details in the play. One day Ibsen was so dissatisfied with his drafts that he destroyed all the preparatory work he had done and began again. It is highly probable that this, so contrary to Ibsen's now ingrained habit, may have had something to do with Hildur Andersen, for at the beginning of May Suzannah returned home and the notes may have borne traces of an intimacy about which Ibsen did not wish Suzannah to know.

That *The Master Builder* is a self-portrait and a self-scrutiny is fairly evident. Others had called him the Master Builder and that was how he had described himself. The play is written in a mixture of arrogance and resignation, a great writer's confession to a young admirer; this is both its strength and its weakness—its strength in that the play, when the main parts are taken by actors of stature and personality, can be moving and lucid, its weakness because behind the effective façade it is very much shallower and simpler than several of Ibsen's previous dramas.

Its use of images and symbolic language is almost obtrusive. The problem is the same as in many of the other plays from his youth onwards—the struggle between external ambition and the search for truth, between aesthetic and ethical demands on himself, between noble endeavours and inner betrayal. All this is there, translated into master builder's language, which in our day seems transparent and with a slightly comical hope to it; even the homes of the people have been tricked out like the churches with towers and spires.

But the Master Builder's guilty conscience looks forward as well as back—back because he knows that in his life he has not been complete and genuine, but has broken his own rules of the game, forward because he knows he has made demands on and aroused expectations in the young, whom he dare not face: he cannot meet his obligations towards them, and that makes him 'dizzy'.

The young come knocking at the door from two directions. First comes the young woman who insists on the kingdom he has promised her. She is more of a personification than a character. She is Miss Bardach, Miss Raff, Miss Hildur Andersen and his own Hilde from *The Lady from the Sea*. As Hildur Andersen's and Ibsen's 'friendship-date' is specifically mentioned in the play, we can perhaps assume that it is dedicated to Hildur Andersen— that it is to her that he speaks the soliloquy on responsibility and moral frailty that *The Master Builder* really is.

From the other side comes the young artist, the new master builder, who is held down by Solness, by this colossus with feet of clay who has his immense authority to defend. Young Brovik is Knut Hamsun, slightly disguised. And here we must digress to mention a matter which gave Ibsen good cause for a guilty conscience.

When Ibsen was in Norway in 1885, after the debate in Parliament on a writer's pension for Kielland, when he discovered how bitterly alone he was in both rightist and leftist circles, he was crying in the wilderness for new contacts. He directed his hopes towards the women, the workers and youth. And he promised youth to be their 'pivot-man' on the extreme left wing.

A couple of years later the rebellion of Norwegian youth took place, politically in that a socialist workers' party was founded, and artistically in that impressionism appeared in painting and writing. Bourgeois anger was white hot, and this gave rise to two prosecutions, one against Hans Jaeger, a philosophical-literary figure, and his somewhat theoretical novel, *From Bohemian Cirles in Kristiania*, and the other against Christian Krogh, the painter and writer, and his novel about a young prostitute, *Albertine*. Both cases should have struck Ibsen to the heart. Both were caused by the authors bringing out into the light taboo subjects of the same kind that Ibsen himself had dealt with. On each occasion the case ended with the author being sentenced because he had rebelled against man's monopoly of double morality. But the 'pivot-man' on the extreme left wing of youth remained silent, he who was still to see his *Ghosts* banned in several places throughout the world. He did not take part in the noisy controversy, as, for instance, Bjørnson did. He kept silent, despite his fine phrases on the transitoriness of ideals.

He had, in fact, good cause for a guilty conscience though, and it should be added in mitigation that he does not let Solness doubt in his mind for one moment that young Brovik has talent and right on his side.

There is, however, one peculiarity of *The Master Builder* that only one literary scholar, oddly enough, has noticed, and no producer, as far as I know, has used on the stage. It is Professor Seip, who writes in the introduction to the play's centenary edition: 'Much of what happens in *The Master Builder* is very vulnerable if one takes reality as a starting-point. The explanation is that most of it takes place in Solness' soul, and these inner events are illustrated by external actions. . . .'

During the winter and spring of 1892, while Ibsen was still struggling in vain with drafts of *The Master Builder* and Suzannah was nursing her health in Italy, important things were nevertheless happening in this small family. Sigurd became engaged to Bjørnstjerne Bjørnson's daughter, Bergliot, who was twenty-two and had trained as a singer in Paris. What started it was that Bjørnson, full of enthusiasm for Sigurd Ibsen's journalistic writing in 1890 and 1891, had invited him to Aulestad to embrace him. But the newspapers and the general public were very interested in visitors to Aulestad and society gossip began to appear in the press on whether the two great writers would now be related by marriage.

Bergliot and Sigurd did, in fact, fall in love and the Bjørnson family, and undoubtedly Suzannah Ibsen too, were delighted about the engagement. That Father Ibsen was not is evident from the following furious letter which Father Bjørnson sent to his daughter in March, 1892:

'My dear Bergliot,

'You are much too young to understand all the *wrong* Ibsen has done me.

'It could all be a thing of the past. But he came here to Norway without even sending me a greeting. Sigurd became betrothed, and he greeted neither my mother nor my brother, and does not speak to Bjørn, except in passing.

'He even repudiated the betrothal itself. He did so repeatedly and most distinctly. To me he said (at Ole Olsen's) that Sigurd had said to his mother, that *if* he were ever married, then it would be to Bergliot.

'I greeted him, and he returned the greeting. And I did not see any more of him, except in company.

'From this one can draw only one conclusion; he wants nothing to do with us. So be it! But then I too want in truth to be a free man and say exactly what I think of him and his recent writing and personality. He has had bad friends who make mischief. Think of tolerating a fellow like Hans Jaeger! And others too! One can never be sure of anyone who takes notice of "such people" and anonymous letters. But I will refrain from all these accusations, I have *not* complained about Ibsen, either to you or to others.

'You can tell Sigurd this just as it is. He is so honest and talented, that I am pleased every time I meet him. . . .

'Very best regards to the Sørensens.

'Your father
'friend B. B.'

But they were married, although without Ibsen's blessing. The letter in which Bjørnson invites the Ibsen family to the wedding at Aulestad on October 11 bears witness to a state of armed neutrality on Bjørnson's part. He suggests that the Ibsens stay at Lillehammer, so that they can travel back again on the day of the wedding; but for the sake of the young and to avoid gossip the Ibsens must come. It appears from the letter that the old Bjørnsons have not considered being present at the church ceremony, because they themselves think that 'it is false', and the young also appear to agree. So it must have been Suzannah who had insisted on a church wedding.

The chilly atmosphere between these two great writers at this time is clearly shown by Ibsen's telegram of good wishes to Bjørnson on December 8, 1892, his sixtieth birthday: 'Henrik Ibsen sends his best wishes for your birthday.'

Meanwhile Ibsen was in Kristiania putting the finishing touches to *The Master Builder*, which was published on December 12 in the usual first edition of 10,000 copies.

It came out almost simultaneously in a large number of languages and for a while was performed at theatres all over the world. This was not a play that would cause controversy. It is evident that the symbols and imagery confused people and led to over-interpretation, but the criticism that appeared was respectful, almost deferential.

During the period that followed Ibsen was very much occupied with helping his son Sigurd, who was having difficulty in finding a political platform. The Norwegian Liberal government was pleased with Sigurd's polemics on Sweden's undervaluation of Norway in foreign affairs. But Norway had no Foreign Ministry of her own, so the government could not find office for him, and it was not possible to live on freelance political journalism in Norway at that time. Both Ibsen and Bjørnson were active on his behalf, and they were by no means nobodies. The lengths to which Ibsen went are shown in a letter to Sigurd in February, 1893. Ibsen had then met Olaus Arvesen, a Member of Parliament, who himself probably had no particular political influence, but who furthered Ibsen's cause with those who had. Ibsen writes to Sigurd:

'I then took the opportunity to express, quietly, but with considerable force, my personal opinion on the government's behaviour towards you. I said that you had now for some time put yourself at the disposal of the government, but that all their fine promises to you had remained unfulfilled. I told him that on his own initiative Steen had already last year told me that the instituting of the political office under the Ministry of the Interior had been decided on, and was to be carried out in the near future. But that hitherto, as far as I knew, nothing had been done, and that I had now therefore lost all belief in or reliance on the government's promises and statements. I ended by energetically, slowly and cold-bloodedly telling him that I was now therefore thinking of deciding to renounce my Norwegian citizenship, leaving the country in the autumn and becoming naturalized in Bavaria, and would suggest that you did the same.'

It is clear that the terrified Arvesen has reported the matter fully to the authorities concerned. The fury of two giants, and the threat of the world scandal it would cause if Ibsen renounced his Norwegian citizenship, were frightening. But the rules of the political game are a world of their own. Ibsen neither bothered about them nor understood them. Bjørnson knew them, but intentionally set himself above them. Anyhow, there was no permanent appointment for Sigurd this time. Then the Steen government fell, so other ways out had to be tried, including applying for a personal professorship for Sigurd.

Ibsen also had another matter to deal with. He wished to follow up his success with *Peer Gynt* and Grieg by turning *The Vikings at Helgeland* into an opera; he started turning the dialogue into verse, and also worked on Grieg, who was at the time at Grefsen Spa, near Kristiania. Grieg took courage and refused.

In the late autumn of 1893 a number of authors had foregathered and agreed to form a Society of Authors. On April 29, 1894, invitations to an inaugural meeting were sent out, to be held on May 7. Henrik Ibsen's name was among those on the invitation, and he went to the meeting. The meeting itself was conducted in a peaceful and orderly manner, but afterwards there was some steady drinking among a number of younger authors and suddenly Nils Kjaer stepped forward and made a speech which developed into a violent attack on the older writers—there could be no doubt to whom this was addressed: 'We hate you! But your day is over'. Ibsen never set foot in the society again, but remained a member.

Not until all this was over did Ibsen continue with his dramatic work. The result was *Little Eyolf*, which was published on December 11, 1894.

With reference to his very last play, *When We Dead Awaken*, which came out in 1899, and which he called an 'epilogue', Ibsen himself has said that it was *not* meant to be an epilogue to all his writing, but to his contemporary dramas. In reality, it is an epilogue to three of them, *The Master Builder*, *Little Eyolf* and *John Gabriel Borkman*. And there is an obvious connection between them. They are plays about men's feelings of guilt, or more specifically, Ibsen's; variations on the same theme, which come to a noble, tragic conclusion in the epilogue.

The first play is about the victorious master who begins to suspect his own motives and stumbles on the fact of his own betrayal, the good cause for his 'guilty conscience'. Then follows *Little Eyolf*, the richest and most various of the three, but at the same time the one that is most marred by external symbols. It is a play on a psychological problem which Ibsen touched on several times before, but which science first discovered and examined. some decades later. It is about a consistent self-deceiver, Hjalmar Ekdal's blood brother, now seen from new and revealing points of view. It concerns the man who, meaning well, makes others believe in him, but who has neither the ability nor the character to fulfil their expectations, and who is brought face to face with his own inadequacy.

Both the play's merits and its weaknesses are directly related to Ibsen's methods of working. To an even greater extent than in Germany, he had become a solitary man. He did sometimes go out in company, especially with the Sontum and Andersen families, whom he considered his nearest contacts. He also attended gentlemen's dinners at the Conservative Club, *Andvake*. After being elected to the Humanist Society he occasionally attended meetings there; and for years he went for his short daily walk to the Grand Café, where he had a drink, sat in his reserved place and read the newspapers, nearly always obviously un-approachable.

When one also knows that at home he lived in a state of armed neutrality with Suzannah, we have a pathetic picture of an ageing genius, with a world reputation which no one since Goethe had attained, voluntarily enclosed in a mental cloister of his own making. He has testified to the fact that during the last nine years of his writing he had had valuable assistance and support from his young 'artist friend', but this does not make his isolation any less. The assistance he had from her was the opportunity to think aloud. And she had listened with almost too great an understanding, unable to offer him any new material from experience, to illuminate a man's feelings of guilt, or any *criticism* of the kind that Suzannah must have been able to give him earlier.

This time too, Ibsen needed an alien element to set the action going, so that one self-scrutiny inevitably leads to the next. He has chosen his catalyst from the old story he heard in his childhood in Skien, about the Rat Woman, a local edition of the Pied Piper of Hamelin. This figure was undoubtedly greeted with enthusiasm by his young friend, as something extremely profound and symbolic, and was indeed given a diversity of interpretations when the play came out. Today the Rat Woman usually seems depressing on the stage, a superfluous and rather cheap symbol in an otherwise profound and totally realistic play.

Little Eyolf's psychology is consistent and clear. The warm-blooded Rita has fallen in love with Alfred and married him, but after a brief spell of sensual ecstasy he moves away from her and she notices that she is constantly losing ground. Her fierce jealousy of everything that binds him elsewhere increases his feelings of guilt at having married her for her money. He clutches at anything which will keep Rita at a distance: at the book with the characteristic title *Human Responsibility*, at his weakly son and at his incestuous love for the younger sister, Asta.

In this situation, the son causes feelings of guilt in both parents. To elucidate matters further it should be mentioned that Ibsen lets the boy change during his progress from working manuscript to final formulation. While right up to the autumn of 1894 Eyolf was thought of as a somewhat ordinary, but weakly lad, he becomes a cripple in the finished play. Thus the parents have yet another reason to feel guilty, since they are directly responsible for his condition, having, out of carelessness and inattention, dropped him on the floor when he was a baby.

To start this psychological avalanche, therefore, Ibsen had to begin the play by doing away with the son. It was for this purpose that the Rat Women was invented, but Eyolf might just as well have drowned in a 'natural' way, caused by some heedlessness or other on the parents' part.

After this external dramatic action, the tension is transferred to an inner level. Alfred and Rita strip each other's pretences away layer after layer, until they reach a state of paralysing resignation. Asta, the sister, is brought to the same condition by being forced to admit that her 'sisterly' love for Alfred has basically been anything but sisterly. She lets Borghejm, the healthy road-builder, take care of her.

At the end of the play there is also a somewhat superfluous symbol in the Norwegian flag, which is hoisted to mark the fact that hereafter Alfred and Rita will devote themselves to responsibility for their fellow-human beings, the poor boys, instead of fostering their own egoism. At the time the flag was also taken as mysterious and profound symbolism.

Has *Little Eyolf* a happy ending? Yes, superficially it has, but Ibsen himself had some doubts. When the play was to be performed for the first time at the Christiania Theatre on January 15, 1895, Ibsen was there, openly in the company of the Andersen and Sontum families—Suzannah was in Italy again. He asked for as many as ten tickets for the first night, but wished to pay for them. Mrs Caroline Sontum had related that at a restaurant afterwards Ibsen asked her: 'Do you think Rita will really take care of those naughty boys. Don't you think that it's just a Sunday mood?' Two people, and especially the man, who have been addicted to self-deception all through their lives, would be expected to deceive themselves even in their new disguises.

Ibsen completed the manuscript in the middle of October, 1894, and the publication date was December 11. By that time the necessary rights would be secured all over the world.

Little Eyolf received extra pre-publication publicity because Thomas Krag, the writer, slipped into Graebe's printing works in

Copenhagen to steal a look at the proofs and told *Politiken* about it. There was a great fuss about this indiscretion, and also a wild race to get hold of *Little Eyolf* on the quay when the boat from Copenhagen to Kristiania arrived on December 11, late in the day, on account of a fog in the fjord.

Two things happened in Ibsen's private life before the book was published. First Sigurd, his son, had proposed that there should be a chair in Sociology at the University of Kristiania; with that began the years of struggle for a chair for Sigurd.

The other was that Suzannah, again accompanied by Sigurd, was to go to Italy for the winter, to spas which were said to be especially good for rheumatic patients. She hated the apartment in Victoria Terrace, which was damp, and in particular she believed that the long dark corridor had made her legs worse. Bergliot says that the apartment had other snags too—it was infested with mice. But Ibsen knew what to do: 'In the evening I take a glass of milk and some rusks into my room. I give the mice a little of this in a bowl and put it in the next room, so that they do not come near me.'

From December, 1894, until the beginning of May, 1895, Ibsen writes no fewer than fifteen letters, some very long, to Suzannah, about this and that, mostly minor matters. Although there had been violent quarrels and outbursts between them for many years, these letters show how totally dependent Ibsen was on their daily companionship and the routine life she had administered for him with the help of their maid. Some examples of the tone of his letters show this. In the first letter, he assures her that everything is perfectly all right with him and that the food which they fetch from the caterer, or the boarding house, is excellent.

'There is plenty of it too, so we have ample for supper if I want it. But I prefer to eat herring with the most delicious hot potatoes Lina cooks in the new machine. She looks after everything for me with the greatest care. Bergliot had dinner here on Sunday. Otherwise no one has been here. The evenings are lonely, of course, but then I sit and read at the dining-table. ...'

This idyll is emphasized so much that it appears almost suspect. I wonder whether before she left, Suzannah had regarded his friendship with the young pianist with some suspicion and told him that when he was alone he was to behave himself? Or whether in the evenings he did not enjoy the diversion of pleasant conversations with Hildur all the same?

The following letters tell of *Little Eyolf*'s overwhelming success, with money streaming in from all over Europe: only a month after publication the play has reached an edition of 13,250 copies with his own publisher alone. He speaks of his fortune, which is growing, and he emphasizes his idyllic solitude.

'Here at home everything is in excellent and regular order. Lina is exemplary in every way. She just seems to live and breathe in order to do everything in the way she knows you would like.'

A little later, Ibsen writes to Suzannah about the purchase of a painting of a certain interest.

'At the big exhibition, I have bought a masterpiece by Chr. Krohg. It is really a portrait of Strindberg, but Sigurd calls it "The Revolution" and I call it "Madness Breaking Out". It was Sigurd who urged me to buy it for the comparatively remarkably low price of 500 kroner.'

This brief passage reveals a great deal about Ibsen's attitude to art, including his own. He does not see a painted portrait as an image of a person, but as a painting of his soul, a portrait of the human being behind the external features. Most people did not see art in this way at the time. But it also says something of Ibsen's attitude to aggressive youth that he wished to have his young 'mortal enemy', August Strindberg, in order to stare at him across his desk for the rest of his life. No writer had opposed Ibsen's view of women so implacably as had Strindberg, ever since the publication of *A Doll's House*.

But the price itself is significant too. Five hundred kroner was, for instance, almost two full months' salary for the head of a government office, and it was a very high price for a painting by a forty-three-year-old painter. Edvard Munch, eleven years younger, sold his paintings at this time for less than a tenth of this price.

Ibsen continues his confidential chat in letters to Suzannah throughout the spring of 1895, about food and money and politics. In a letter of April 13 he exclaims: 'We now have 166,000 kroner invested. Even I dare to say that that is well done.' He is right in that. Until the middle of the 1890s he had had to take all possible precautions to protect himself against literary pirates in every country, and had nevertheless managed to accumulate a fortune which is the equivalent of several million kroner in Norway today. The Berne Convention first came into being during these years and protected the copyright of cultural works, anyhow in most countries of importance to Ibsen. But Denmark, where his own publisher was, did not sign the Berne Convention until 1903, so he still had to see to the protection of his copyright personally. But he could take his precautions and the money poured in.

Then in May, 1895, a new crisis arose in his married life. Biographically speaking, its only interest is that it is puzzling how he was able to continue his friendship with Hildur Andersen, whom Suzannah from now on would not tolerate in her home. As late as September, 1900, he thanked her for nine years' uninterrupted collaboration when, after his first stroke, he sent her a bouquet with the words: 'Nine red roses for you. Nine rose-red years for me. Accept the roses in gratitude for the years.'

This controversy has its human interest, because it throws light on the old writer's attitude to those around him. It was in the spring of 1895 that his step-mother-in-law, the meddlesome Magdalene Thoresen, had heard the gossip in Kristiania, where rumour had it that Ibsen was still going about with his thirty-one-year-old friend. As usual two and two made five and collating this with Suzannah's long absence abroad, people said that he was now seeking a divorce. Magdalene soon reported this to Suzannah in Italy, and though Suzannah had trouble with her legs, her spirit and temperament did not fail her over the years, so she sent her Henrik a powerful volley across the bows. In the previously mentioned letter of May 7, 1895, Ibsen replies for the defence:

'My dear Suzannah,

'It has hurt me acutely to read your latest letter dated May 1. And I hope that you now, after due consideration, are sorry that you sent it to me. It is your stepmother, the damned old sinner, who once again has been busy and trying to cause unhappiness by inciting us against each other. But it is easy to see who is behind that poor dotty creature. . . .'

A little later he says,

'I do not understand your stepmother's bombastic mode of expression and artificial profundities. Have never understood them. But when she writes something about my "wanting to be free at any price"—then I can solemnly assure you and explain that I have never seriously considered or meant any such thing and neither shall I ever think or mean any such thing. What I may have blurted out to you in the excitement when outbreaks of your moods and temper have been driving me to momentary despair is another matter and nothing to set any great store by. But my earnest advice is that if you wish to preserve your peace of mind, which is necessary for your health, then you should cease all kind of correspondence with your mentally confused stepmother. It is possible that she means everything for the best for you. But that woman's interference in any matter or in a relationship has always shown itself to be fatal. . . .'

The words speak for themselves and any comment is superfluous. But six weeks go by before he writes another letter, and then they come thick and fast, as if nothing had happened. And fundamentally that is probably true.

In a letter of June 21, he tells her about their new apartment:

'I have given up the apartment in Victoria Terrace and rented two floors in the new building the Hoff brothers are fitting out on the corner of Arbiens Street and Drammens Road. Sigurd and Bergliot were the ones to suggest it and I think you will find you are satisfied with it. I shall have a large study with direct access to the entrance, so that people who come to see me will not need to enter any other room in the apartment. So you will have free and exclusive use of the big corner drawing-room with a balcony, and beside this an almost equally large living-room with a door into the dining-room, where there is room to seat twenty to twenty-two people, with a niche for a sideboard which I shall buy. From the dining-room, you go directly into a spacious library, and from there into your bedroom, which is considerably larger than mine is here in the Terrace. My bedroom is next to it, and has a balcony. You need not use the corridor except when you go to the bathroom. . . .'

What Suzannah was perhaps never allowed to know was that it was Hildur Andersen who helped the unpractical Ibsen to furnish the new apartment.

Of Ibsen's daily life during these years, it is worth noting that he was pestered by visitors. Not only did his literary champions from all over the world come to confer with him, but also leading painters and sculptors wished to paint and model him, and he patiently sat for them for hours over weeks and months. Inquisitive and curious admirers also plagued him. Bergliot relates an amusing episode. An American rang the bell and asked to see Ibsen and his study, but was refused. The next day he came again and said that he had travelled all the way from America for this purpose alone. So Suzannah took pity on him, and she tells Bergliot:

'I opened the door and the American came in and bowed. Ibsen was standing in the doorway of his study in complete silence, glaring at him in absolute fury. The American did not say anything either. He just sneaked cautiously along the wall, past Ibsen and into the study. He sneaked on and up to the desk, snatched up a pencil and rushed out. Without a greeting, without a word.'

After which Ibsen berated Suzannah for letting foreign thieves come in and steal his pencils.

So he sat through the winter and spring of 1895 in his grand, icy and mouse-ridden apartment in Victoria Terrace, meditating and thinking, with Lina looking after him. That he had not at this time any new play in preparation appears from a letter to William Archer, as late as the end of June, in which he indicates that he hopes to have a new work ready the following year. His reading that winter includes Georg Brandes's book on the aged Goethe's love affair with Marianna von Willemer. This took place when Goethe was roughly the same age as Ibsen was now. He thanks him for the book and writes:

'When I think of the character of Goethe's work during the years in question, his resurgence of youth, then it seems to me that I ought to have been able to guess that he must have been blessed with something rather wonderful for him, like meeting Marianne von Willemer of all people. Destiny, chance, opportunity can in fact still be benevolent and kindly forces occasionally.'

One can draw one's own conclusions. But at the same time, he seems genuinely honest in his anxiety over Suzannah's health, although his motives are perhaps not quite so honest when throughout the summer and autumn he constantly emphasizes that it is exclusively for the sake of Suzannah's health that she should stay in Italy for a longer period, and anyhow not return home until the move to Arbiens Street is complete.

In the summer of 1895, he was again defeated in his fight for Sigurd's future. The University in Kristiania did not include a chair in Sociology in its budget proposals. But Sigurd's father and father-in-law again trod the path of personal pressure on politicians. Ibsen personally visited the city's two most influential rightist editors, Beatzmann and Vogt, but although they were very willing to help, they had to explain to him that the Conservatives in Parliament would be unlikely to follow them and neither were the Liberals especially willing to set up a 'parliamentary chair', so there the matter had to rest.

On October 15 Ibsen moved into his new apartment and a few days later Suzannah came home after nearly a year's absence. It looks as if her jealousy had also included the incomparable Lina, whom in a letter she insists be dismissed. Ibsen protested, saying that in any case it must not happen before the move was over. But she must have left by October 30, as on that day Ibsen writes a very favourable reference for her.

Not until April, 1896, in a letter to Georg Brandes, does Ibsen mention that 'now I am occupied with preparations for a big new piece of work. . . .' In July, he reports to Jacob Hegel that an exceptionally warm summer is making the work easier for him and on September 6 that he has completed the manuscript and has started the clean copy; and on October 20 he sends the manuscript in.

John Gabriel Borkman is the third in the series of his 'self-examinations'. As with Solness and Allmers, Borkman carries a burden of guilt which he cannot escape and which has undermined and destroyed him inwardly, because he has used different moral yardsticks, one for what he wants out of life, and another in his personal relationships. But whilst the Master Builder openly acknowledges his guilty conscience, which makes him dizzy, and Allmers is extremely reluctantly forced to admit to the self-deception behind which he has hidden, Borkman consistently denies all guilt.

It seems paradoxical at first sight that Ibsen, the arch-individualist, who let Brand, the priest, drive everything and everyone round him to destruction because his vocation demanded it, has now such a guilty conscience in his old age. But in reality this is both psychologically and logically consistent, as will become evident from a brief recapitulation of the course of his development. He begins with *Catiline*, in which he shows the rebel placed between the forces of good and evil. He continues writing about 'ideals', but broadly speaking they were ideals and aesthetic requirements he had learned from reading. The fact that sharp characterization emerged from this at times is proved by the fact that some of his early dramas still have dramatic tension and are performed all over the world today.

Then his own immense inner contrasts, his *ideas*, exploded into the two revolutionizing dramatic works *Brand* and *Peer Gynt*. Although they contain an excessive profusion of human features and living characters, they were meant to be poems about the ruthless demand of individualism for truth and wholeness.

After these two 'messages' from some of the best and weakest elements in himself, he occupied a central position, in the middle of his own day, and was able to write comprehensively about the defects and weaknesses of contemporary society and individual people. With the help of intuition and intelligence and fantastic powers of observation, but without any profound knowledge of the psychological research of his day, he became incontestably the greatest psychologist and dramatist of his time.

It is illuminating that for many years he came to concern himself chiefly with the destinies of women, not only because women were an oppressed minority in society, but also because, still under the pressure of social conditions, they covered such an immensely wide range of stages of development that they especially captivate the first explorer of human psychology.

As a person, Henrik Ibsen had been tormented by a secret ambition of immeasurable dimensions, hidden at first, but later clearly visible. A writer who can say of his own writing that if this is not poetry, then the concept of poetry will come to adapt itself to his writing, and be right, knows his own worth. And his ambition had been satisfied to saturation point, right up to the moment when he exclaims in a letter that it now no longer gives him any happiness.

It was when he had come so far that he was able to return to his native country and guard his solitude and contemplate, where no one could hurt him any longer. And it was then that he started the work of his old age, a minute scrutiny of the psychology of *men*, in different variations.

There is one more point to mention before we return to a brief outline of *John Gabriel Borkman*. It has often been said that Ibsen constantly uses variations of his earlier dramatic characters, and this is to a great extent true. It should also be noted that almost all great artists continue variations of their original themes, and expand on them throughout their lives. Although it can be said that Borkman, for instance, is a relative of Consul Bernick, as Alfred Allmers is of Hjalmar Ekdal—and there are many other parallels—this is not because Ibsen sought fresh inspiration by re-reading his old works again and again. On the contrary, he often said that he had usually completely finished with a work once he had sent it in. That he had to revise one or two of his earliest works for new editions is another matter; and it is also clear that during the years when he still travelled a great deal he was constantly reminded of his earlier works by having to see them on the stage.

But during his voluntary monastic existence, this incredibly rich gallery of characters haunted his mind. The characters, both major and minor, have almost all been conceived as whole people, three dimensional, each with his or her own destiny; but because of the stern demands on conciseness of a dramatic situation the spectator has only been able to see single sides of them, often only to hear a few words when they influence the plot. Even when it comes to main rôles, characters which he has had to change and which are discarded after the earlier drafts of the play, have continued their independent lives in his mind and imagination. All the indications are that it was this multitude of unused dramatic characters that he played with in his old age, new acquaintances interesting him less.

John Gabriel Borkman is a black, pessimistic play. Borkman is right when he compares himself to a Napoleon who has been crippled by a shot in his first battle. He is related to Napoleon, to Adolf Hitler too, for that matter. His self-confidence is fanatical, his greed for power and ambition boundless and his conscience is blunted from the first. The dramatic tension in this play, therefore, does not lie in the fact that the main character is forced to self-acknowledgement, for this does not happen; he dies irreconciled in his last attack of self-deception, which breaks out into madness. The tension is in the struggle between the two women whose lives he has destroyed.

In the manuscript, the two were only sisters, and in the completed play they are twin sisters. In his thrusting way to the top, Borkman loved Ella, but the man who was able to make him a bank manager also loved her, so Borkman let him have her and took Gunhild, her twin sister. Later when Borkman had become a bank manager, the rival for Ella's affections, angry at being rebuffed by her, revealed Borkman's grand embezzlement, so that the new bank manager spent many years in prison. The only valuable bonds that Borkman did not use to his own advantage were Ella's. I personally believe he did this deliberately; he knew Ella's kind heart and that she would not want to leave his wife and children (and himself) in the lurch if everything were to go wrong.

So we see the struggle between the twin sisters, the vengeful Gunhild, who has been made malevolent by the scandal and who dreams of bringing up Erhart, her son, to clear the name of Borkman; and the milder Ella, whose life has also been wrecked, fighting to secure at least Erhart's happiness. Both lose.

With great dexterity, Ibsen unfolds these intrigues, and minor intrigues with Borkman's Sancho Panza, Foldal and his daughter, Kaja. Nevertheless, this play is not one of Ibsen's best. Every character is so over-simplified that we have only the smallest idea of the immense complications which made them as they are. And all the praise of the author's use of symbols and images has made him fasten on to the play a symbolic fourth act which is technically almost impossible to stage. But it might well be that *John Gabriel Borkman* could have a successful stage revival, in which the main characters were played with such strong Napoleonic or Hitlerian fanaticism that the spectator believed that the tyrant might conceivably obtain redress, and again become dangerous.

Towards Evening

John Gabriel Borkman followed the pattern of many of Ibsen's previous plays. At Gyldendal's, the play came out in two first editions simultaneously, amounting to 15,000 copies, and in the course of a few days it was published in a number of languages. In a few months it had been performed in theatres all over the world.

There is *one* thing that Ibsen scholars have never investigated, because it has nothing to do with his writing, only his private life. This was the question of how Ibsen found the time to administer his world fame from a practical point of view. In our day, every mildly successful entertainer has his own agent, his public relations officer, his fan club and often secretaries. As far as is known, Ibsen had not even a skilful lawyer to arrange things for him. He did indeed have his champions in Germany, France and Great Britain and they looked after his rights, very often in their own financial interest. But otherwise Ibsen evidently must have been his own secretary and that must have taken time.

But during the winter and spring of 1897 he did not have time for such matters. He was then fully occupied with his interests in Sigurd's future. Nothing had come of the possibility of a chair. But as a salve for his wounds, a government grant was offered him, so that he could give a series of lectures in sociology at the University of Kristiania during the winter of 1896–97. They were extremely well attended, with old Ibsen always sitting in the front row. As for the result, it is enough to quote from Wilhelm Keilhau's article on Sigurd Ibsen in the *Norwegian Biographical Dictionary*:

'But the much diminished grading committee set up, which anyhow was remarkably constituted and included at least two people without the slightest expert knowledge, after having heard the lectures did not wish to recommend him for a professorship. The university authorities let the matter drop and they still have not set up a faculty in Sociology.'

Keilhau wrote this thirty-eight years later.

In any case Sociology was not really Sigurd Ibsen's special subject, anyhow not in the sense that we use the word today. Halvdan Koht was himself present as a student at Sigurd Ibsen's lectures and was not particularly impressed. He writes nearly seventy years later: 'I had done some reading in this subject during my studies, and I must honestly say that I thought these lectures had nothing to offer me that I did not know before.'

A compromise was suggested. Sigurd Ibsen was to give another series of lectures, but in open competition with other possible candidates for the chair, a suggestion he rejected with contempt. So two whole years went by before the country made use of him—in a field in which he really was among our foremost experts.

The decision over the chair was made in the summer of 1897, when Sigurd was in Italy with his mother, and Henrik Ibsen sent them indignant bulletins. And to Bjørnson, he writes reviving his threat to emigrate.

'If I leave, then I leave for good. And if all ways are barred to Sigurd, then I cannot see that I have anything else to do here. And I have other refuges to escape to. I have lived long enough in Munich to be able to become naturalized in Bavaria, where I am certain to be favourably received. In Italy too. And I must say that Norway is a difficult country to be a native of.'

Had he been serious in his threat, it would have been a world sensation of a truly dramatic kind. Fortunately he was not. It goes without saying that he did not get started on his next drama under such disturbing circumstances. Meanwhile, his seventieth birthday was approaching, and that occupied his time for months beforehand and months afterwards.

It was to be celebrated, and celebrated in a grand manner. Dr Julius Elias in Germany and Jacob Hegel in Copenhagen were publishing large editions of his collected works, memorial publications were in preparation and all over the world the theatre was to do him honour.

It was in connection with this jubilee that Gyldendal made the greatest publishing coup in its history. Bergliot Ibsen has written about it, gently but clearly, in her memoirs. First she describes how Henrik Ibsen, and the other great writers, throughout their long lives, were cheated by publishers and theatres in every country. She hastens to assure her reader that Gyldendal and the Hegel family were no worse than any other publishers, and describes the touching gratitude Ibsen, like Bjørnson, felt towards Frederik Hegel:

'... who so often in the needy years had sent meagre advances, that would have been unnecessary if Ibsen had only received reasonable royalties. And so now Gyldendal, for his seventieth birthday, wished to honour Henrik Ibsen by proposing a contract for the rights to all his works. Similar terms were offered Father. Father was to have 200,000 kroner and Ibsen 150,000, for Father's writing and stories were, despite everything, more saleable than Ibsen's dramas. Later on Sigurd had this changed, so that Ibsen should have the same sum as Father.

'It was the suave Peter Nansen who came to Kristiania, bringing the offers with him. He would have preferred to acquire the stage rights for Hegel too, but I had that stopped on Father's behalf, and Ibsen did not agree to it either.'

So much for Bergliot Ibsen. Two hundred thousand kroner was no doubt a great deal of money at the time, but it was not to be paid in cash that Ibsen could have invested, but in annual payments over twenty years, and without the publishers paying interest on the sum. That the publishing firm, who knew that Ibsen was the world's most often-played dramatist, also expected to acquire the stage rights in the same swoop, until fifty years after the author's death, is the most unbelievable part of this coup. But Ibsen sold his book-rights and so did Bjørnson. Kielland sold his for a tenth of what the other two received. It became a million-kroner deal for the Danish Gyldendal, both in the next few years and later with sales to Sweden and the Norwegian Gyldendal, founded twenty-five years later. So his publisher had good cause to celebrate Ibsen's jubilee in a grand manner.

He was honoured in periodicals and newspapers all over the world. On the actual birthday, plays by him were performed at, amongst others, two theatres in Oslo, two in Copenhagen, six in Berlin, four in Vienna, as well as in towns and countries all over the world, even in Japan.

Describing the day itself, Bergliot Ibsen writes:

'I can remember that from early in the morning there was a stream of telegrams from all over the world, and a profusion of flowers and handsome gifts stood all round the rooms. During the course of the day, one deputation after another came to offer their good wishes. Naturally there was a deputation from Kristiania Theatre, too. There was to be a gala performance the following evening, with a prologue by Lorentz Dietrichson, a friend since his youth, and this was to be recited by our unforgettable actress, Mrs Laura Gundersen. The deputation now came to request Henrik Ibsen and his wife to do the theatre the honour of gracing it with their presence. Mrs Ibsen thanked them, but requested one box for him and one for her. "Ibsen shall sit alone," she said. Ibsen himself would have preferred to have her at his side. But she insisted. "This is your evening, and it would not be my place to be there." And so it came about that they each sat in separate boxes. I still remember them. Just as I do the evening of his actual birthday, when the great torchlight procession came. . . .'

Here Mrs Bergliot Ibsen's memory is slightly at fault. At first there was naturally the gala performance at the theatre on his actual birthday, with, amongst other things, scenes from *Peer Gynt*, then the next day another gala performance of *The Master Builder* with Ibsen present, and the day after that came the torchlight procession. On the fourth day of the celebrations, March 23, the official banquet was held for him.

It was in his speech of thanks at this banquet that he announced his autobiography, 'a book which binds my life and my work together into an explanatory whole'. Nothing came of this. It was in the same speech that he said that there was no

'. . . unconditional feeling of happiness connected with this fairy-tale destiny of mine; gaining fame and a name in so many countries. And I have won warm, understanding hearts out there too. *That*, first and foremost.

'But this real inner happiness—it is no discovery, no gift. It must be earned at a price, which is often oppressive enough. For *this* is the point: that *whoever* gains a home in so many countries, deep down inside him, does not feel wholly at home anywhere—not even in his own country of birth.

'But it may still come. And I wish to look on this evening as a starting point. . . .'

And so to Copenhagen to be honoured there. He chose Nils Vogt, editor of *Morgenbladet*, as his travelling companion and adjutant, for Ibsen was already even by today's standards a very old man, who needed help. It should be mentioned that the trains of the time had no dining-cars and arrangements had to be made at the highest level for Ibsen to take his meals in his compartment, in contrast to the other passengers, who had to get down and eat at the stations.

The celebrations in Copenhagen were to continue over a whole week. They began with a comical interlude over the Grand Cross of Danebrog. First Ibsen received a case containing a copy of the order, as was customary, to signify that the receiver of the order should himself pay for this expensive decoration. Ibsen was terrified and thought they were joking, but next morning a deputation was dispatched to the Court Jewellers to obtain the actual decoration, after which the Minister for Cultural Affairs personally appeared with yet another decoration, as a gift from King Christian IX.

The festivities during this first week of April, 1898, have been humorously described by Peter Nansen, in his book *Portraits*. He says amongst other things:

'On the evening of April 1st, there was the gala performance at the Royal. Ibsen was not really enthralled at the prospect of what was to come. For the theatre had not been able to find anything else to put on except *The Wild Duck*, which the theatre had already performed for him twice before—with exactly the same cast. . . . And it was probably also doubtful whether the production had become any better with the years. Anyhow, Mrs Hennings, whose Hedvig had originally been a masterpiece of delicate and splendid youthfulness, was now somewhat elderly for the part.'

She was then forty-eight.

But the auditorium was a festive sight. In the massive royal box sat the Royal Family and among King Christian's children who were present were the Russian Tsarina and the future Queen of England. In the equally massive 'court ladies' box, Ibsen sat enthroned, alone with his Grand Cross. Behind the scenes, however, there was turmoil. And here it must be mentioned that the acting director of the Royal Theatre was no other than Peter Hansen, Ibsen's friend from their gay and festive trip to the Nile cataracts in 1869, when Ibsen had been forty-one and Hansen twenty-nine. As had been the custom in the Danish National Theatre for many generations, up to the Second World War and after, the theatre had at its head a member of the senior civil service, often someone from the nobility, and in addition an executive director. Hence the appointment of this literary historian, theatrical consultant, and titular professor that Peter Hansen now was.

After the gala performance there was to be a torchlight procession to honour Ibsen in the theatre, but Peter Hansen had put a notice up, ordering actors and actresses to pay their respects after the performance and before the torchlight procession. This had caused a mutiny. None of these prominent figures was going to be ordered about by anyone. Only a few young ballet dancers came forward. But Peter Hansen carried the situation off.

' "May I, my dear Ibsen, present to you"—a bashful little ballet dancer was pushed forward—"Miss N. N. Very promising. One of our most talented."

'And thus it went on with between ten and fifteen young ladies and gentlemen.'

Fortunately, Ibsen did not notice anything, for now the torch-light procession arrived and the whole of the enormous King's Square outside was packed with people. And he was cheered and cheered. Peter Hansen, meanwhile, had escaped with his wife to the Hotel Angleterre.

'We had hardly ordered a little food and drink before an infernal racket occurred outside in the square. We heard yells and cheers for Ibsen, mixed with screams from women who were nearly being trampled underfoot. And suddenly the main door burst open and into the place, as if shot from a cannon, came *Ibsen*, somewhat ruffled, his top coat torn and his broad-brimmed stove-pipe hat on the back of his head, the ribbons of his order dangling outside his overcoat, and Peter Hansen and his wife. . . .'

The good Peter Hansen had in fact, in the confusion at the theatre, forgotten to secure a cab for the hundred yards or so across the square, so when the great writer was to go to the hotel, he was literally almost trampled to death by the homage being paid to him. That same evening Professor Hansen had also received the resignation of one of the theatre's principal actresses, so he forgot Ibsen when they arrived at the hotel, too, and had to be reminded to ask the celebrity if he would like something to eat.

Next day was the great gala banquet. That also became an exceptionally scandalous occasion as far as arrangements were concerned. The price of inclusion was set as astronomically high as twenty-five kroner per person, which corresponds to more than ten times that sum in kroner today. The guests were dissatisfied with what they got for their money; but even so the manager of the hotel had in fact gambled his prestige on *losing* on the banquet. He served kingly culinary and alcoholic delicacies which cost him far more than the guests had paid, but they were still not satisfied.

K

But the great scandal came with Professor Peter Hansen's banquet speech. Every cultural personality in Denmark had been thoroughly scrutinized to single out who should pay homage to Ibsen. Brandes was away, and most of the others were rejected, so that it should be no one from either the right or the left. Eventually a suitable professor was found. But in a panic, he reported just before the banquet that he was ill. Again Peter Hansen had to step into the breach. He had prepared a little speech on what fun he and Ibsen had had in Egypt a generation beforehand. This he could not use now. Instead, he said a few halting words about Ibsen, who had brought his theatre so many full houses.

Consternation! Ibsen's written speech of thanks has not been preserved. He did have to admit that Professor Hansen's speech had confused him, and then he thanked Denmark in equally confused terms. After this, some highly inebriated writers stood up and tried to repair the damage, but only made matters worse.

The homage to Ibsen continued. He travelled on to Stockholm, where there was another Grand Cross to collect, an audience with King Oscar, a dinner at the Palace, an official banquet, a gala performance and a dinner given by the Swedish Society of Authors. Finally two women's organizations, united by annoyance at the fact that only men had had access to the celebrations so far, wrung a promise from Ibsen that he would put off his journey home and be their guest of honour at a celebration at Hasselbacken on Saturday, April 16.

This last dinner was to become the most memorable for Ibsen. At the table, he was seated between two pillars of the feminist movement, and one of them, Ellen Key, made a speech to him which he did not like, so he was grumpy and forbidding. But afterwards there was folk-dancing, performed by the Friends of Folk-dancing, and Ibsen was so taken by one of the young dancers that one might well call it his last romantic infatuation. They agreed she should come to the station to see him off next day.

This young lady was called Rosa Fitinghoff, and Ibsen started an almost ardent correspondence with her soon after his arrival home at Arbiens Street. He complains that it was not until his last evening in Stockholm that they had met, and begs her to write letters and send her photograph. This she did, and the correspondence continues throughout the spring and summer, amongst other things about the possibility of Miss Fitinghoff and her mother making a detour to Kristiania on their way home to Stockholm, after their summer holiday in Lysekil.

Nothing came of this. But the year after their little flirtation at Hasselbacken, she writes again and reminds him of it, and he replies: 'I shall never forget that day. Be certain of that!—Your letters live in a special space in my desk, and when I go to work in the mornings, then I always look into this little space and greet Rosa. Yours sincerely, H. I.'

The reason why Ibsen did not get started on his next play that year was not only because of the months of festivities and many practical business matters, but also because the German edition of his collected works caused him a great deal of work. In addition Sigurd Ibsen was once again very active politically. He started his own political weekly, *Ringeren*, which had great influence during the two years of its existence. The editorial board consisted of Sigurd Ibsen himself, Bjørnstjerne Bjørnson and Ernst Sars—a very formidable three-leafed clover.

In 1899, Sigurd succeeded in obtaining the position he had so long deserved. As mentioned before, Norway had no Foreign Service of her own, but now the Trade and Consular Department of the Ministry of the Interior was expanded into a department of its own, with Sigurd Ibsen at the head of it. It now became the Consular Service, which came to the forefront in the struggle for an independent Norwegian Foreign Service, in fact against Sigurd Ibsen's own wishes; and it was the preparatory work that he did here which six years later caused the break between Sweden and Norway.

The appointment was made on July 14, 1899, and on the following day Sigurd Ibsen writes to Bergliot, who was at Aulestad with her parents: '. . . when I saw the appointment in print in *Morgenbladet*, and there could no longer be any doubt about it, then I sent my telegram to Aulestad. . . . After that I drove to my parents . . . My parents were quite transfigured with happiness. . . .'

Ibsen had been brooding over a new play ever since *John Gabriel Borkman*. He knew what kind of play it was to be and he had mumbled about it to someone. But, as he himself said, for a long time only one of the play's characters was clear to him. Not until late in the winter of 1899 did he write a few scanty notes, and it was not until the end of that summer that he seriously started on it. It seems that by then the structure of the play was quite clear. The names were changed a little, the main character began by being called Strubow, then became Strubeck and finally Rubek. Then the minor characters surrounding the action are firmly removed, and they may just as well remain out of view. This includes the 'gossipy wife from the capital, considered extremely amusing by the visitors at the spa. Malicious out of thoughtlessness'. This might have been a rewarding character on the stage, which in a practised director's production might have become an effective factor in the plot, but she is ruthlessly eliminated because she could draw attention away from the focal point.

And *that* focal point is one single thing: Henrik Ibsen's pathetic summing up of his own life, the insoluble contrast between life and literature. He does not make the slightest attempt to camouflage himself.

Many people reckon that *When We Dead Awaken* is one of Ibsen's weaker contemporary dramas; and on the stage it has had difficulty in coming into its own. As with *John Gabriel Borkman*, it begins with sheer realism and then swings over to symbolism and ends in a totally abstract last act. It has proved difficult to find an appropriate style of acting for it. Both the more recent symbolists and the experimenters in the theatre of the 'absurd' have in their own ways used the abstract with greater ingenuity and consistency, both when they really have had something to say and when now and again they have done their conjuring tricks with marked cards.

It has also been pointed out that the problem in *When We Dead Awaken* is clearer and more strained than in his earlier dramas. The play's character of pessimistic self-confession and self-scrutiny is so clear there is not much temptation to study it, because it interprets itself.

But is this self-scrutiny less profound and less gripping because Ibsen, now unmasked, is dissecting his own mind? It does not seem so to me; I am one of those who are intensely interested in this play and I find new things every time I read it.

When Ibsen asserts that Solness is a brilliant architect, or implies that Allmers could perhaps write something new and important on human responsibility, or finds it explicable that a man of Borkman's type is allowed to become a bank manager, we cannot entirely suspend our disbelief. They do not become any less interesting as people for that, but their situations in life can sometimes appear to be mere postulations. But when it comes to Professor Rubek, there is no shadow of doubt that he is both a human being and an artist of stature commensurate with the praise given to him.

Every word he says carries the message that he has put the whole of his soul into creating art: he has sacrificed everything to his genius; he has become his own God. Only thus could he reach his goal.

But therefore he also knows inwardly exactly what it has cost him. And he knows more! though he has paid the price, he has not reached the goal. If others have not managed to see through his small compromises, his small rearrangements of the whole truth, in the final artistic result, at least he himself has been aware of it. He has renounced life to worship his enormous artistic ambition—he has walked over both his own and others' corpses—but it is only his purely external ambition that is satisfied. His own self-realization judges him. Was it worth the price?

In my opinion, *When We Dead Awaken* is not only a study of the ruthless self-realization of an ageing genius and therefore one of the most interesting autobiographical documents in art of modern times. It is also as literature, in form and content, one of the plays which will absorb readers, and perhaps audiences, for generations to come.

This is no small nut that Ibsen gave his reader to crack. For the devil himself is in the nut, and with his seventy-one years Ibsen was still full of explosive force. In a very decisive way, it bears the stamp of his age. He had become too old to experiment, to wish to perfect himself. He did not give a hang for the demands of realism and symbolism; he did not court understanding any longer. Right up to the last, he insisted that he wrote for human beings about human beings; but this epilogue was written for and about himself.

Rubek is an artist through and through. Maja is the little life he has been able to buy himself after he has become famous. Irene is inspiration itself, 'the model', the life he has loved and wished to create, and at the same time has longed secretly to be allowed to live himself. It is this life, the reality of inspiration, for which he must now answer. Irene sees through him as a person, and will also come to see through him as an artist if she is allowed to see his work.

For a long time the play was entitled *The Day of Resurrection*. This perhaps indicates that the love affairs of his old age, small in themselves, had nevertheless given him new hope of being able to live once more. Then the title became *When We Dead Awaken*. Then at least he still had a faint hope that it is only the dreamed of life which wakens, and he will be able to defend himself against it in some way or other. But then comes the key; the final lines between Rubek and Irene:

'Irene: We only see the irretrievable first when——
Professor Rubek: When——?
Irene: When we dead awaken.
Professor Rubek: Well, what do we actually see?
Irene: We see that we have never lived.'

Rubek is a sculptor, or 'image-master', as he is also called. But when he tries to explain away to Irene his falsification of his own work, she catches him red-handed:

'Irene: (hard and cold) Fictionist!
Rubek: Why fictionist?
Irene: Because you are spineless and lethargic and full of forgiveness for all your life's deeds and for all your thoughts. You have murdered my soul, and so you model yourself in repentance and

penance and confession—(smiles)—and with that you say your accounts are balanced.

Professor Rubek: (defiantly) I am an artist, Irene. And I'm not ashamed of the weakness that perhaps adheres to me. For I was *born* an artist, you see—and so I'll never be anything else but an artist, anyhow.

Irene: (looking at him with a malevolent, concealed smile and speaking gently and softly) You're a fictionist, Arnold. (Strokes him gently over his hair.)

Professor Rubek: (annoyed) Why do you keep calling me a fictionist?

Irene: (with watchful eyes) Because there is something apologetic in the word, my dear. Something forgiving—which spreads a cloak over all weakness. . . .'

Can a great writer judge himself more ruthlessly?

Irene is one of Ibsen's most exacting roles to act and it is not difficult to see that she has much in common with Ellida Wangel. Both are women with over-intense, sensitive spirits. Rubek has not seduced, but transported Irene, literally terrifying her into a mixture of longing and fear at the thought that her ecstatic spiritual life may become reality.

Her spirit, though perhaps the more dignified word soul is more suitable here, has been crushed by it and she has spent many years locked up as a mental patient. Ibsen leaves it open whether what she tells of her past from the time she left Rubek is truth or obsession; most of it is undoubtedly fantasy. But she is on her way back to real life. Rubek's source of inspiration is 'revived'—at the same time a desperate hope and a mortal threat.

Her words may appear disconnected; now they are messages from a great, deep darkness, now from a transfiguring light; and nearly everyone who tries to create her character on the stage either under- or over-acts her outbursts. But, at least in reading the play any experienced psychiatrist recognizes her and has met her in his profession, at one moment distant and 'dead', at the next violently involved, on her way back in to reality.

If *When We Dead Awaken* is ever made into a film, using very exceptional actresses and actors who suit Rubek and Irene, and the mixture of abstraction and realism which films can give better than the stage, then Ibsen's dramatic epilogue could be the world sensation it deserves.

Naturally *When We Dead Awaken* was soon translated and widely performed. But it was not particularly successful on the stage and the critics divided themselves as usual between homage, deference, confusion and dislike.

Ibsen himself said that the play was meant as an epilogue to a series of contemporary dramas, a fact which indicates that he had something else on his mind, in another form, which he wished to write. It is clear from a letter to Count Prozor in March, 1900, that he himself doubted whether he could write any more, for in it he says:

'Whether I shall write another drama or not I do not yet know, but if I am still allowed to keep the mental and physical powers which I still enjoy, then in the long run I would probably not be able to keep away from my old battlefields. But in that case, I should want to toil on with new weapons and new armour.'

But this did not come about. Koht dates Ibsen's first stroke as in 1901, but it most probably occurred as early as the middle of March, 1900. Ibsen himself says, in a short letter of thanks for a birthday greeting from Nils Vogt, dated April 2: 'I have been very unwell since the day of the Palace ball and still have to stay indoors.' In a letter to August Larsen, his agent at Gyldendal's, he writes on April 20th: 'But ever since the middle of March, I have been unwell (though not bed-ridden), and my doctor has forbidden me use of pen and ink.'

The symptoms are clear enough: loss of power in his right arm and leg. His physician, Dr Sontum, ordered massage and a period at a spa and in the summer of 1900 Ibsen went to Sandefjord Spa. Bergliot's memory must be at fault when she says that he took Suzannah with him, for on June 13 he wrote from Sandefjord the last letter he ever wrote to his wife. It begins:

'Thank you for your letter, which I have just received. Everything is going excellently. Sleeping well. Appetite ravenous at every mealtime. I have massage daily and it does me an incredible amount of good. Not a trace of pain. I can already walk as far as I want to, without feeling fatigue in my foot.'

Then he goes on with some domestic admonitions and wishes her a good trip—undoubtedly to Italy.

The rest is silence.

From Ibsen's return from Sandefjord at the end of August 1900 until his last written word, dated February, 1904, there are altogether sixteen letters from him, seven of them written during the autumn of 1900—of which none is more than six lines long. Four letters were written in 1901, three of them of three lines or less—and a slightly longer loving New Year letter to Rosa Fitinghoff, in which he tells her that he has been ill for the first time in his life. (In this letter he compares her to 'a young princess from the world of fairy-tales'.) From 1902, there remain altogether two telegrams and one letter, none longer than two lines. From 1903, a letter to Jacob Hegel of two lines; and in 1904 Ibsen placed a laconic full-stop at the end of his writing. It is a letter written to Doctor Edvard Bull, the physician who looked after him during his last years, after the death of Doctor Sontum and after the family had tried another doctor who never came when he was summoned. The letter is written on February 14, 1904, and runs: 'Thank you. H. I.'

But we know from other sources how during the last years of his life he fought against illness and approaching death with grim defiance. Both he and the family behaved for a long time much as most families would in similar circumstances. They were optimists; everything was going so well. In the autumn and winter he returned to his walks to the Grand, his drink, his walk home again, setting his watch by the university clock: in short, he continued to be the city's unapproachable notable.

After his second stroke in 1901 he no longer liked walking along Karl Johan's Street, but was pleased about the key to the Queen's Park which King Oscar II had personally given him—a part of the Palace park which was the royal family's private and enclosed domain. This park was just across the road from Ibsen's apartment. So he went there, unlocked the gate with his royal key, and was able to be in peace there. But even after the family had engaged a permanent nurse for him, Bergliot says that he sometimes *wanted* to go out for a walk on his own, and when the nurse accompanied him down the street, he struck out at her with his stick and insisted on going alone.

Two outsiders have told stories of interest, after visiting him during these years. One of them is Peter Nansen, who visited him on business—probably in 1901, or anyhow after his second stroke. Nansen realized as soon as he was on the threshold that his visit was a strain and a torment to Ibsen, so he wanted to withdraw swiftly and said that he could settle the matter with Ibsen's son.

' "Yes, do that," Ibsen replied. "It will be a nice little income. But I'm very tired in the daytime. I can't manage business matters. Talk to my son. And thank you for coming, and please convey my thanks to the firm."

'His voice was that of an aged and very sick man. It was difficult for him to form his words and sentences correctly. They came out in a mumble and as if from far away.'

In 1903 Ibsen had his third stroke, and the rumour went round the whole world that his death was imminent. But he held out for three more years. As late as in 1904 he received a visit from Halvdan Koht, the young literary scholar who had then just published a collection of Ibsen's letters. Koht says:

'Then I thought it was altogether absurd that I had never even spoken to him. So I was allowed a conversation with him in his home. But he was a wreck by then. This was two years before his death. He had had strokes, and he suffered from aphasia, so it was very difficult to talk to him. When I went in to him, he had a masseur sitting with him, who was with him constantly and who was so used to him that he could interpret what Ibsen meant when he used all kinds of incorrect words. So when I went in and greeted him, he said: "Yes, you are the man who has published this dictionary." "Letters, he means," said the masseur. And thus the conversation went on, with Ibsen saying only a few words, and I sat and talked to him and looked at him.'

For some time longer Ibsen insisted on getting out and with the help of his masseur, Arnt Dehli, he was assisted up into a landau and then the two of them drove round the town. After Ibsen's death Dehli was of course interviewed, so that posterity should know what pearls of wisdom the genius may have let fall when à deux, but Dehli spoke with great tact and discretion. Only two small episodes will be mentioned here. Dehli was asked what Ibsen had talked about on their drives together:

'About everything under the sun, according to his impulse. He often joked. Once we passed Fridtjof Nansen, and turned back soon afterwards. Then Ibsen said: "Brr, it's been cold here, since we met that polar explorer." Another time we met Professor Ludvig Ludvigsen Daae far down Drammens Road. Ibsen, who was in a specially good mood that day, waved to him and called out good-day. But Daae neither saw nor heard, although Ibsen called good-day three times. Then Ibsen turned to me and said: "I can tell you that he's offended, because he thinks he's the model for Rektor Kroll. But I hadn't thought of him." '

From 1905 onwards, his physical strength came to an end. But despite his weakness and aphasia, he still possessed his mental powers, so he was able to follow Sigurd's great contribution to the consular controversy, first as a departmental head, then as a Cabinet Minister and finally as Norwegian Minister in Stockholm, right up to the spring of 1905, when he refused to take part in Michelsen's government because he disagreed with the procedure being used to achieve the break up of the Union between Sweden and Norway.

On May 23, 1906, Henrik Ibsen died. There are several legends about his last words on earth. According to his daughter-in-law, Bergliot, the night before he had said to Suzannah: 'My sweet, sweet wife, how kind and good you have been to me,' but as recently as 1956, Koht in his great biography of Ibsen maintains that his last words were a reply to a few words from Suzannah to the nurse to the effect that he would now no doubt soon be well again: Ibsen is said to have turned and said grimly: 'On the contrary.'

His funeral was the most pompous Norway had ever seen, with the young King of Norway, Parliament, the government, the Corps Diplomatique in the lead, supported by everything else the country had to offer in the way of authority. It was Christopher Bruun, the alleged model for Brand, who officiated. Bruun had in fact been at the Ibsens' a good deal during the last few years. Bergliot Ibsen implies that he must have made some attempts to convert the stubborn old free-thinker, whereupon Ibsen had snubbed him with: 'That's my own business.' Anyhow he died as irreconciled as he had lived, and the biting irony of this great rebel's pompous funeral—to which only writers on the whole had failed to receive invitations—made such an impression that Gerhard Gran, twelve years later, gave a detailed description of it: the list of notables present alone runs into a whole page.

With that the last line is drawn of the portrait of Henrik Ibsen, as the author of this book believed he was. In conclusion it is fitting to quote the visionary lines with which another Norwegian dramatist, Helge Krog, ended his memorial to Henrik Ibsen on his centenary on March 20, 1928:

'We know that the light from space does not reach us until a certain time after it has left the stars. It is the same with the light from the works of great authors. The source is the same, and the light pours continuously, but it is always a new light. And so it is with Ibsen's great dramas. Fifty years, a hundred years after their creation there open from inside them new sources of light, which astonishingly illuminate our life and give us the joy of first experience. And there is undoubtedly light *on the way* to us from Ibsen's writing.'

Chronology

HENRIK IBSEN

Henrik Johan Ibsen was born in Skien on March 20, 1828, father Knud Ibsen, mother Marichen (Marchen) née Altenburg.

Family moved to Venstøp in Gjerpen in 1835.

Confirmed autumn, 1843.

Apprentice apothecary in Grimstad, January, 1844. Lived there until April, 1850.

Catiline. (Published 1850. World première at New Theatre, Stockholm on December 3, 1881.)

Visited Skien in April, 1850, on his way to Kristiania.

Went to Heltberg's cramming school in Kristiania for about three months during summer of 1850. Took school leaving exam in August, 1850.

The Warrior's Barrow. (World première at Christiania Theatre on September 26, 1850. Revised in 1853 and published in *Bergenske Blade* in 1854.)

Supported himself as free-lance writer in Kristiania until November, 1851.

Winter of 1850–51 teacher at Thranite Movement's 'Sunday School'.

Appointed by Ole Bull as resident dramatist at the Norwegian Theatre in Bergen and moved there in November, 1851.

Lived in Bergen until summer of 1857. In the spring of 1852, received grant to study theatre conditions in Copenhagen, Berlin, Hamburg and Dresden.

St John's Night. (World première at the Norwegian Theatre in Bergen on January 2, 1853. Published in *Posthumous Writings* in 1909.)

Lady Inger of Østråt (World première at the Norwegian Theatre in Bergen on January 2, 1855. Published 1857.)

The Feast at Solhaug. (World première at the Norwegian Theatre in Bergen on January 2, 1856. Published 1856.)

Engaged to Suzannah Daae Thoresen, spring, 1856.

Olaf Liljekrans. (World première at the Norwegian Theatre in Bergen on January 2, 1857. Published in German in 1898, in Norwegian in 1902.)

Appointed director of the Norwegian Theatre in Møllergaten, Kristiania, July, 1857.

Married to Suzannah Daae Thoresen in June, 1858.

The Vikings at Helgeland. (Published 1858. World première at the Norwegian Theatre in Kristiania on November 24, 1858.)

Son Sigurd born December 23, 1859.

Walking tour to Gudbrandsdalen, Sogn and Møre on a grant in summer, 1862, to collect folk-lore.

Ceased to be director of theatre when the Norwegian Theatre in Møllergaten went bankrupt.

Love's Comedy. (Published 1862. World première at Christiania Theatre on November 24, 1873.)

Artistic consultant at Christiania Theatre from January, 1863.

Took part in student rally in Bergen in June, 1863.

The Pretenders. Published 1863. (World première at Christiania Theatre on January 17, 1864.)

Left Norway in April, 1864, with his family, to live in Rome.

Brand. Published 1866. (World première at New Theatre in Stockholm on March 24, 1885; fourth act performed at Christiania Theatre on June 26, 1867.)

Artist's salary, 1866.

Peer Gynt. (Published 1867. World première at Christiania Theatre on February 24, 1876.)

Went to live in Dresden in 1868.

The League of Youth. (Published 1869. World première at Christiania Theatre on October 18, 1869.)

Visit to Stockholm in summer of 1869 to take part in Scandinavian Orthographic Conference. Selected by King Carl XV as one of the two delegates from Norway-Sweden to official opening of Suez Canal.

Poems. (Published 1871.)

The Emperor and the Galilean. (Published 1873. World première at Civic Theatre in Leipzig on December 5, 1896. Norwegian première at National Theatre on March 20, 1903.)

Visited Kristiania in 1874.

Moved to Munich in 1875.

Pillars of Society. (Published 1877. World première at the Royal Theatre in Copenhagen on November 18, 1877. Norwegian première at the Norwegian Theatre in Bergen on November 30, 1877.)

Moved to Rome in 1878. Back to Munich in 1879.

A Doll's House. (Published 1879. World première at the Royal Theatre in Copenhagen on December 21, 1879. Norwegian première at Christiania Theatre on January 20, 1880.)

Again went to live in Rome from 1880–85.

Ghosts. (Published 1881. World première at Aurora Turner Hall in Chicago on May 20, 1882. Norwegian première at Møllergaten Theatre (August Lindberg's Company) on October 17, 1883.)

An Enemy of the People. (Published 1882. World première at Christiania Theatre on January 13, 1883.)

The Wild Duck. (Published 1884. World première at the National Stage in Bergen on January 9, 1885.)

Visit to Norway 1885—Kristiania, Trondhjem, Molde, Bergen.

Lived in Munich from 1885–91.

Rosmersholm. (Published 1886. World première at the National Stage in Bergen on January 17, 1887.)

Summer holiday in Jylland, travelled to Gothenberg, Stockholm and Copenhagen in 1887.

The Lady from the Sea. (Published 1888. World première at Christiania Theatre on February 12, 1889.)

Hedda Gabler. (Published 1890. World première at Christiania Theatre on February 26, 1891.)

Journey to North Cape in summer of 1891. Lived in Victoria Terrace in Kristiania from September, 1891 until October, 1895.

The Master Builder. (Published 1892. World première at Lessing Theatre in Berlin on January 19, 1893. Norwegian première in Trondhjem (William Petersen's Company) in January, 1893.)

Little Eyolf. (Published 1894. World première at Deutsches Theatre in Berlin on January 12, 1895. Norwegian première at Christiania Theatre on January 15, 1895.)

Moved to Arbiens Street in Kristiania in 1895 and lived there until his death.

John Gabriel Borkman. (Published 1896. World première simultaneously at the Swedish Theatre and the Finnish Theatre in Helsinki on January 10, 1897. Norwegian première at Drammen (August Lindberg's Company) on January 19, 1897.)

Honoured with great festivities in Kristiania, Copenhagen and Stockholm from March to April, 1898.

When We Dead Awaken. (Published 1899. World première at Court
Theatre in Stuttgart on January 26, 1900. Norwegian première at
National Theatre on February 6, 1900.)

Henrik Ibsen died in Kristiania on May 23, 1906.

Index